P9-COO-392

▪ INDIANA ▪

The Hoosier Heritage Quilt, Indiana's official state quilt, was created by piecing together quilt blocks from each of the state's 92 counties. This beautiful work of art, which is exhibited at the State Museum in Indianapolis, honors the rich heritage of our state.

JAMES H. MADISON

PROFESSOR OF HISTORY
INDIANA UNIVERSITY, BLOOMINGTON

MACMILLAN/McGRAW-HILL SCHOOL PUBLISHING COMPANY

NEW YORK   CHICAGO   COLUMBUS

PROGRAM AUTHORS

Dr. Barry K. Beyer
Professor of Education and American Studies
George Mason University
Fairfax, Virginia

Jean Craven
Social Studies Coordinator
Albuquerque Public Schools
Albuquerque, New Mexico

Dr. Mary A. McFarland
Instructional Coordinator of Social Studies,
  K–12 and Director of Staff Development
Parkway School District
Chesterfield, Missouri

Dr. Walter C. Parker
Associate Professor, College of Education
University of Washington
Seattle, Washington

CONTENT CONSULTANTS

Dr. Darrel Bigham
Professor of History
University of Southern Indiana
Evansville, Indiana

Eleanor Roach
Fourth Grade Teacher
Arlington Woods School
Indianapolis, Indiana

Candace Carr
Sheila Kelly
Bev Tibbetts
Classroom Teachers
W. D. Richards Elementary School
Columbus, Indiana

GRADE-LEVEL CONSULTANTS

Nancy Augustine
Fourth/Fifth Grade Teacher
Harper Elementary School
Evansville, Indiana

Joyce Chambers
Fourth Grade Teacher
John F. Nuner Elementary School
South Bend, Indiana

Don Dewey
Fourth Grade Teacher
Slate Run School
New Albany, Indiana

Gloria Jones
Fourth Grade Teacher
Robert Lee Frost School
Indianapolis, Indiana

Kay J. Stover
Fourth Grade Teacher
Vohr Elementary School
Gary, Indiana

Bonnie Terry
Fourth Grade Teacher
La Fontaine Elementary School
La Fontaine, Indiana

CONTRIBUTING WRITERS

Kathlyn Gay
Joanne Landers Henry

ACKNOWLEDGMENTS

The publisher gratefully acknowledges permission to reprint the following copyrighted material:
"On the Banks of the Wabash, Far Away," by Paul Dresser and compiled, arranged, and edited by John W. Schaum. Copyright © 1982 by Schaum Publications. Used by permission of the publisher. Excerpts from A HOME IN THE WOODS: PIONEER LIFE IN INDIANA, as related by Howard Johnson. Copyright © 1978 by Indiana University Press. Used by permission of the publisher. Excerpt from "Follow the Drinkin' Gourd," words and music by Paul Campbell. Copyright © 1951 by Folkways Music Publishers, Inc. Used by permission. Excerpt from "Smokey the Bear" by Steve Nelson and Jack Rollins. Copyright © 1952 by Chappell & Co. Used by permission. Excerpt from "In the Spring of the Year" by James Buchanan Elmore, quoted in WILD FOOD PLANTS OF INDIANA AND ADJACENT STATES by Alan McPherson and Sue McPherson. Copyright © 1977 by Indiana University Press. Used by permission of Indiana University Press. Excerpt from "Indiana" in THE POEMS OF MAX EHRMANN, edited by Bertha K. Ehrmann. Copyright © 1976 by Robert L. Bell. Used by permission of Robert L. Bell. Excerpt from THE BEST OF GEORGE ADE, selected and edited by A. L. Lazarus. Copyright © 1985 by Indiana University Press. Used by permission of the publisher. "Students Write New Bill," Associated Press, January 10, 1990. Used by permission.

Copyright © 1991 Macmillan/McGraw-Hill School Publishing Company
All rights reserved. No part of this book may be reproduced or transmitted in any form or by any means, electronic or mechanical, including photocopying, recording, or by any information storage and retrieval system, without permission in writing from the publisher.

Macmillan/McGraw-Hill School Division
866 Third Avenue
New York, New York 10022

Printed in the United States of America
ISBN 0-02-144103-0
9 8 7 6 5 4 3 2

CONTENTS

UNIT 5 Indiana Today   202

SPECIAL SECTION 270

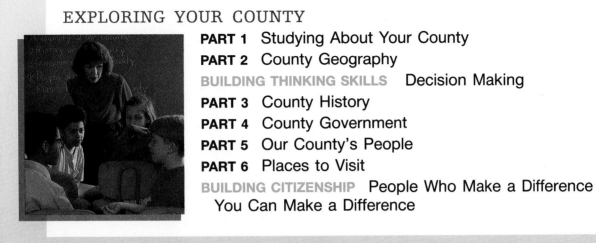
REFERENCE SECTION 287

Building Citizenship

Building Skills

Charts, Graphs, Diagrams, and Time Lines

Maps

WHAT IS A Hoosier?

Dear Students:

This book is about us—about all of us who live and have lived in Indiana. All of us share many things in common.

One important thing we share is a name. Anyone who lives in Indiana is called a Hoosier. We use this name with pride. Yet no one knows for sure what the name means or where it comes from.

Some people suggest the word Hoosier came from a man named Samuel Hoosier. He came to Indiana to hire men to help him build a canal near the Ohio River. The Indiana men who worked on the canal were called Hoosier's men and then just Hoosiers.

Another story was told by Indiana's most famous poet, James Whitcomb Riley. He said that once there was a terrible fight. Men were hitting, scratching, and even biting noses and ears. When the fight was over, someone reached down and picked something up from the dirt floor. "Whose ear?" the man asked. From that question came the word Hoosier. Although Riley told this story as a joke, many Hoosiers like it because it

reminds them of the early days when Indiana was part of the rough and tumble West.

The more likely meaning of the word Hoosier is that it was a very old word that meant a large hill. Many of the people who came to Indiana long ago came from the hills of Kentucky and Tennessee. The word Hoosier may have been used to describe people from hilly areas.

We really do not know what the word Hoosier means. We do know, however, that Hoosiers share many things in addition to a name. They share geography—the land and water of our state. This book will help you understand our state's varied geography. It will help you learn more about this state which stretches from the rolling hills near the Ohio River to the open flat land of the north.

Hoosiers also share a history. This book will help you learn more about that history. It will help you understand why we have a special feeling about our past and a special pride in being Hoosiers.

From Tecumseh and George Rogers Clark to farmers, factory workers and teachers, it is the people who make our state special. And it is you and your classmates, along with many other Hoosiers, who will continue to make Indiana a strong, growing state.

This book will tell you about our history as a state and what it means to be a Hoosier. It is an exciting story.

Sincerely,

James H. Madison

James H. Madison

On the Banks of the

by Paul Dresser
Arranged by John W. Schaum

Andante
espressivo

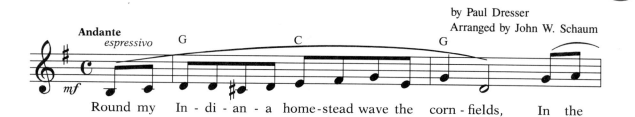

Round my In - di - an - a home-stead wave the corn - fields, In the

dis - tance loom the wood - lands clear and cool. Of - ten

times my thoughts re - vert to scenes of child - hood, Where I

first re - ceived my les - sons, na - ture's school. Oh, the

Wabash, Far Away

moon - light's fair to-night a - long the Wa - bash, From the

fields there comes the breath of new mown hay. Thru the

syc - a-mores the can - dle lights are gleam - ing On the

banks of the Wa - bash, far a - way.

USING YOUR TEXTBOOK

TABLE OF CONTENTS

Lists all parts of your book and tells you where to find them

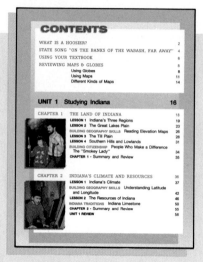

CONTENTS

Your textbook contains many features that will help you understand and remember the geography, history, and people of Indiana.

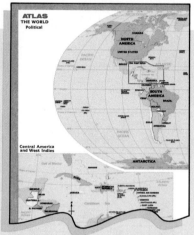

ATLAS
THE WORLD
Political

ATLAS

Maps of the world, the United States, and Indiana

REVIEWING MAPS & GLOBES

REVIEWING MAPS AND GLOBES

Reviews skills that will help you use the maps in your book

LESSON OPENER

Important vocabulary, people, and places introduced in the lesson

Lesson introduction

Asks you to think about what you already know from your book or from your own experience

Question you should keep in mind as you read the lesson

LESSON
1 Early Explorers

READ TO LEARN

Key Vocabulary		Key People	Key Places
colony	trading post	Robert La Salle	New France
explorer	missionary	White Beaver	Kankakee River
fur traders	religion		South Bend
trade goods			

Read Aloud

[We found] only great open plains, where nothing grows except tall grass, which is dry at this season, and which the Miami had burned while hunting buffalo.

   A French traveler wrote these words to describe his first visit to what is now northern Indiana. As you will read in this lesson, the French would play an important role in this part of the world.

Read for Purpose

1. **WHAT YOU KNOW:** Who were the first people to live in Indiana?
2. **WHAT YOU WILL LEARN:** Why did the French come to Indiana?

NEW COLONIES

   Native Americans were the only people living in North America until te 1500 ... the early ... 00s,

colony is a place that is ruled by another country. They began colonies for many reasons. Some ... land ... new ...

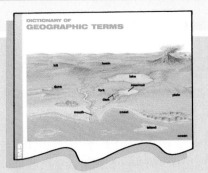

DICTIONARY OF GEOGRAPHIC TERMS

Definition, pronunciation, and picture of major geographic terms

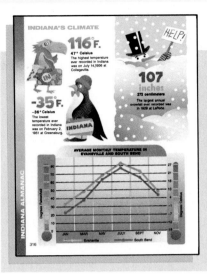

INDIANA ALMANAC

Important and interesting facts about Indiana

GAZETTEER

Location and pronunciation of all key places and page where each is shown on a map

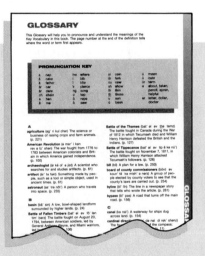

GLOSSARY

Definition and pronunciation of all key vocabulary and first page where each is found

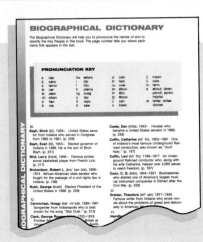

BIOGRAPHICAL DICTIONARY

Identifies and pronounces names of key people and lists first page where each is found

INDEX

Alphabetical list of important subjects and pages where information is found

REVIEWING MAPS & GLOBES

Using Globes

Key Vocabulary

continent   equator
ocean   prime meridian
hemisphere

In social studies this year you will be reading the story of Indiana, the Hoosier State. You will read about how Indiana is an important part of the United States and the world.

As you study our state, you will discover that maps and globes can be of great help to you. Maps and globes show many of the places around us. The students below are using a globe to find the location of Indiana. By using the globe, they can also find countries, cities, rivers, lakes, and mountains.

Maps and globes show a great deal of information at a glance. They can be thought of as special "tools." Let's review how to use them.

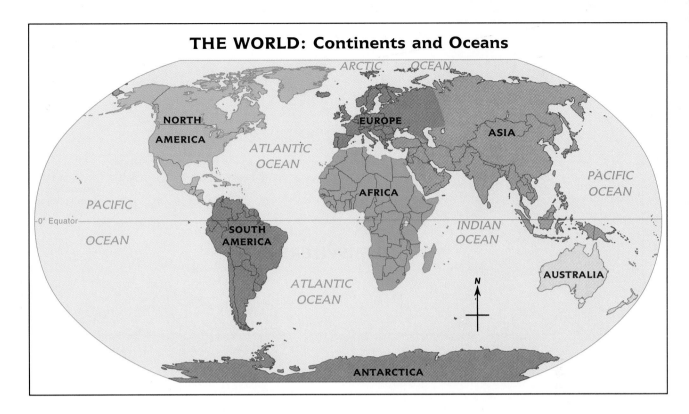

THE WORLD: Continents and Oceans

Continents and Oceans

You know that the earth is round. Another word for a round body is *sphere* (sfîr). A globe, like the earth, is a sphere. A globe is a model, or small copy, of the earth, in the same way that a toy train is a model of a real train. Both models look like the originals, only they are much smaller.

Globes show the land and water of the earth. Very large bodies of land are called continents. The earth has seven continents. They are North America, South America, Europe, Africa, Asia, Australia, and Antarctica. The students in the picture used a globe to find out that Indiana is located in North America.

From the map on this page you can see that the continents are separated by large bodies of water. Actually, when you look closely at a globe, you will see that all the large bodies of water on the earth are part of one larger, connected body of water.

This one large body of water is divided into smaller parts called oceans. The earth has four oceans: the Atlantic, the Pacific, the Indian, and the Arctic.

Hemispheres

No matter how you turn a globe you can see only half of it at one time. Since a globe is a sphere, what you see is half a sphere. Another word for half a sphere is hemisphere. *Hemi* means "half."

The maps on page 10 show you that the earth can be divided into different hemispheres. Each map shows half of the earth.

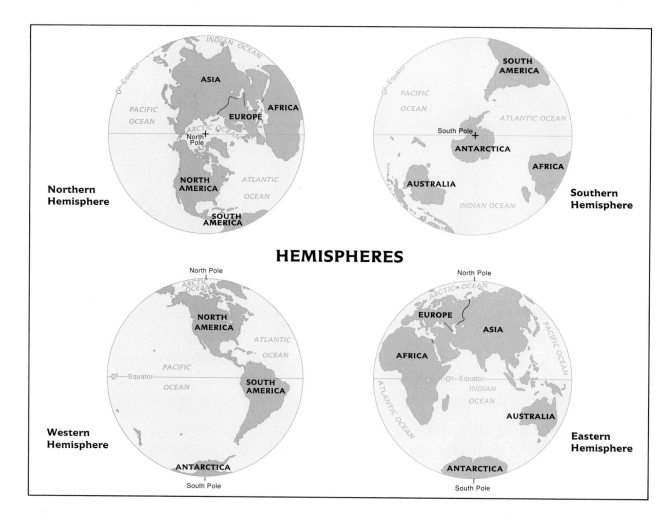

HEMISPHERES

The northern half of the earth is divided from the southern half of the earth by the equator. The equator is an imaginary line that lies halfway between the North Pole and the South Pole. The equator divides the earth into the Northern Hemisphere and the Southern Hemisphere.

How many continents are found in the Northern Hemisphere? How many continents are found in the Southern Hemisphere?

The earth can also be divided into the Eastern Hemisphere and the Western Hemisphere. These hemispheres are separated by another imaginary line called the prime meridian. You will read more about the prime meridian in the skills lesson beginning on page 42.

1. Name two things you can learn about the earth from looking at a globe.
2. What is a continent? Name two continents that border on the Atlantic Ocean.
3. What does the word *hemisphere* mean?
4. What is the equator?
5. In which two hemispheres can North America be found?

Using Maps

Key Vocabulary

compass rose	symbol
cardinal directions	map key
intermediate directions	scale

Maps are drawings that show all or part of the earth's surface. Maps are very useful. A map, unlike a globe, can show the whole earth at one time.

Compass Rose and Directions

How can you find directions on a map? Many maps have a **compass rose**. A compass rose is a small drawing with lines showing directions.

North, east, south, and west are the **cardinal directions**, or main directions. Look at the compass rose on the map of the United States. The letters N, E, S, and W stand for the cardinal directions.

The compass rose also has lines that mark **intermediate directions**. Intermediate directions always lie halfway between the cardinal directions. Northeast is the intermediate direction between north and east. The other intermediate directions are southeast, southwest, and northwest. The letters NE, SE, SW, and NW stand for the intermediate directions. Look at the map again. In which direction is Indiana from New Mexico?

Not all maps have a compass rose. Instead, some maps have a north pointer. A north pointer is an arrow that shows which direction is north on a map.

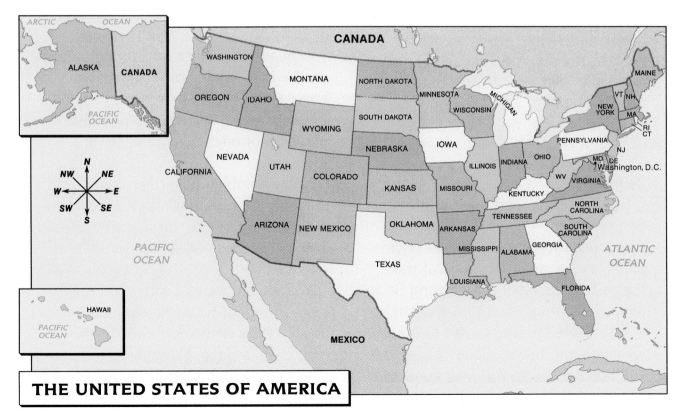

THE UNITED STATES OF AMERICA

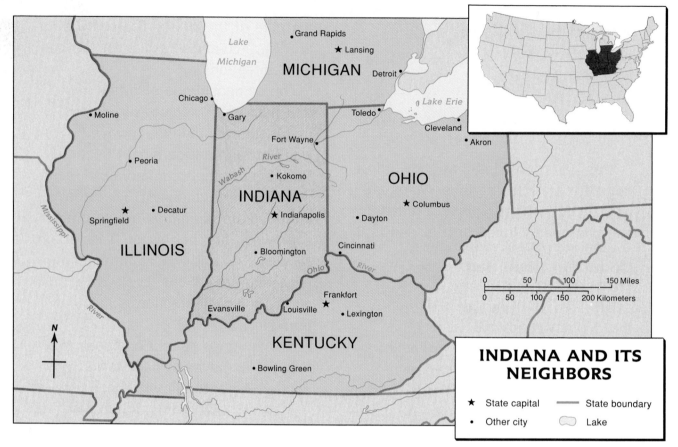

INDIANA AND ITS NEIGHBORS

★ State capital   ── State boundary

• Other city   ⬭ Lake

If you know where north is, you can easily find all the other directions. Look at the map titled "Indiana and Its Neighbors." In which direction is Ohio from Indiana? In which direction is Chicago, Illinois, from Fort Wayne, Indiana?

Symbols

Symbols are used to give information on maps. A symbol is anything that stands for something else. Symbols may be small drawings of the things they represent. A drawing of an airplane is often used to represent an airport. Dots are often used to stand for cities and towns. Color is also used as a symbol. You may know that blue is usually a symbol for water.

Map Keys

To understand, or "read," a map, you must know what the symbols used on the map represent. Most maps have a map key. The map key, sometimes called a legend, explains the meaning of each symbol used on the map.

Some symbols have the same meaning on different maps. For example, ★ often stands for a state capital. The symbol • often stands for another city or town.

You should always check the map key to find out what the symbols used on that map represent. Look at the map on this page. What does the star stand for? What does the gray line stand for?

Scale

Maps do not show sizes and distances as they really are. To show real sizes and distances, maps would have to be as large as the part of the earth they show. Maps can, however, give you a very accurate idea of what the real sizes and distances are.

They do this by having short distances, such as inches or centimeters, represent much larger distances, such as miles or kilometers. Scale is the relationship between the distances shown on the map and the real distances on the earth.

In this book map scale is shown by two lines, the top one for miles and the bottom one for kilometers. Look at the map on this page. The map's scale shows you that 1 inch on the map represents 80 miles on the earth. Two centimeters on the map represent 100 kilometers on the earth.

You can use a ruler to measure the distance between two places on a map. Another way to measure distances on a map is with a scale strip. To make a scale strip, use the map scale on the map of Indiana as a guide. Take a strip of paper with a straight edge. Place the paper below both scale lines and, moving the strip along, mark the distances. Your strip might look like this:

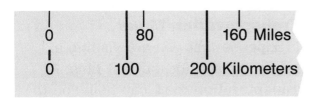

Now use the scale strip to find the distance between South Bend and Bloomington. The map key shows that a black dot stands for cities. Place the 0 (zero) edge of the scale strip on the black dot next to South Bend. Then read the number that is closest to Bloomington. You will see that the distance between South Bend and Bloomington is about 180 miles (290 km).

1. Why is a compass rose useful?
2. Name the four cardinal and the four intermediate directions.
3. What is the difference between a compass rose and a north pointer?
4. What does a map key explain on a map?
5. What do map scales show?

13

Different Kinds of Maps

Key Vocabulary

grid map

transportation map

There are many different kinds of maps. Some maps show continents, oceans, countries, or states. Other maps can help travelers to find their way. Each kind of map is useful and can help you to better understand the places you are studying.

Map Titles

When you use a map, first look at the map title. The title tells you what is shown on the map. It may also tell you the kind of information that is shown on the map. What is the title of the map on this page?

Grid Maps

Grids make it easier to find places on the map. A grid map is made up of two sets of lines that cross each other to make squares. One set of lines crosses the map from left to right. The spaces between these lines are marked with letters. The other set of lines crosses the map from top to bottom. The spaces between these lines are marked with numbers. Each square on the map can be identified by its letter and number. This makes it easy to find places on the map or to give their locations.

Look at the grid map on this page. You can find Fort Wayne easily if you

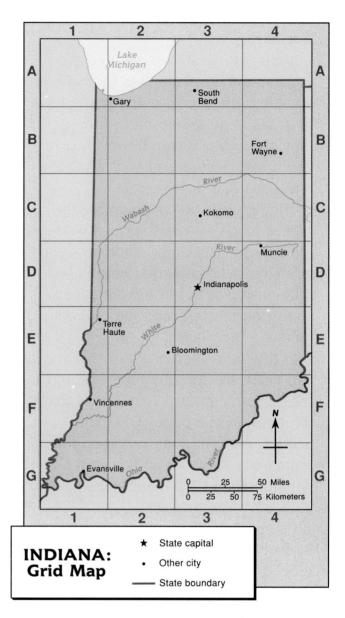

INDIANA: Grid Map

★ State capital

• Other city

— State boundary

know that it is located in square B-4. What is the letter and number of the square in which Terre Haute is located? What is the letter and number of the square in which Kokomo is located?

Transportation Maps

Suppose that you are visiting a city in Indiana for the first time. A transportation map can help you to

14

find your way around. A transportation map shows the different ways you can travel from one place to another. Different kinds of transportation maps may show roads and railroad, subway, or bus routes.

Look at the map of the METRO on this page. The METRO is the name of the transportation system in Indianapolis. This map shows major roads and bus routes in downtown Indianapolis. If you live in or ever visit Indianapolis, this map might help you to get to the many interesting sites in our state's capital.

The map key shows that the green line stands for express bus routes and the red line stands for local bus routes. The black circles and black squares show where the buses stop.

Describe one route you might take from the City County Building to the State Capitol. What route would you take from the State Museum to the State Office Buildings?

1. What is a transportation map?
2. Look at the map on page 14. In which square is Muncie located?
3. Describe a bus route you might take from Senate Avenue to the Market Square Arena.
4. Why do you think there are so many different kinds of maps?

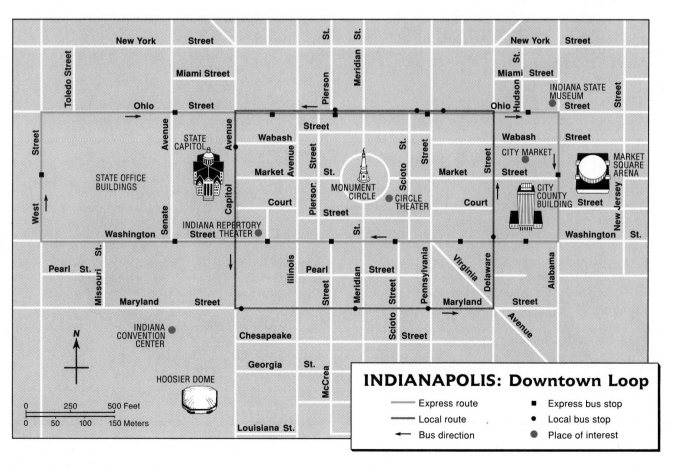

INDIANAPOLIS: Downtown Loop

—— Express route	■ Express bus stop
—— Local route	● Local bus stop
← Bus direction	● Place of interest

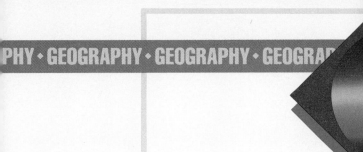

UNIT 1

STUDYING INDIANA

WHERE WE ARE

The state that we call home is in the part of the United States known as the Middle West. In our state you can walk in the sand at Dunes State Park, hike through the woods in Hoosier National Forest, cheer for the racers in the Indy 500, and much more. Let's find out about Indiana—its land and its people.

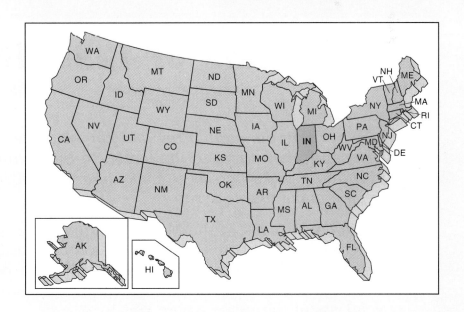

17

CHAPTER 1

THE LAND OF INDIANA

FOCUS

I gather walnuts so that my dad can grow new trees and plant them in the forest. In the summer our family picks berries to make jam, and in February we make maple syrup.

Susie Lauck lives in the Martin County State Forest, near Shoals, where her father is a forest ranger. When Susie thinks about Indiana's geography, her first thoughts are of trees and rolling hills. What is special about the place where you live?

1 Indiana's Three Regions

READ TO LEARN

Key Vocabulary

landform
geography
natural feature
sand dune
region

Lake Michigan
Wabash River
Ohio River

Read Aloud

Lovely are the fields and meadows,
That reach out to hills that rise
Where the dreamy Wabash River
Wanders on through paradise.

These words are from Indiana's state poem, "Indiana." In a beautiful and poetic way, they describe two wonderful things about our state: its land and its water. In this lesson you will read about three different parts of Indiana and how the land and water vary in each of these parts of our state.

Read for Purpose

1. **WHAT YOU KNOW:** What is the land like in the area where you live?
2. **WHAT YOU WILL LEARN:** What are the major geographical features of Indiana?

INDIANA AND ITS NEIGHBORS

Indiana is one of the 50 states that make up our country. Turn to the map on page 11 in the Reviewing Maps and Globes section. It shows that Indiana is located in the middle part of the United States. How would you describe the shape of our state?

The map on page 12 shows our neighboring states. Ohio is located to the east of Indiana, and Illinois is

These three views show how different Indiana can look. Which view looks most familiar to you?

located to the west. Michigan is our northern neighbor, and Kentucky is our southern neighbor.

Among the 50 states, Indiana is ranked thirty-eighth in land area. Although it is not one of the largest states, Indiana is certainly one of the most beautiful. Let's take a closer look at our land.

DIFFERENT VIEWS OF INDIANA

Benita Clarkson, Jason Miller, and Darlene Burns are friends. They come from different parts of Indiana. Benita lives in Gary, Jason's home is in Kokomo, and Darlene is from New Albany.

Recently Benita, Jason, and Darlene were asked these questions: What does Indiana's land look like? What kinds of lakes and rivers are in our state?

"That's easy," said Benita. "Indiana has sand hills and a huge lake."

Jason shook his head. "That's not right. Indiana's land is flat with small rivers weaving through it."

"You're both wrong," said Darlene. "Indiana has rolling hills and a long, winding river."

Which person do you think is right?

INDIANA'S GEOGRAPHY

Benita, Jason, and Darlene are all correct. Indiana has all the different kinds of land and water they described and more.

Look at the map on this page. It shows the landforms of our state. Landforms are shapes that make up the earth's surface. Mountains, hills, plains, and plateaus (pla tōz') are some common landforms.

The map also shows that the northwestern part of our state is located next to Lake Michigan. The sand hills that Benita spoke of can be found along Lake Michigan.

The flat land and small rivers that Jason talked about are found in the middle of our state. Here you will also find part of the Wabash River—Indiana's longest river.

Darlene talked about the southern part of Indiana. Here you will find rolling hills and a long, winding river, called the Ohio River.

All these landforms are important parts of Indiana's geography (jē og' rə fē). Geography is the study of the earth's land and water, and of its plants and animals. It also includes the study of the ways of life of the people who live on and use the land.

NATURAL FEATURES

Land and water are two kinds of natural features that make up our state's geography. Natural features are those parts of the earth that are

MAP SKILL: Indiana's land is made up of three types of landforms. Which landform covers most of our state?

made by nature. Rivers, forests, and mountains are examples of natural features. We would not call buildings or bridges natural features because they are made by people.

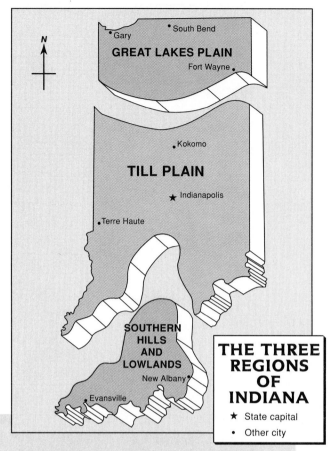

THE THREE
REGIONS
OF
INDIANA

★ State capital
• Other city

MAP SKILL: In which of Indiana's regions is the state capital located? In which region is Gary located?

area with common features that set it apart from other areas.

In our state there are three separate physical regions: the Great Lakes Plain, the Till Plain, and the Southern Hills and Lowlands. Benita lives in the Great Lakes Plain, the northernmost region. Jason lives in the Till Plain. The Till Plain is in the middle of our state.

Find the Southern Hills and Lowlands region on the map on this page. Darlene's home is in this region of Indiana.

THE HOOSIER STATE

The Great Lakes Plain, the Till Plain, and the Southern Hills and Lowlands have natural features that make each region's geography special. All these features make the Hoosier state one of great beauty.

Check Your Reading

1. What is geography?
2. What is a natural feature? Give two examples of natural features found in Indiana?
3. Name the three regions of Indiana. In what part of the state is each region found?
4. **GEOGRAPHY SKILL:** Which of Indiana's regions is located next to Lake Michigan?
5. **THINKING SKILL:** Think about the region where you live. List three natural features that are found there.

Benita talked about hills of sand found near Lake Michigan. She was talking about a natural feature called a sand dune. Sand dunes are hills of sand that are shaped by the wind. A sand dune is another example of a landform.

THE REGIONS OF INDIANA

When Benita, Jason, and Darlene talked about Indiana, each one described the natural features of her or his region. A region is a large

2 The Great Lakes Plain

READ TO LEARN

Key Vocabulary

plain
glacier
till
moraine
basin

Key Places

Great Lakes
Indiana Dunes State Park
St. Joseph River
St. Marys River

Read Aloud

Lakes, streams, and springs are . . . plenty. In the grove where I have built there is an abundance of [many] *crab apple, plum, and cherry trees. . . .*

This is how Solon Robinson described northwestern Indiana. Robinson was a farmer, traveler, and writer. During the 1830s he often wrote about living in the Great Lakes Plain. In this lesson you will read more about the many "lakes, streams, and springs" in this region.

Read for Purpose

1. **WHAT YOU KNOW:** Which water activities do people who live near Lake Michigan enjoy during the summer months?
2. **WHAT YOU WILL LEARN:** What is special about the geography of the Great Lakes Plain?

NAMING THE GREAT LAKES PLAIN

Do you remember in which region Benita Clarkson lives? It is the Great Lakes Plain. This region has "Great Lakes" as part of its name because it borders Lake Michigan, one of the five Great Lakes.

If the Great Lakes were combined, they would make up the largest body of fresh water in the world. The water in all of these lakes could cover the United States with a flood that would measure 10 feet (3 m) in depth. That's more than twice the height of most fourth graders.

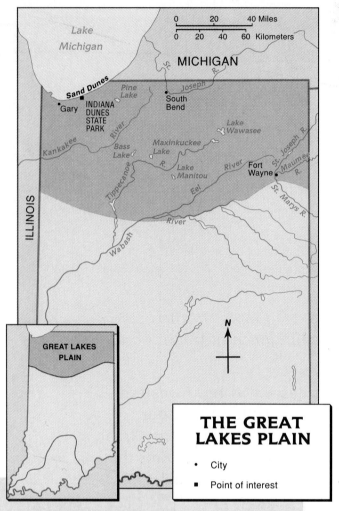

THE GREAT LAKES PLAIN

- • City
- ▪ Point of interest

MAP SKILL: What major city is found closest to Lake Michigan?

An easy way to remember the names of the Great Lakes is to remember that the first letters of their names spell the word *HOMES*: *H*uron, *O*ntario, *M*ichigan, *E*rie, and *S*uperior.

The Great Lakes Plain is also named after a landform. A **plain** is a large area of flat or gently rolling land. Look at the map on this page. How much of Indiana is covered by this plain?

Indiana's geography did not always look the way it does today. Natural forces changed the land. An important change occurred when **glaciers** (glā′ shərz), or huge, moving masses of ice, traveled over the land we now call Indiana.

GLACIERS SHAPED THE LAND

Glaciers moved south from Canada. Find Canada in the Atlas on page 288. As the glaciers moved through northern Indiana, they flattened the hilly land.

Like giant bulldozers, the glaciers scooped up rocks, gravel, clay, and dirt. When the glaciers melted, they left these substances, or **till**, behind. Till filled in land that was low or uneven and made the Great Lakes Plain flat.

Sometimes till formed into huge piles or mounds. We call these piles of till **moraines** (mə rānz′). In the Great Lakes Plain there are moraines 100 miles (160 km) long and 500 feet (150 m) thick. Look at Lake Michigan on the map on this page. The rounded southern tip of the lake is shaped by moraines.

HOW THE GREAT LAKES WERE FORMED

Sometimes glaciers carved out deep **basins**. A basin is a low, bowl-shaped area. When the glaciers melted, the basins filled with water and became lakes. This is how the Great Lakes were formed.

24

Along parts of the shores of the Great Lakes, melted glaciers left behind large mounds of sand. In Lesson 1 you read that sand dunes are found along Lake Michigan. In 1925 Indiana Dunes State Park was opened to the public. This park has trails that run through the vast dunes, which many people enjoy.

RIVERS

In addition to creating lakes, glaciers also formed rivers. As the glaciers melted, rushing water wore away land and created riverbeds.

Many rivers flow throughout the Great Lakes Plain today. You can see some of them on the map on page 24. These rivers add great beauty to this region of our state. They also help the region in an important way.

Rivers provide water for farms in the Great Lakes Plain. Rich farmland lies along the St. Joseph River and along the St. Marys River. For many years farmers have raised dairy cattle and grown such crops as corn and beans.

NORTHERN LAKE COUNTRY

Glaciers played an important role in shaping the beauty of the Great Lakes Plain. Today much of northern Indiana is dotted with small lakes that were also made by melted glaciers. It is no wonder that this region is also called the "Northern Lake Country."

The Great Lakes Plain offers a variety of activities for Hoosiers.

 Check Your Reading

1. Why is the northern part of Indiana called the Great Lakes Plain?
2. What is a glacier?
3. How did glaciers help shape the geography of the Great Lakes Plain?
4. GEOGRAPHY SKILL: Look at the map on page 24. Near which natural features are most of the region's cities located?
5. THINKING SKILL: How do you think your life might change if the earth's climate suddenly became much warmer?

Reading Elevation Maps

Key Vocabulary
elevation

In the last lesson you read about the land and regions of our state. You learned that Indiana has many different kinds of land. The landform map on page 21 shows this land. In this lesson we will look at another kind of map.

Landforms
You know that the surface of the earth is not flat. It varies in shape from place to place. The many different shapes that make up the earth's surface are called landforms.

In Lesson 1 you read about the different landforms found in Indiana. Hills are landforms that are lower and less rugged than mountains. Sand dunes are landforms that are shaped into hills by the wind. Plains are large areas of flat or gently rolling land.

Hills, sand dunes, and plains are just some of the earth's major landforms. The map on page 21 shows that all of these landforms are found in our state. Which kind of landform is found throughout the central part of Indiana?

Elevation
Landform maps help you to see how the land varies from one part of our state to another. But they do not show how high the hills are or how low the plains are. They do not show anything about elevation (el ə vā′ shən). Elevation is the height of land above sea level. It is measured in feet or in meters. Elevation at sea level is 0 feet (0 m).

An Elevation Map
Look at the map on the next page. It is an elevation map of Indiana. How is this map different from the landform map on page 21?

Like a landform map, an elevation map uses different colors to show different areas of land. But the colors of an elevation map only show how high the land is. They do not show what kind of land it is.

Using an Elevation Map
Look at the elevation map key. Which color is used to show elevations between 400 feet (120 m) and 1,000 feet (300 m)? Which range in elevation is shown by the color yellow?

As you can see, elevation maps can be very useful in showing many things about an area of land. They show where the land is highest, where it is lowest, and how it changes in different places. They also show where mountains are found. What does this elevation map tell you about the land of Indiana?

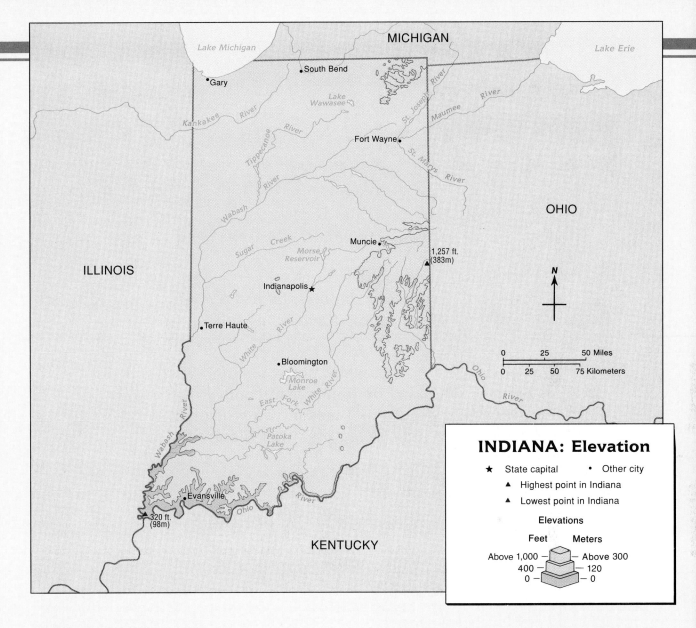

INDIANA: Elevation

★ State capital • Other city
▲ Highest point in Indiana
▲ Lowest point in Indiana

Elevations

Feet	Meters
Above 1,000	Above 300
400	120
0	0

Reviewing the Skill

Use the map above and the information in this lesson to help you to answer these questions.

1. What is the main difference between a landform map and an elevation map?

2. Is Muncie at a higher or lower elevation than Evansville?

3. Which cities shown on the map have an elevation of between 400 feet (120 m) and 1,000 feet (300 m)?

4. Where is the lowest point of elevation in Indiana? Where is the highest point of elevation in Indiana?

5. If you were to travel from Bloomington to Evansville by car, would you be traveling mostly uphill or mostly downhill?

6. Why is it helpful to be able to read an elevation map?

3 The Till Plain

READ TO LEARN

Key Vocabulary

fertile   tributary
source   fork
mouth

Key Places

Terre Haute
White River
East Fork White River

Read Aloud

The husky, rusty russel of the tossels of the corn,
And the raspin' of the tangled leaves, as golden as
the morn. . . .

These lines are from a well-known poem, "When the Frost Is on the Punkin" by James Whitcomb Riley, a famous Hoosier poet. In this lesson you will read about some of the natural features that inspired him as he wrote his poetry.

Read for Purpose

1. **WHAT YOU KNOW:** In which region of Indiana do you live?
2. **WHAT YOU WILL LEARN:** What is special about the geography of the Till Plain?

NAMING THE TILL PLAIN

One feature of the Till Plain that may have inspired Riley's poetry is the flatness of the land. This is how one Hoosier student once described the Till Plain.

The traveler may ride upon the railroad train for hours without seeing a greater elevation than a haystack or a pile of sawdust.

This region is named the Till Plain because it is made up of thick, flat till. As you read in Lesson 2, till is a layer of rocks, gravel, clay, and soil left behind by melted glaciers. It is easy for farmers to grow large amounts of crops on the flat land in this region.

The soil that glaciers left behind long ago is very fertile (fûr' təl). This means that the soil is good for

growing crops. Today farmers use this fertile soil to grow large crops of corn, soybeans, wheat, and oats. Together, the flat land and fertile soil make it possible for farmers to grow food that is shipped to people all over the world.

THE WABASH RIVER

In Lesson 2 you read that long ago melting glaciers formed rivers. The Wabash River is one of many rivers that run like silver ribbons throughout the Till Plain. Our state song, "On the Banks of the Wabash," tells about its beauty.

The Wabash is the longest river in Indiana. Find the Wabash River on the map on this page. Trace its path through our state. Then look at the bar graph on page 30. It shows the five longest rivers in our state. Which of these rivers is closest to your home?

The source of the Wabash is in western Ohio. A river's source is the place where it begins. From its

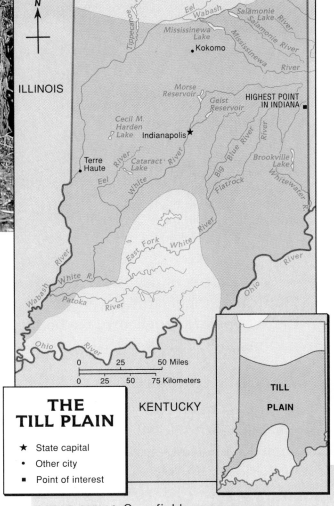

MAP SKILL: Corn fields are very common in the Till Plain. Name three of the region's rivers.

source, the Wabash River flows southwest across our state for 475 miles (764 km). Just south of Terre Haute, the Wabash forms the border between Indiana and Illinois.

From the map on this page, you can see that the mouth of the Wabash is found at the southwestern tip of Indiana. The mouth is the place where a river empties into another body of water.

29

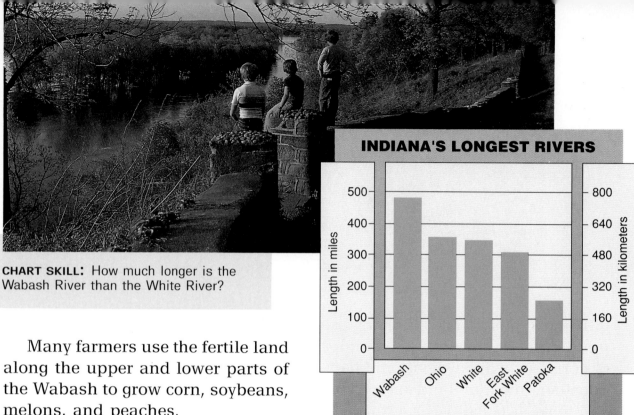

CHART SKILL: How much longer is the Wabash River than the White River?

INDIANA'S LONGEST RIVERS

Length in miles: 0, 100, 200, 300, 400, 500

Length in kilometers: 0, 160, 320, 480, 640, 800

Wabash, Ohio, White, East Fork White, Patoka

Figures represent river's lengths within Indiana.

Many farmers use the fertile land along the upper and lower parts of the Wabash to grow corn, soybeans, melons, and peaches.

TRIBUTARIES OF THE WABASH

There are various small rivers in the Till Plain that flow into the Wabash River. A stream or small river that flows into a larger river is called a tributary (trib′ yə ter ē).

The map on page 29 shows some of the tributaries of the Wabash River. One tributary is the White River. It begins in eastern Indiana and flows southwest. Near Petersburg the river branches, or forms a fork. This branch is called the East Fork White River. Thousands of acres of land all along the banks of the White River are used for farming.

THE HEARTLAND

The Till Plain is found in the center, or heart, of our state. As you have read, the flat, fertile land of the heartland makes it a perfect farming region. In the next lesson you will read about the Southern Hills and Lowlands.

Check Your Reading

1. Which substances left by glaciers help farmers grow crops in our state?
2. What is the source of a river? What is the mouth?
3. GEOGRAPHY SKILL: Look at the map on page 29. Name two tributaries of the Wabash.
4. THINKING SKILL: How do you think life in our state would be different if the soil that glaciers left behind was not fertile?

4 Southern Hills and Lowlands

READ TO LEARN

Key Vocabulary

silt   limestone
sinkholes   erosion

Key Places

Wabash Lowland
Whitewater River
Lost River

Read Aloud

As we left the valley . . . I could well grasp the painter's desire to live and paint in this region. . . .

Theodore Steele, a famous Hoosier painter, said this about the southern region of our state. He felt that many artists like him would come here to work. In this lesson you will read how the landforms in southern Indiana differ from those of the other regions.

Read for Purpose

1. **WHAT YOU KNOW:** Which beautiful place in your region might an author describe or an artist like to paint?
2. **WHAT YOU WILL LEARN:** What is special about the geography of the Southern Hills and Lowlands?

NAMING THE SOUTHERN HILLS AND LOWLANDS

You have read about how glaciers shaped the geography of our state. Glaciers flattened the hills that once covered the Great Lakes Plain and the Till Plain. However, glaciers never reached much of southern Indiana. They melted, leaving the hills untouched. For many years painters like Theodore Steele have captured the beauty of these tree-covered rolling hills.

Not all of southern Indiana is hilly. This region also has valleys and plains. In Lesson 3 you read about the Wabash River. As the Wabash flows across our state, it picks up silt from the Till Plain. Silt is tiny bits of soil picked up and then deposited by the water in rivers and streams.

SOUTHERN HILLS AND LOWLANDS

- • City
- ■ Point of interest
- Hoosier National Forest

MAP SKILL: These beautiful sights can all be found in southern Indiana. Which two rivers border the Wabash Lowland?

The Wabash leaves silt along the river valley in the southwestern part of our state. This area is called the Wabash Lowland. Find the Wabash Lowland on the map on this page. Because the silt of the Wabash Lowland is picked up from the Till Plain, it is very fertile. This silt makes the land in the Wabash Lowland the most fertile farmland in southern Indiana.

Another important river that carries silt to surrounding lands is the Whitewater River. The Whitewater has two forks, the east and west forks. The river flows close to In-diana's border with Ohio in the southeastern part of our state.

THE MYSTERY RIVER

Many rivers wind through the Southern Hills and Lowlands. One of the most interesting rivers in this region is the Lost River. The Lost River flows for miles and then, as if by magic, it suddenly disappears.

Actually the river "disappears" into sinkholes. Sinkholes are holes worn in rock by water. In just 1 square mile (2.6 sq km) of the Lost River valley, there are over 1,022 sinkholes. When the river flows over all these sinkholes, the water swirls down into each one like water draining from a bathtub.

These photos show the Lost River in southern Indiana. How do you think it got its name?

EROSION CAUSES SINKHOLES

Sinkholes are often found in a type of rock called limestone. The sinkholes found in limestone are caused by erosion. Erosion is the slow wearing away of rock and soil by water, wind, or ice.

The water erosion that takes place in the limestone bed of the Lost River causes more than small sinkholes to form. Over thousands of years, erosion also carves out large underground caves and tunnels.

As the Lost River disappears into the many sinkholes, it flows through these underground tunnels. Eventually the water bursts back to the surface in a bubbling spring.

A VARIED STATE

Benita Clarkson, Jason Miller, and Darlene Burns each described our state differently. Throughout this book you will read about how Indiana's varied geography plays an important role in our lives.

Check Your Reading

1. What effect did glaciers have on landforms in southern Indiana?
2. Why do farmers value the land in the Wabash Lowland?
3. What is erosion?
4. **GEOGRAPHY SKILL:** Why is the Lost River different from other rivers in our state?
5. **THINKING SKILL:** Compare the geography of the Southern Hills and Lowlands with that of the Great Lakes Plain.

THE "Smokey Lady"

With a ranger's hat and shovel
And a pair of dungarees
You can find him in the forest
Always sniffin' at the breeze.

People stop and pay attention
When he tells them to beware.
That's why they call him Smokey—
He's the fire preventin' bear.

Beverly Stout, an Indiana forester, has sung these words about Smokey the Bear more times than she can remember. Stout refers to Smokey the Bear often when she talks to school and civic groups about preventing forest fires. During her programs, Stout may wear the Smokey costume and play the role of Smokey the Bear. In fact, students often call her the "Smokey Lady."

Stout helps her audiences understand that "we have to protect the forests needed to make wood products and prevent the loss of homes for wildlife." She has won many awards for her work, including a top national honor, the Bronze Smokey. She entertains groups as she explains the serious "Do's and Don'ts" of fire prevention.

Fires can start naturally, or they can be caused by carelessness. Lightning is one natural cause of forest fires. But others start because people forget to put out cigarettes or campfires. When a fire breaks out, Stout will work with other Indiana foresters. Sometimes she volunteers to fight fires in other states.

Fighting a forest fire is dangerous, difficult work. Firefighters may have to dig a ditch around the fire, rake up leaves, or chop down brush to keep the flames from spreading.

Stout spends many hours beyond her working day at the fire headquarters of the Morgan-Monroe State Forest trying to prevent fires before they start. Everywhere she goes, she spreads Smokey the Bear's message: "Only you can prevent forest fires."

REVIEWING VOCABULARY

erosion	plain	till
geography	silt	tributary
glacier	sinkhole	
mouth	source	

Number a sheet of paper from 1 to 10. Beside each number write the word from the list above that best matches the definition.

1. The study of the earth's land and water, its plants and animals
2. An area of flat or rolling land
3. A huge, moving mass of ice
4. The rocks, gravel, clay, and dirt that a melting glacier left behind
5. The place where a river begins
6. The place where a river empties into another body of water
7. A stream or small river that flows into a larger river
8. Tiny bits of soil deposited by water
9. A hole in rock made by water
10. The slow wearing away of rock and soil by water, wind, or ice

REVIEWING FACTS

1. What are the three regions of our state?
2. How were the Great Lakes formed?
3. What is the soil like on the Till Plain?
4. What is Indiana's longest river?
5. What region is also known as the Northern Lake Country?

WRITING ABOUT MAIN IDEAS

1. **Writing a Descriptive Paragraph:** Write a paragraph that describes the geography of the part of Indiana in which you live.
2. **Writing a Travel Booklet:** Travel booklets are written to make people want to visit an area. Write about your favorite part of our state. Be sure your booklet tells why people might enjoy visiting that area.
3. **Writing a List:** Make a list of the bodies of water that you have seen in our state.

BUILDING SKILLS: READING ELEVATION MAPS

Use the map on page 27 to answer these questions.

1. What is the difference between what is shown on a landform map and what is shown on an elevation map?
2. Is Evansville at a higher elevation or lower elevation than Gary?
3. Name another city with about the same elevation as Bloomington.
4. What could an elevation map of Indiana teach someone who has never visited our state before?

CHAPTER 2

INDIANA'S CLIMATE AND RESOURCES

FOCUS

The weather in Indiana is very different from the weather in Mexico. I like the change of seasons here and the snow. Playing in the snow is fun.

Julio Amador moved to Indianapolis from Mexico two years ago. Recently he visited the weather station at the Indianapolis International Airport to learn more about weather. In this chapter you will read about how the weather affects life in our state.

1 Indiana's Climate

READ TO LEARN

Key Vocabulary

weather   precipitation   tornado

climate   humidity   growing season

temperature

Read Aloud

One morning it was snowing; one of [those] heavy wet snows that sticks to the trees and everything else it falls on. Things [were pretty] white when we started out, but we noticed that the trail was getting harder to see all the time.

These words were spoken by a young boy who lived in Indiana many years ago. The snowstorm kept him and his sister from getting to school that day. Natural forces like snow, rain, and wind can keep us from doing things that we want to do. But they also help our lives in important ways, as you will read in this lesson.

Read for Purpose

1. **WHAT YOU KNOW:** How would you describe the worst storm you remember? How would you describe a "perfect" summer day?
2. **WHAT YOU WILL LEARN:** How does the climate of Indiana affect our lives?

WEATHER PATTERNS

One July day in 1936 the people of Jasper County sweated through 116°F. (47°C) weather. Barely two weeks later, they woke up to find frost on the ground!

Clearly, Indiana's weather can change quickly. The weather is how hot, cold, wet, or dry a place is. Weather can change from hour to hour, or day to day.

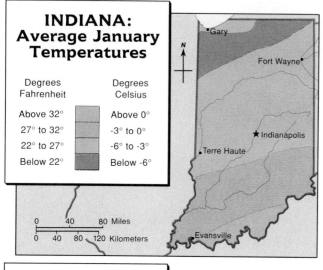

INDIANA: Average January Temperatures

Degrees Fahrenheit | Degrees Celsius
Above 32° | Above 0°
27° to 32° | -3° to 0°
22° to 27° | -6° to -3°
Below 22° | Below -6°

Gary
Fort Wayne
★ Indianapolis
Terre Haute
Evansville

0   40   80 Miles
0 40 80 120 Kilometers

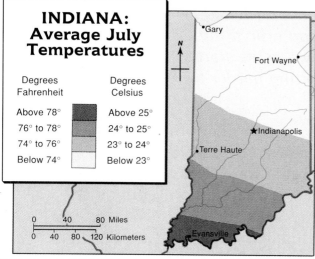

INDIANA: Average July Temperatures

Degrees Fahrenheit | Degrees Celsius
Above 78° | Above 25°
76° to 78° | 24° to 25°
74° to 76° | 23° to 24°
Below 74° | Below 23°

Gary
Fort Wayne
★ Indianapolis
Terre Haute
Evansville

0   40   80 Miles
0 40 80 120 Kilometers

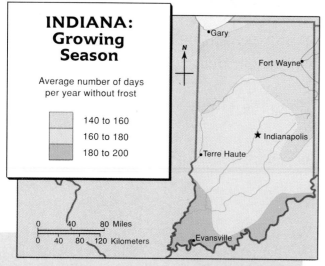

INDIANA: Growing Season

Average number of days per year without frost

140 to 160
160 to 180
180 to 200

Gary
Fort Wayne
★ Indianapolis
Terre Haute
Evansville

0   40   80 Miles
0 40 80 120 Kilometers

MAP SKILL: How long is Terre Haute's growing season each year?

OUR STATE'S CLIMATE

Even though Indiana's weather changes every day, it follows a pattern over a long period of time. We call this pattern climate. Our climate pattern changes with each of the four seasons: winter, spring, summer, and fall.

Our state's climate is almost the same as that of most of the states that are located across the middle of the nation. Winters are not as harsh as in states farther north. There are not often long, intense periods of heat as there are in the South.

TEMPERATURE

Why are some places very cold and others very hot? Temperature (tem′ pər ə chər) is affected by how far a place is from the equator. It is also affected by how high or low a place is from the level of the sea. Temperature is how cold or hot the air is in a place. Temperatures in Indiana can be very hot and very cold.

Look at the world map on page 9. Places along the equator get the full force of the sun's rays. Those farther away get weaker rays. Since Indiana is a long way from the equator, we have a colder climate than southern states.

Look at the climate maps on this page. They will show the average temperature where you live. What is the average temperature in January? In July?

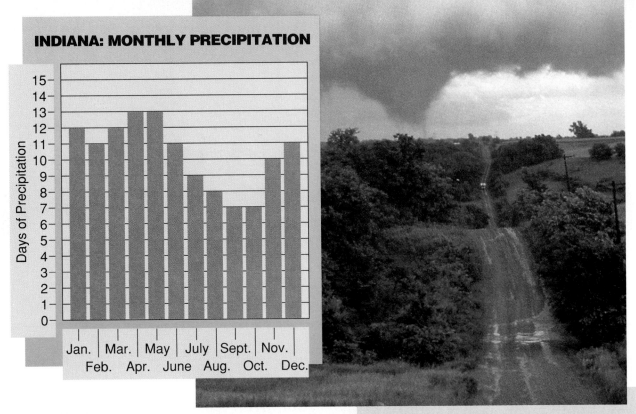

INDIANA: MONTHLY PRECIPITATION

Days of Precipitation

Jan. Feb. Mar. Apr. May June July Aug. Sept. Oct. Nov. Dec.

PRECIPITATION

Another important part of Indiana's climate is its precipitation (pri sip i tā′ shən). Precipitation is any form of water, usually snow or rain, that falls to the earth.

As you can see from the precipitation graph on this page, Indiana has about 11 days of precipitation in June. Phoenix, Arizona, by contrast, has only about 1 day of precipitation in June. Indiana gets just enough precipitation for farmers to grow corn and other crops.

Even when there is little rain or snow, there still can be a great deal of humidity in the air. Humidity is moisture, or dampness, in the air. When humidity is high in the summer, the air seems warmer.

GRAPH SKILL: Indiana's weather varies greatly throughout our state. The chart shows how many days of precipitation occur each month. Which months have the most precipitation?

During the summer the central region of Indiana is usually hot and humid. But such weather does not last long. Usually cooler air with less humidity moves in from the north during the fall.

WIND PATTERNS

"Quick Dorothy!" she screamed. "Run for the cellar!" Dorothy caught Toto . . . and started to follow her aunt. . . . There came a great shriek from the wind, and the house shook so hard that she lost her footing. . . .

These words describe what happened to Dorothy when a **tornado** struck her home in the book *The Wizard of Oz*. A tornado, often called a twister, is a dangerous storm that whirls in a dark cloud shaped like a funnel. Tornadoes can harm people and animals and do great damage to buildings.

Tornadoes are only one example of the wind patterns that Indiana experiences. For example, in the northwestern part of our state, winds blow directly across Lake Michigan for most of the year. This creates what is commonly known as "lake-effect" weather.

Winters along the shores of Lake Michigan are usually a little warmer than in other northern regions of the state. This fact is due to the "lake effect."

Most winds over Indiana come from the west. Sometimes during the summer or spring months, western winds sweep far south and bring warm air toward Indiana and other states in the Middle West. When this happens, warm air hits cold air that has come from the far north.

Such mixtures of cold and warm air often make thunderstorms. In turn, tornadoes can form during thunderstorms. Since warm, humid western winds and chilly northern winds often mix over Indiana, thunderstorms and tornadoes often happen in our state.

CLIMATE AFFECTS PEOPLE

You read in the beginning of this lesson that snowstorms can keep us from doing things. Other kinds of weather and climate also affect us. Floods caused mainly by heavy rain may damage homes, roads, and farmland in the winter and spring. But when there is not enough precipitation, crops may fail. Farmers depend on the weather in a special way. Enough rainfall and sunshine are necessary for them to grow crops.

If you live in northern Indiana, you will probably see more snow this winter than will someone living in the southern part of our state. But the southern region has hotter and more humid summers. Farmers in the south can grow more kinds of

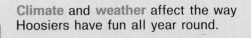

crops because their growing season is longer. A growing season is a period of the year when the weather is warm enough for plants to grow.

Look at the map on page 38. Does Evansville or Fort Wayne have a longer growing season?

A VARIETY OF WEATHER

Even though the weather in Indiana changes from north to south, the climate is similar within each region. Temperature, precipitation, and wind patterns are all important parts of our climate. No matter where you live in Indiana, climate affects your life.

Check Your Reading

1. In what ways is weather different from climate?
2. Why does the land near Lake Michigan have warmer winters than other northern regions of the state?
3. Describe two ways in which climate affects people's lives.
4. **GEOGRAPHY SKILL:** Look at the maps on page 38. Which cities are coldest in January and warmest in July?
5. **THINKING SKILL:** What are three questions that you could ask to learn more about the climate of a region?

41

Understanding Latitude and Longitude

Key Vocabulary

latitude	meridian
parallel	prime meridian
degree	global grid
longitude	

Have you ever tried to describe the location of Indiana to people who have no idea where it is? How would you begin to explain where our state is located? You could identify the states that border Indiana, but how could you be more exact?

Mapmakers thought about this problem hundreds of years ago. They invented a system of imaginary lines on maps and globes to describe a location. Together, these lines provide an "address" for any place on earth. Let's look at how they work.

Lines of Latitude

You already know about one of these imaginary lines—the equator. Look at the map on this page and put your finger on the equator. Notice the other lines of latitude. They run in the same direction as the equator. These lines are called parallels. Parallel lines never meet and are always the same distance apart.

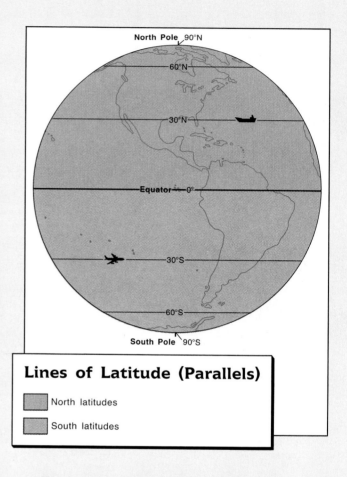

Lines of Latitude (Parallels)

☐ North latitudes

☐ South latitudes

Each line of latitude also has a number. Notice that the equator is labeled 0°, meaning zero degrees. Degrees are used to measure the distance between the lines. The symbol ° stands for degrees. The latitude of the equator is 0°.

Now look at the lines of latitude north of the equator. These parallels are labeled N for "north." The latitude of the North Pole is 90°N. There are 90 degrees north of the equator and there are 90 degrees south of the equator. The parallels south of the equator are labeled *S* for "south." The latitude of the South Pole is 90°S.

Parallels of latitude measure degrees north and south of the equator. But, as the map shows, the parallels run east and west. Find the small ship on the map. The ship is moving west. Along which parallel is it traveling? Now find the small airplane on the map. On which parallel is it traveling? Is the airplane going east or west?

Lines of Longitude

Now look at the map on this page. It shows lines of longitude. These lines are also called meridians. Find the line on the map marked 0°. This line is called the prime meridian. *Prime* means "first." The prime meridian is the first line or starting place for measuring lines of longitude.

Look at the meridians to the west of the prime meridian. These lines are labeled *W* for "west." The lines to the east of the prime meridian are labeled *E* for "east."

Longitude is measured up to 180° east of the prime meridian and up to 180° west of the prime meridian. Since 180° east and 180° west fall on the same line, this line is marked with neither an *E* nor a *W*.

Unlike latitude lines, meridians are not parallel to each other. They are

not always the same distance apart. Look at the map again. As you can see, meridians are far apart at the equator, but they come together to meet at the North Pole and at the South Pole.

Meridian lines measure degrees east and west. But, as the map shows, the meridians themselves run north and south. Look at the ship on the map below. The ship is moving south. Along which meridian is it traveling? In which direction is the airplane on the map traveling?

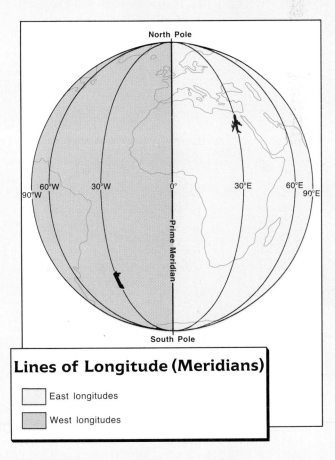

Lines of Longitude (Meridians)

East longitudes

West longitudes

The Global Grid

Together, lines of latitude and lines of longitude form a grid. A grid is a set of crisscrossing lines. The grid on the map below is called a global grid because it covers the whole earth. On this map it is possible to find any place in the world if you know its latitude and longitude.

For example, the "address" of New Orleans can be given as 30°N, 90°W. To find New Orleans on the map below, first put your finger on the point where the equator and the prime meridian cross. Now move your finger north to the parallel labeled 30°N.

Next move your finger west along this parallel to the point where it crosses the meridian labeled 90°W. Did you find New Orleans?

When a place is not exactly at the point at which two lines cross, you have to use the closest lines. For example, look at the map of the United States on page 45. Find the city of Pierre, South Dakota. It is not found at a point where two lines cross. You must find the lines it is closest to on the map. It is closest to 45°N, 100°W. We can say that the "address" of Pierre, South Dakota is about 45°N, 100°W.

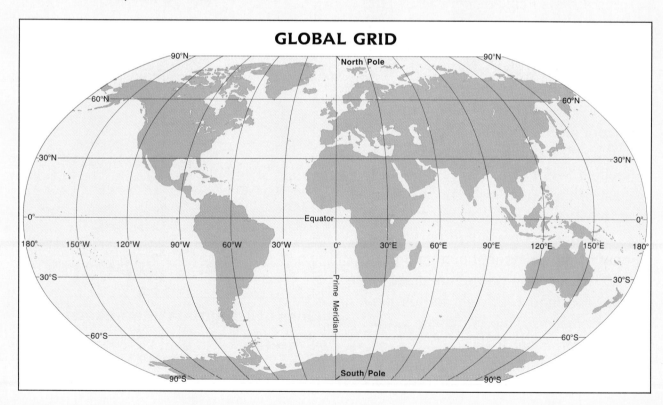

GLOBAL GRID

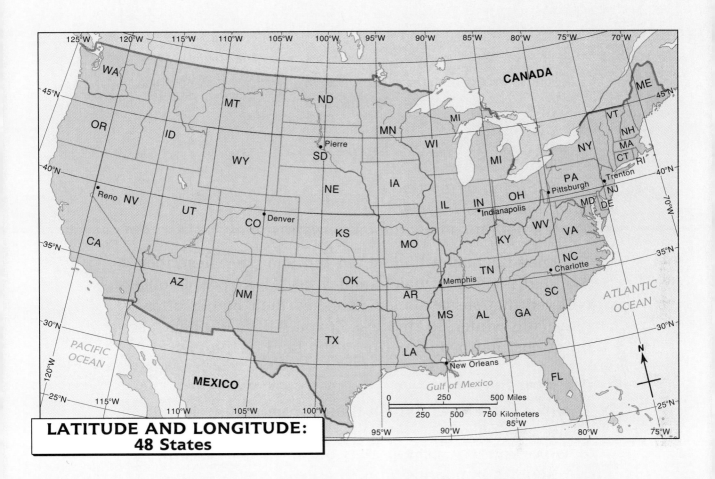

LATITUDE AND LONGITUDE:
48 States

Reviewing the Skill

1. What are lines of latitude and longitude? What do they help you to do?

2. Which line of latitude runs through the state of New Mexico? Which line of longitude?

3. Which city shown on the map is located at 35°N latitude, 90°W longitude?

4. To the nearest degree, what is the latitude and longitude of our state capital?

5. Why is it important to understand latitude and longitude?

2 The Resources of Indiana

Key Vocabulary

natural resources   ground water
minerals   conservation
fuel

Key Places

Hoosier National
Forest

Read Aloud

In the Spring of the year,
when the blood is thick,
There's nothing so good as a sassafras stick.

James Buchanan Elmore, an Indiana poet, described a root that is used to make a spicy tea. Many people once believed that sassafras tea refreshed their bodies after a long, cold winter. In this lesson you will read about useful things that people get from the land of Indiana.

Read for Purpose

1. **WHAT YOU KNOW:** Which things from nature do you use every day?
2. **WHAT YOU WILL LEARN:** Why are Indiana's natural resources important to us?

NATURAL RESOURCES

What do boxes, tape, and paper have in common? They are all made from parts of trees.

Trees are just one example of Indiana's many natural resources. A natural resource is something found in nature that is useful to people. This means that people can use or enjoy things they find in nature. Trees can be used to build furniture that people need. They can also live in a beautiful forest where people camp or hike.

SOIL

Rich soil is one of Indiana's most important natural resources. Farmers use it to grow corn, soybeans, wheat, and other vegetables and grains. They also grow hay and feed for beef cattle and for milk cows.

The rich soil found throughout Indiana is just right for growing corn, the state's biggest crop. Look at the map on this page. Where is corn grown in Indiana?

MINERAL RESOURCES

Indiana's land also contains another valuable natural resource, minerals, which are found in the earth. Coal is a mineral that comes from the remains of dead plants that over millions of years have hardened like rocks.

The map on this page shows that coal is mined, or dug, from the ground in southwestern Indiana. Most Indiana coal is used for fuel. We burn fuel to get heat or energy for factories or homes.

Petroleum (pə trō' lē əm), or oil, and natural gas are two fuels found in the southwestern region of Indiana. Other important mineral resources in the area are gypsum (jip' səm) and limestone. Both of these are used to make cement and many other building materials.

Limestone, which you first read about in Chapter 1, comes from thick deposits of materials that once lay at the bottom of a sea.

It is dug from a quarry, or huge open pit. Most of the limestone used in the United States comes from southern Indiana, as you can see from the map on this page.

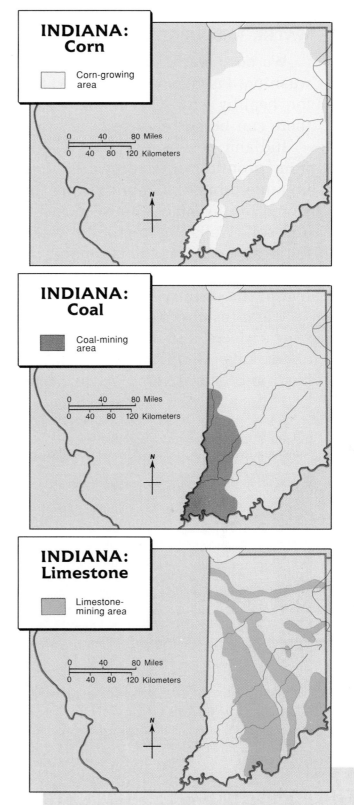

INDIANA: Corn
Corn-growing area
0   40   80 Miles
0   40   80   120 Kilometers
N

INDIANA: Coal
Coal-mining area
0   40   80 Miles
0   40   80   120 Kilometers
N

INDIANA: Limestone
Limestone-mining area
0   40   80 Miles
0   40   80   120 Kilometers
N

MAP SKILL: In which area of Indiana is the most coal found?

47

WATER RESOURCES

We need water for drinking and washing. Farmers depend on water for healthy crops. Without water there can be no life.

Indiana gets some of its water from ground water, or water that is underground. Ground water is stored in tiny spaces between rocks and soil. Wells pump ground water to the surface. It is the main source of drinking water for people who live in the country.

Water resources also include our state's rivers and lakes. You read about Lake Michigan and the Wabash and Ohio rivers. We also use these natural resources for transportation, fishing, and swimming.

FOREST RESOURCES

As you have read, Indiana's trees are also natural resources. Oak, maple, walnut, tulip, and other trees are used to make furniture and other products. How many objects can you find in your classroom that are made of wood?

At one time much of Indiana was covered with forests. But people cut down many trees to plant fields and build things. As a result, there are few large forests left in our state.

Today our government protects trees in state and national forests. Hoosier National Forest in southern Indiana is one example of a forest that the United States government protects. It is the largest forest in Indiana.

HUMAN RESOURCES

Indiana is famous for its rich soil, limestone, and other natural resources. But people need to work with many of these resources before they become useful to us. The people of Indiana are probably our state's biggest natural resource.

Farmers plan how and when to plant their crops. Miners run machines to get coal and limestone out of the ground. Foresters plant trees and protect our forests. People use natural resources in many different and interesting ways.

Indiana's forests are often enjoyed for their beauty.

One of Indiana's most important natural resources is corn. Hoosier farmers produce food for all Americans.

CONSERVING NATURAL RESOURCES

Some natural resources, such as water, can be used more freely than others because nature puts back what we use. Natural resources like coal, however, cannot be reused. Once taken from the earth, minerals, fuels, and other resources cannot be replaced.

As a result more and more people are trying to protect our natural resources. This effort is called conservation. People who practice conservation use natural resources wisely and carefully.

Many farmers work hard to conserve soil. Some plant crops in strips that follow the shape of the land. Others plant new crops between the remains of old ones. Farming methods like these keep soil from being washed or blown away during storms.

RESOURCES FOR THE FUTURE

Soil, minerals, water, and forests are Indiana's greatest natural resources. People are also an important natural resource. Because many natural resources can never be replaced once they are used, it is up to all of us to use our state's resources wisely.

 Check Your Reading

1. What are three natural resources found in Indiana?
2. How do many people in the country get their drinking water?
3. Why is it important to protect our natural resources?
4. GEOGRAPHY SKILL: In which part of Indiana is most of the state's limestone found?
5. THINKING SKILL: How would our state change if most of its soil were to wash or blow away?

READ TO LEARN

Key Vocabulary

monument

Read for Purpose

1. **WHAT YOU KNOW:** What are Indiana's most valuable mineral resources?
2. **WHAT YOU WILL LEARN:** Why is Indiana's limestone important?

INDIANA LIMESTONE

On a hill in southern Indiana, in Lawrence County, lies a cemetery. If you were to walk to the far edge of the cemetery, beyond the row of maple trees, you would find a long, gaping pit. Its sides of solid stone look like a giant staircase. At the bottom of the pit is a mirror-like surface of deep, green water. Heaps of limestone rubble spill into the pit at both ends. Limestone from this pit was used to build the Empire State Building in New York City. For a long time it was the tallest building in the world.

The pit, or quarry, near the cemetery is now abandoned. Hundreds of other abandoned quarries are scattered throughout southern Indiana, especially in Monroe and Lawrence counties. Some quarries are still in operation, producing what many people believe to be the finest limestone in the world for building. The limestone found near Bedford is called Indiana limestone. The quarries in southern Indiana are the only places in

50

The National Cathedral, Pentagon, and Empire State Building are some of our most famous limestone buildings.

the world that produce this strong building stone.

Indiana limestone has been used in buildings and monuments all over our nation. A monument is something that is built in memory of a person or an event. In addition to New York City's Empire State Building, buildings in other major cities were also made with Indiana limestone.

In Washington, D.C., our nation's capital, the National Cathedral is made from Indiana limestone. Just outside Washington, D.C., in Arlington, Virginia, is our country's largest office building—the Pentagon. The Pentagon is the headquarters for the Department of Defense. Imagine how much Indiana limestone was used in constructing a building in which about 23,000 people work. The Baltimore Cathedral, the Chicago Museum of Fine Arts, and Pittsburgh's Mellon Institute are just a few of our country's other famous buildings that were created from the quarries of beautiful southern Indiana.

Limestone is quarried from deep pits such as this one near Bedford, Indiana.

Hoosiers have used Indiana limestone to construct many buildings and monuments in their own state. Part of the State House, scores of county courthouses, and many buildings on the Indiana University campus at Bloomington are made with Indiana limestone. In Mitchell a 44-foot (13-m) high spaceship made of limestone was built to honor Indiana's Gus Grissom. You will read more about Gus Grissom in the Traditions Lesson in Chapter 12.

LIMESTONES OF INDIANA

Indiana limestone is just one kind of limestone found in Indiana. Monroe and Lawrence counties contain this limestone, which is easily carved after it is first quarried. Later this limestone becomes hard and long lasting, making it perfect for building. This limestone is then shipped all over the United States and to other countries.

Some limestone found in Indiana is used to make cement and lime. Cement is made of clay and limestone. Can you think of ways in which cement is used?

Lime is a white powder that is made from burning limestone and other ingredients. It is used on fields to improve the soil. Lime is also used to make mortar. Mortar is a mixture of lime, cement, sand, and stone that is used for holding bricks together. Imagine how many homes and fireplaces across our country have a little piece of Indiana in them!

THE HISTORY OF INDIANA LIMESTONE

The limestone of Indiana became famous after the great fire of Chicago in 1871. This fire, which destroyed over 17,000 buildings in 24 hours, is said to have been started by a cow that kicked over a lighted lantern in a barn. The barn caught fire and the flames spread from building to building. Most of the buildings in the center of the city were destroyed. The people of Chicago decided that they should rebuild their city using a building material that wouldn't burn. They chose limestone.

You can find out more about the history of Indiana's limestone in White River State Park in Indianapolis. The park has a walk called the Riverwalk Promenade that is made out of about 1,200 limestone blocks. The

This beautiful carved limestone is found along the Riverwalk Promenade in Indianapolis.

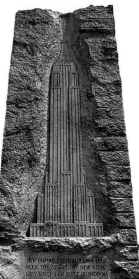

The magnificent rose window (above) was carved by a master craftsman (left) from limestone found in southern Indiana.

history of the limestone industry in Indiana is carved on 14 of these blocks. There you can see Indiana limestone while you read about it.

HOOSIERS DO THEIR PART

Hoosiers are proud that Indiana limestone is one of the finest building materials in the world. They work hard to quarry the stone and transport it to places all over our country and the world. Hoosiers work together so that others may enjoy the beauty and strength of Indiana limestone.

Check Your Reading

1. Which kind of limestone is quarried only in Indiana?
2. In what ways can limestone be used?
3. Name three famous buildings that were made with Indiana limestone.
4. **GEOGRAPHY SKILL:** Which counties in Indiana contain the best limestone for building?

REVIEWING VOCABULARY

climate	mineral
conservation	precipitation
fuel	temperature
humidity	tornado
ground water	weather

Number a sheet of paper from 1 to 10. Beside each number write the word or term from the list above that best matches the definition.

1. How hot, cold, wet, or dry a place is
2. The pattern of heat, cold, wetness, or dryness over a long period of time
3. The air's heat or coolness in a place
4. Any form of water, usually snow or rain, that falls to the earth
5. The moisture, or dampness, in the air
6. A dangerous, funnel-shaped storm
7. Something burned to produce heat or energy
8. Water that is stored in tiny spaces between rocks and soil
9. A natural resource that is found in the earth
10. The wise use of natural resources

REVIEWING FACTS

1. Why is Indiana's average yearly rainfall good for farmers?
2. What is a natural resource?
3. How are coal, petroleum, and natural gas alike?
4. What is a growing season?
5. Why does Indiana have few large forests today?

◖▬▶ WRITING ABOUT MAIN IDEAS

1. **Writing a Weather Report:** Write a weather report that describes today's weather.
2. **Writing a Radio Commercial:** Write a radio commercial encouraging people to practice conservation.

BUILDING SKILLS: UNDERSTANDING LATITUDE AND LONGITUDE

1. What are lines of latitude? What are lines of longitude?
2. Look at the map on page 45. Which line of longitude runs close to Indiana's eastern border?
3. Why would an airline pilot need to understand latitude and longitude?

REVIEWING VOCABULARY

conservation	glacier
erosion	mineral
fertile	natural resource
fuel	precipitation
geography	tributary

Number a sheet of paper from 1 to 10. Beside each number write the word or term from the list above that best completes the sentence.

1. The study of the earth's land and water, plants, and animals is known as _____.
2. A _____ is a huge, moving mass of ice.
3. Soil that is _____ is good for growing crops.
4. A _____ is a stream or small river that flows into a larger river.
5. Wind, water, and ice cause _____, the wearing away of rock and soil.
6. Rain, snow, and sleet are forms of _____.
7. A _____ is something found in nature that people find useful.
8. Gypsum is an example of a _____ that is found in the earth.
9. Petroleum is a _____ that is used to produce heat and energy.
10. To save natural resources, people practice _____.

WRITING ABOUT THE UNIT

1. **Writing a Diary Entry:** Write a diary entry that describes how the weather in Indiana has affected you today.
2. **Writing an Essay:** Which region of Indiana would you like to visit? Write a short essay explaining why you would like to visit that region.

ACTIVITIES

1. **Keeping a Weather Chart:** Chart the weather for three weeks. For each day note the high and low temperatures and any precipitation, sunshine, and so on. At the end of the three weeks, decide if the weather was typical of Indiana's climate. Write a paragraph explaining your conclusion.
2. **Working Together to Make a Bulletin Board Display:** With a group of classmates, prepare a visual display about the geography of Indiana. Divide your group's display into the state's three regions. Be sure to include at least one map as well as pictures and written descriptions.

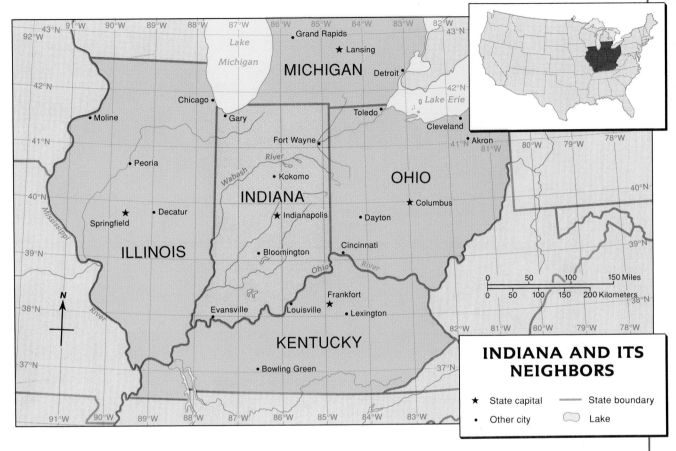

INDIANA AND ITS NEIGHBORS

★ State capital   ～～～ State boundary
• Other city   Lake

BUILDING SKILLS: UNDERSTANDING LATITUDE AND LONGITUDE

Use the map on this page to answer the following questions.

1. Which city is close to 41°N, 85°W?

2. What is the approximate latitude of Evansville?

3. What is the approximate longitude of Indianapolis?

4. What is the latitude and longitude of Columbus, Ohio?

 **LINKING PAST, PRESENT, AND FUTURE**

Today Indiana has few forests because people who lived long ago did not practice conservation. Which of our state's resources must we be careful to conserve today? How can we work to conserve these resources so that future Hoosiers may also enjoy them?

57

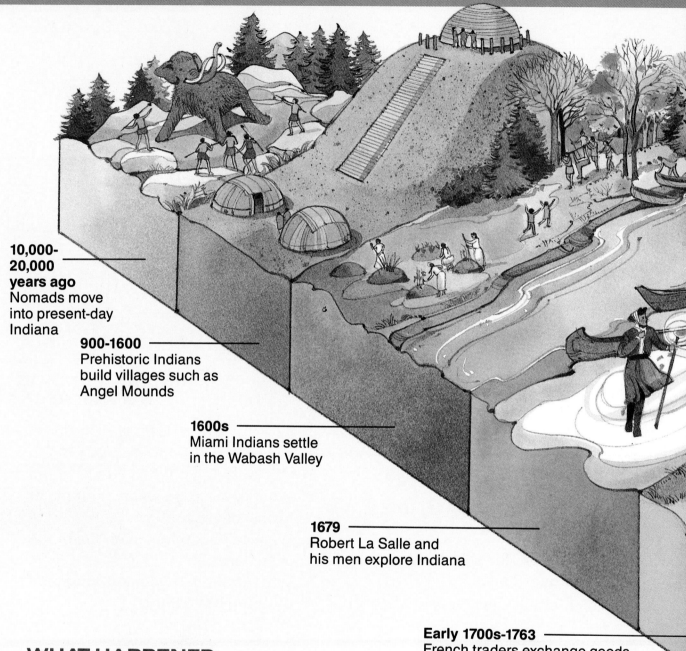

10,000-20,000 years ago
Nomads move into present-day Indiana

900-1600
Prehistoric Indians build villages such as Angel Mounds

1600s
Miami Indians settle in the Wabash Valley

1679
Robert La Salle and his men explore Indiana

Early 1700s-1763
French traders exchange goods for furs with Indians

1763
Great Britain controls Fort Ouiatenon after the French and Indian War

WHAT HAPPENED

The story of our state reaches far back into the past and stretches far into the future. The early part of it is the story of Indians, French traders, British soldiers, and settlements that slowly became towns. In this unit you will read about the people who helped to build Indiana.

UNIT 2

EARLY INDIANA

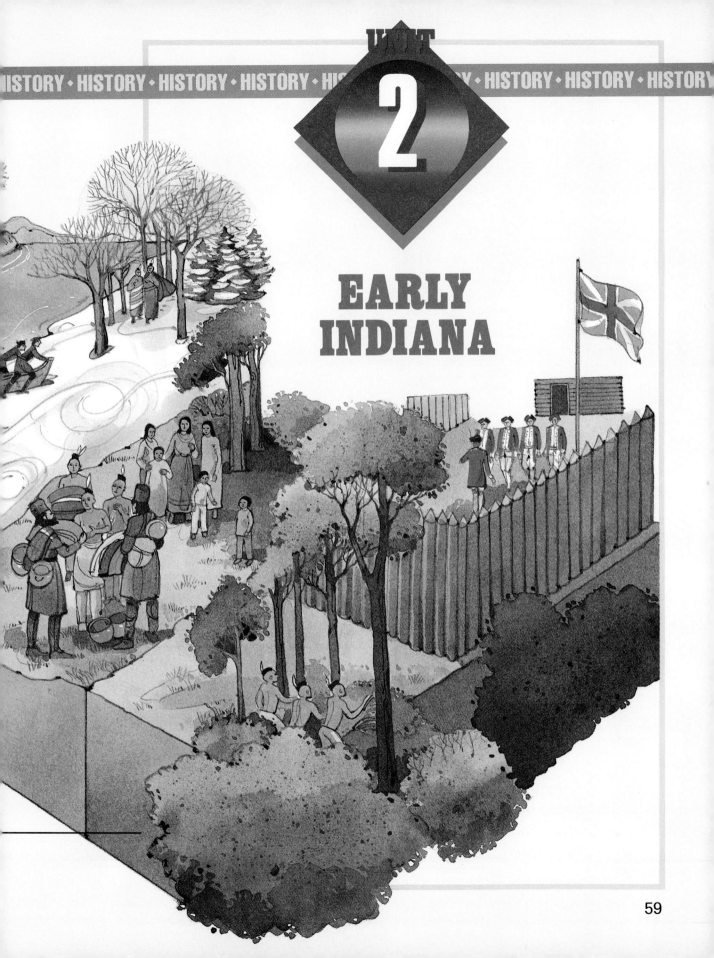

CHAPTER 3

INDIANA'S FIRST PEOPLE

FOCUS

At school I made a doll of an Indian chief. I was the only one in the class who had a real chief for an uncle.

Pam Gann is proud of her Indian background. Her great-uncle is a Cherokee chief. In this chapter you will read about Indians who lived in our state long ago.

1 The Early Indians

READ TO LEARN

Key Vocabulary

artifact   land bridge
archaeologist   nomad
prehistoric   mound
mammoth

Key Places

Beringia
Mounds State Park
Angel Mounds State
  Historic Site

Read Aloud

November 26, 1940, was one of the most exciting days in Glenn Black's life. Black and other scientists had been digging in the earth near Evansville. Suddenly Black's shovel struck something hard. After more digging he found a statue of a man carved out of stone. The stone carving excited Black because it would tell him more about how Indiana's first people lived.

Read for Purpose

1. **WHAT YOU KNOW:** How did glaciers change the shape of the land?
2. **WHAT YOU WILL LEARN:** What was life like for the early Indians?

CLUES FROM THE PAST

Can you imagine what life might have been like thousands of years ago? The stone figure that Glenn Black found is an example of an artifact. Artifacts are objects, such as pottery and tools, that were made by people long ago. They are clues that help us to learn about how people lived long ago.

Archaeologists (är kē ol′ ə jists) are people who search for and study artifacts. Glenn Black was Indiana's most famous archaeologist. Beginning in 1938, Glenn Black discovered many artifacts in Indiana. Every time he discovered an artifact, he learned something new about Indiana's first people.

61

THE FIRST PEOPLE

Archaeologists have learned that the first people came to the area we know now as Indiana more than 10,000 years ago. These people are called the prehistoric Indians. *Pre* means "coming before." History is the story of the past. Prehistoric Indians came to Indiana long before people began to write down the story of our past.

Indians are sometimes also called Native Americans. The word *native* means "one of the first people to live in a land."

WHERE THEY CAME FROM

Many scientists believe that the prehistoric Indians probably fol-

lowed animals to North America from Asia. One animal that they hunted was called the mammoth. The mammoth was a huge, woolly animal that was similar to an elephant. The prehistoric Indians used the mammoth for food and clothing. They also used the mammoth's bones for tools.

To get from Asia to North America, early people probably walked across a land bridge. This land bridge is called Beringia (ber' ən gēə). It was a wide, marshy plain that connected Asia and North America. Use the Atlas map on page 288 to find the narrow strip of water that separates Asia and North America near Alaska. Many scientists believe that this is where the land bridge was once found.

FROM HUNTING TO FARMING

Because the prehistoric Indians depended on animals like the mammoth, they had to live as nomads. Nomads are people who move from place to place in search of food.

Since they depended on animals for food, the early Indians needed to make good hunting weapons. Archaeologists have found stone tips from spears that Indians used to hunt large animals like the mammoth. Later, Indians learned to make bows and arrows to hunt smaller and faster animals.

In addition to being expert hunters, early Indians had other ways of

The wooly mammoth was hunted by prehistoric Indians for food, clothing and tools.

Indian mounds, such as those found near Evansville, help us to learn more about the people who lived in Indiana long ago.

ANGEL MOUNDS
Site of a palisaded Middle Mississippi Indian village occupied circa 1500 A.D. This 450 acre site includes eleven man-made mounds, town plaza and village area for a population of about 1,000. Excavated by the Indiana Historical Society, 1939-1965.

finding food. They caught fish using fishhooks made from animal bones. They also learned to eat certain plants. Gatherers collected wild berries, nuts, and fruits.

Over 1,000 years ago Indians who lived in what is now Indiana stopped living as nomads. Each group began to choose a place to farm the land. As farmers, they grew corn, beans, squash, and tobacco. Because they stayed in one place, villages and towns began to grow.

THE BUILDERS OF MOUNDS

Almost 3,000 years ago, the Indians began working together to build the first mounds. Mounds are huge piles of earth. We call these early Indians mound builders. They built these large piles of earth for many reasons. Archaeologists have found clues that tell us that the first mounds were used as places to bury their dead and to worship. Later, mounds were also built as homes for the chiefs.

Glenn Black is shown working at the Angel Mounds where this artifact, one of our state's greatest treasures, was found.

Many mounds remain in Indiana today. Some can be seen at **Mounds State Park**, near Anderson. At the **Angel Mounds State Historic Site** near Evansville you can walk to the top of a mound. Try to imagine Indian children of your age climbing on and exploring these mounds thousands of years ago.

TREASURES OF THE PAST

As you have read, much of Indiana's history can be learned by studying artifacts. In the next lesson you will read more about Indiana's history through the story of one important Indian group.

At Indiana University in Bloomington, you can see some of the artifacts that Glenn Black found at Angel Mounds. They are on display in a museum that is named after him. Among the artifacts is the beautiful stone man shown above that Dr. Black found in 1940. It is one of Indiana's greatest treasures.

Check Your Reading

1. What is an artifact? What is an archaeologist? What can artifacts teach us?
2. In what way did life change for prehistoric Indians when they began to farm?
3. What were three reasons that the prehistoric Indians built mounds?
4. **THINKING SKILL:** What are three questions you might ask to learn more about the prehistoric Indians of Indiana?

64

2 The Miami Indians

READ TO LEARN

Key Vocabulary

portage
clan
wigwam
heritage

Key Places

Wabash Valley
Kekionga
Fort Wayne

Read Aloud

The chiefs are generally friendly . . . and their houses are open to every Indian. . . . It is the duty of the chief to maintain peace as long as possible.

This is the way a visitor described Miami Indian chiefs. In this lesson you will learn about this important group of Indian leaders and their people.

Read for Purpose

1. **WHAT YOU KNOW:** What can we learn from studying artifacts?
2. **WHAT YOU WILL LEARN:** What was life like for the Miami Indians?

MANY DIFFERENT INDIANS

In the last lesson you read about prehistoric Indians who lived before people began writing about the past. We know much more about later groups of Indians because of written records. By the 1700s there were many different Indian groups living throughout what is now the state of Indiana.

Two of the most important Indian groups to live here were the Potawatomi (pot ə wä′ tə mē) and the Miami (mī am′ ē). Look at the map on page 66. It shows the names of different Indian groups and where they lived. You can see that the Potawatomi lived in the northernmost part of Indiana. Where did the Miami live?

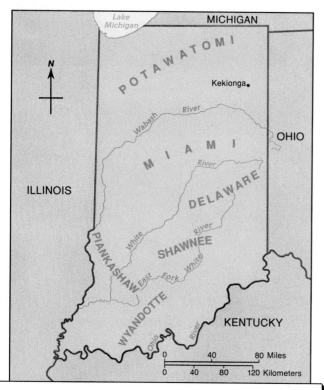

NATIVE AMERICANS OF INDIANA

Present-day boundaries are shown.

MAP SKILL: Which two Indian groups lived in what is now northern Indiana?

THE MIAMI AND THE WABASH VALLEY

Before railroads and highways were built, people often traveled by canoe on rivers. The Wabash River was part of a vast river route that connected the Great Lakes and the Mississippi River. This river route allowed trade to develop between people who lived far away from one another but who shared the river's waters.

The Miami were experts in using canoes to travel on the river. They traded with other people along the Wabash River. Because river travel was an important part of their daily life, they built villages near the river in the Wabash Valley.

The Wabash Valley was also an excellent place to live for other reasons. The Miami found that the land in the valley was very fertile. The Miami grew pumpkins, a variety of beans, melons, and, most important of all, corn in this fertile soil.

Corn grows well in the Wabash Valley because of the fertile soil and the long, hot summers. Even today, farmers there continue to plant thousands of acres of corn each year.

AN IMPORTANT MIAMI VILLAGE

The most important of all the Miami villages was Kekionga (kē kē on gä'), in northeastern Indiana. Look at the map on this page. Find Kekionga north of the Wabash River.

Kekionga was located along an important portage (pôr' tij) between the Maumee and the Wabash rivers. A portage is a path across land over which people can carry boats and goods from one body of water to another. The portage at Kekionga made it the most important of all the Miami villages.

Today the place that the Miami called Kekionga is called Fort Wayne. It is one of Indiana's largest cities. Like Kekionga, it serves as a center of travel and trade.

MIAMI CORN HARVEST

Perhaps Sweet Breeze's and Tall Oak's village looked like this.

LIFE AMONG THE MIAMI

The Miami lived in clans, or large families made up of mothers, fathers, aunts, uncles, grandparents and, of course, children. The following story is about two children who were part of a Miami clan.

Sweet Breeze woke up early to the smell of freshly baked corn bread. She was sure that her grandmother made the best corn bread in the village. The ten-year-old girl squinted at the sunlight peeking through the opening in her family's wigwam. A wigwam is a house made of long, bent poles. These poles are covered with bark. An opening in the roof lets the smoke from the fire escape.

"Wake up!" Sweet Breeze called to her eight-year-old brother, Tall Oak. "You'll be late!"

"I'm coming," Tall Oak said as he wiped the sleep from his eyes. "What's the hurry, anyhow?"

"The harvest festival begins tomorrow," Sweet Breeze reminded him. "We still have to collect more nuts from the forest."

The two children greeted their grandmother and quickly ate their pieces of delicious corn bread. Sweet Breeze picked up a basket to carry corn. Then they hurried to join their mother in the fields. They passed many rows of corn, with squash and pumpkins growing in between the cornstalks. Finally they saw their mother working with the other women of the clan in the cornfields.

Sweet Breeze and Tall Oak worked for hours with their mother. Like all Miami children they learned many different things, such as planting crops and hunting, by watching and listening to their parents and other members of the clan.

67

INDIAN WAY OF GROWING CROPS

Cornstalk acts as beanpole.

corn

beans

squash

Squash plants keep soil from washing away.

DIAGRAM SKILL: Unlike Hoosiers today, the Miami mixed crops, which they grew together. What crops did the Miami grow?

"Mother," Tall Oak asked when they had reached the far field, "why do we celebrate the harvest festival each year?"

"That's a good question," his mother replied. "We celebrate the harvest festival to give thanks for all the crops grown throughout the year. When we sing and dance at the festival, we are celebrating how happy we are that the earth and sun have been good to us."

The children walked with their mother back to the wigwam in the late afternoon. Soon the day would be over, and the next morning would bring the big celebration!

OUR STATE'S INDIAN HERITAGE

Our state has a very special Indian **heritage** (her' i tij). Heritage is a group's history and traditions. Even our name shows how important Indian life has been throughout our state's history. *Indiana* means "Land of the Indians."

The Miami Indians are an important part of our state's heritage. In the next chapter you will read about other important groups of people who came to Indiana and the various changes that they brought to life in our state.

 Check Your Reading

1. Name two Indian groups that lived in Indiana.
2. Why was the Wabash Valley a good place to live?
3. Describe some events that you think might have happened during a day in the life of a Miami child of your age.
4. **GEOGRAPHY SKILL:** On the map on page 66, find the Indian group that lived between the Wabash and the White rivers.
5. **THINKING SKILL:** How do you think life would have been different for the Miami Indians if they had not settled in the Wabash Valley?

READ TO LEARN

◼ Key Vocabulary

myth

◼ Read for Purpose

1. **WHAT YOU KNOW:** Where did the Miami Indians live?
2. **WHAT YOU WILL LEARN:** How did the Miami explain the way in which corn was discovered?

THE GIFT OF CORN

In the last lesson you read about the Miami Indians. They chose to live in Indiana because they were farmers. One of their most important crops was corn.

Because corn was so important to the Miami, they told a myth about it. A myth is a story that explains the beliefs of a group. This myth was told to explain how corn came to be grown on the earth.

THE SEARCH FOR A GUIDE

One spring, long ago, a chief's son came of age. "You must leave the village now, my son," the chief said. "It is time for you to meet the spirit that will guide you through life. You must begin your fast. You must not eat or drink. Soon your guiding spirit will come to you in a dream."

The youth traveled for a day and a night through the forest. At last he came to a wide clearing where the sun shone. He built a shelter of tree branches and leaves

there. It was finished near sundown. He entered and began his fast.

The next morning he did not eat or drink. He watched the squirrels eat from their store of nuts. He thought of how his people gathered food from the forest and clearings. During some summers there were many plants that gave them food, while during others there was little to be found. The gathering from last summer had been the smallest of all. There was much hunger in the village.

"How can the plants that give us food be made to grow every year?" he wondered. "How can the people in the village help the plants to grow?"

By evening he felt very hungry and his mouth was dry from thirst. He sat in the opening of his shelter and dozed as the lights of sunset began to fade. His thoughts wandered and he began to dream.

Suddenly he felt the warmth of the sun on his skin, as if it were midday. He opened his eyes and saw a tall stranger standing beside him. The stranger was wrapped in a bright green robe. The robe clung closely to the stranger's body, covering it from head to foot. From the stranger's scalp grew fine hair the color of a pale-yellow sun.

The stranger raised a hand in greeting. "The sun has read your thoughts and sent me to you."

"What is your name?" the youth asked.

"I am Corn Spirit," the stranger answered. "I bring a gift from the sun, which you worship above all others."

"You bring nothing in your hands. What is the gift, Corn Spirit?"

"You will find out. But first you must prove that you are worthy of this gift. You must wrestle with me in the clearing and take from me my robe of green. Before the sun sets for the third time you must throw me to the ground."

"I will try, Corn Spirit."

Corn Spirit continued. "If I lose, you must do the following. Make a resting place for me in the rich soil on the spot where I fall in the clearing. Return to this spot after the third full moon. Your gift will be ready to harvest. Take it back to your father's village and place it in the coals of your fire. You will know what to do next."

Though weakened by his fast, the youth prepared to wrestle with Corn Spirit. Swiftly he took hold of Corn Spirit's arms and held tight. Locked in combat, they moved back and forth. The youth strained to overcome Corn Spirit, but he could not.

"Enough!" cried Corn Spirit as the sun began to disappear below the horizon. "I will return again tomorrow."

The following evening at sunset, Corn Spirit reappeared. Again they wrestled. The youth felt weaker than before, but he struggled with Corn Spirit, catching at the robe whenever he could.

"Enough!" cried Corn Spirit as

the sun began to disappear below the horizon. "I will return tomorrow. If you do not take the robe from me then, the gift will not be yours."

The following day Corn Spirit again appeared. Though the youth was very weak, he forced himself to his feet. For the last time he locked arms with Corn Spirit.

As they wrestled, each tried to throw the other off balance. The youth could hardly stand. With one final effort he took hold of Corn Spirit's robe. Suddenly he felt strong—stronger than he had ever felt before. He pulled as hard as he could. The robe was his.

Robbed of his strength, Corn Spirit toppled to the ground just as the sun disappeared beneath the horizon. The youth cleared the roots and grass away from where Corn Spirit fell. He hollowed out a resting place and then put Corn Spirit in it. He covered Corn Spirit with a thin blanket of soil. Then he returned to the village and told his father what had taken place.

His father nodded and said, "You have done well, my son. Now you must ask for the sun's blessing and wait."

THE GIFT IS RECEIVED

The son did as he was told. After the third full moon, he returned to the clearing in the forest. He went to the place where he had left Corn Spirit. There he found a plant taller than the tallest person in the village. Attached to the plant's stalk were three likenesses of Corn Spirit. Each was no larger than the youth's hand. These likenesses of Corn Spirit were ears of corn.

He remembered what Corn Spirit had said. So he picked the green-robed ears of corn and carried them

back to the village. He kept one in memory of Corn Spirit. The other two he placed in the coals of the fire. He was certain that they would burn to ashes. But they did not catch fire. Instead, beneath their green robes of leaves, they turned a yellow-brown. When he pulled them from the coals, he found that their kernels had become soft and tasted sweet.

Surprised, he ran to show his father. "This is Corn Spirit's great gift—food from a plant that we can grow ourselves, summer after summer!"

From that point on, the youth's father called him Corn Grower. Corn Grower planted the seeds from the ear that he had saved. He taught the people of the village to plant and care for the new food. He showed them how to harvest it. The people in the village took care to respect the earth. By working together, and taking care of the land, they always had plenty to eat.

Check Your Reading

1. Why was corn so important to the Miami Indians?
2. Who was the stranger who spoke to the chief's son?
3. What was Corn Spirit's gift?
4. **THINKING SKILL:** What was life like for the Miami before they received the gift of Corn Spirit? What was life like for them after they received this gift?

Decision Making

Key Vocabulary

decision

Imagine that you are having a test tomorrow on the early history of Indiana. You want to get a high score to improve your grade. You can study in the afternoon when you arrive home from school or you can play with friends and then study after dinner.

You have to make a decision about what to do. Making a decision is the same thing as making a choice.

Trying the Skill

Imagine that you are the leader of a Miami Indian clan. You live in the village of Kekionga with many other Miami clans. Some other clans are moving west along the Wabash to another village. You need to decide whether to move your clan or remain in Kekionga.

Your goal is to find the best way of life for your group. Listed below are some things that might happen as a result of your decision. Consider whether each result would help you to achieve your goal. Then make your decision.

- Your clan might find better land on which to farm.
- The new village might be less comfortable than Kekionga.
- You will leave many of your friends from other clans.
- It might be more beautiful in the new village than in Kekionga.

1. What is your decision?
2. What did you do to make this decision?

HELPING YOURSELF

The steps on the left will help you to make good decisions. The example on the right shows one way you can use these steps to make a decision about leaving Kekionga.

One Way to Make a Decision	Example
1. State your goal, or what it is you want to do.	Your goal is to find the best way of life for your clan.
2. Identify some things you could do to reach your goal.	You could leave Kekionga or you could stay.
3. Identify what might happen as a result of each choice.	You might find better farmland, but you must leave friends behind.
4. Choose the action that is most likely to help you reach your goal.	You decide to leave Kekionga.

Applying the Skill

Now apply what you have learned. Imagine that you are a Miami boy. Your uncle has asked you to take a trading trip. You will be away for five days and will miss the first day of the Harvest Festival. You have waited all year for the festival because you plan to compete in the annual children's games.

Your goal is to win the games. Missing the first day would put you at a disadvantage. However, the chance to travel to other villages is very exciting. You must decide whether to stay at home or to go on the trip.

Which decision is most likely to help you reach your goal? Choose the best ending for the following sentences.

1. To make your decision, you should first
   a. talk to your friend.
   b. think about your choices.
   c. decide which is the best way to reach your goal.
2. Your decision should help you to
   a. reach your goal.
   b. make up your mind.
   c. see new places.
3. One reason not to take the trading trip is that
   a. your uncle is traveling with someone you do not know.
   b. you would miss one day of the festival and may not win the games.
   c. something bad may happen.

Reviewing the Skill

1. What are some other words that mean *decision making*?
2. Which steps could you follow to make a good decision?
3. Why is it important to make good decisions?

HELPING *the* HOMELESS

As Joyce Marks Booth drove through Indianapolis on her way to church every Sunday, she passed by people who lived on the streets. These people had no homes to live in and not much to eat.

Booth, who is a Miami Indian, felt that she wanted to do something to help homeless people. "When I was growing up, it was a Miami tribal tradition to take care of one another," she explains. "I knew I had to find a way to feed some of the hungry in our city."

Leaders of her church agreed to begin a food program, using the church kitchen to prepare hot meals. At first, Booth and a friend planned the meals, shopped for groceries, and cooked the food. Then other church members began to volunteer. Soon they were serving meals to about 200 people each day.

Some of the people who came for meals had lost their jobs and did not have enough money to pay for their own needs. They did not know where to seek help. Others were too proud to ask for help.

The number of homeless people in Indianapolis continued to grow. Some people slept in the downtown parks. Others found places to stay in empty buildings. Booth thought that church leaders could help by welcoming homeless people to stay inside the church.

Some church members volunteered to keep the building open at night so that people could sleep on the pews. But the homeless also needed a place to bathe as well as a place to stay during the day.

Booth decided to ask church leaders for help in building a shelter for the homeless. The leaders agreed that it could be built on church land. After many months of hard work, the shelter was finally built. Called Dayspring, it now houses 50 people who have no other homes.

Today Booth continues to help people in need. She lives by the beliefs of her Miami ancestors: "We must take care of each other."

REVIEWING VOCABULARY

archaeologist   nomad
clan   portage
heritage

Number a sheet of paper from 1 to 5. Beside each number write the word from the list above that best completes the sentence.

1. A _____ is a large family that includes parents, grandparents, cousins, aunts, and uncles.
2. A _____ is a route or place on land that people use to carry boats from one body of water to another.
3. An _____ searches for and studies objects made by people long ago.
4. A group's history and traditions make up their _____.
5. A _____ moves from place to place searching for food.

REVIEWING FACTS

Number a sheet of paper from 1 to 5. Beside each number write **T** if the statement is true. If the statement is false, rewrite it to make it true.

1. Some foods grown by prehistoric people were corn, beans, and squash.
2. Prehistoric Indians used steel-tipped spears to hunt animals.
3. The two most important Native American groups in Indiana were the Miami and the Kekionga.
4. Rivers were important routes for travel long ago.
5. Miami children learned by attending school.

◀═▶ WRITING ABOUT MAIN IDEAS

1. **Writing a History Paragraph:** Write a paragraph describing what nomads ate and how they got their food.
2. **Writing a Journal:** Imagine that you are an archaeologist in the year 2090 searching for artifacts in a 100-year-old schoolroom. Describe three artifacts that you find.

BUILDING SKILLS: DECISION MAKING

Imagine that you collect Indian artifacts. Suppose that you were asked to donate your collection to a museum. Many people visit the museum, which is located far from where you live. Should you donate your collection?

1. To make a decision, you should first
   a. talk with your teacher.
   b. think about your choices and the possible results of each one.
   c. visit the museum.
2. Your decision should help you to
   a. make money.
   b. reach your goal.
   c. make friends.
3. Why is it important to know how to make good decisions?

77

CHAPTER 4

THE FRENCH AND BRITISH IN INDIANA

FOCUS

I like the food, the music, and how people dress up at The Feast of the Hunter's Moon.

Brooke Compliment used these words to describe the yearly gathering that takes place at an old French fort near Lafayette. In this chapter you will read about French and British settlement in our state.

1 Early Explorers

READ TO LEARN

Key Vocabulary

colony   trading post
explorer   missionary
fur traders   religion
trade goods

Key People

Robert La Salle
White Beaver

Key Places

New France
Kankakee River
South Bend

Read Aloud

[We found] only great open plains, where nothing grows except tall grass, which is dry at this season, and which the Miami had burned while hunting buffalo.

A French traveler wrote these words to describe his first visit to what is now northern Indiana. As you will read in this lesson, the French would play an important role in this part of the world.

Read for Purpose

1. **WHAT YOU KNOW:** Who were the first people to live in Indiana?
2. **WHAT YOU WILL LEARN:** Why did the French come to Indiana?

NEW COLONIES

Native Americans were the only people living in North America until the late 1500s. By the early 1600s, however, new groups of people began arriving in North America from Europe.

These Europeans, from countries like England and France, came to North America to begin colonies. A colony is a place that is ruled by another country. They began colonies for many reasons. Some wanted land to build new homes. Others were looking for riches. Many wanted more freedom than they had in Europe.

Thirteen English colonies were located along the coast of the Atlantic Ocean. The French colonies,

79

The Granger Collection

Robert La Salle claimed a large area of North America, including present-day Indiana, for France.

called New France, were located along the Saint Lawrence River north of the English colonies.

ROBERT LA SALLE

As the colonies grew, explorers began to travel farther into North America. An explorer is someone who travels to unknown lands. Robert La Salle was one of France's greatest explorers. In 1679 he became the first known European to explore what is now Indiana.

On December 3, 1679, La Salle left the southeastern shore of Lake Michigan and traveled up the St. Joseph River. He hoped to find a portage that would connect the St. Joseph River to the Kankakee River. If he could find this portage, he might also be able to make his way to the sea. The king of France had asked La Salle to find a route to the sea and to claim it for France. You can trace La Salle's route on the map on page 81.

La Salle and White Beaver, his Mohegan (mō hē′ gən) Indian friend and guide, and 26 other men paddled up the St. Joseph River in 8 long canoes. For two days they struggled against the river's strong current. It was cold and snowing when they finally found the bend in the river that was near the portage. They called it the "south bend" of the St. Joseph River. Later the city of South Bend would be located there. With White Beaver's help La Salle found the portage.

In 1681 La Salle traveled down the Kankakee River again. This time he continued down the Illinois River and then down the Mississippi River. He claimed all the land from the Great Lakes to the end of the Mississippi for France. This land included what we now call Indiana.

That same year La Salle met with leaders of the Miami and other Indian groups. La Salle spoke to them about trading with the French. He also promised that French soldiers would protect them from any unfriendly Indian groups. This meeting took place under a large oak tree, called the Council Oak, which still stands in South Bend today.

In the early 1700s many French men came to the lands La Salle had claimed for France to work as fur traders. The fur traders gathered large numbers of furs and sent them back to France to be sold. The fur of animals such as raccoon, fox, and beaver was valuable and could bring a good price in Europe.

The fur traders also learned that Native Americans would exchange furs for certain goods, called trade goods. Trade goods included hunting knives, guns, hoes, blankets, needles, thread, ribbons, and glass beads.

Sometimes fur traders went to Indian villages to exchange trade goods for furs. Other times the Indians traded furs at a trading post. A trading post was a place where people met to exchange goods.

For the French, fur trading was a good business. They were able to sell the furs for much more money than the trade goods had cost them. Some of them became very wealthy from fur trading.

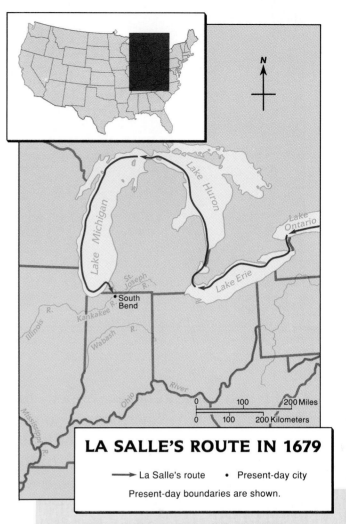

LA SALLE'S ROUTE IN 1679

→ La Salle's route   • Present-day city

Present-day boundaries are shown.

MAP SKILL: Through which of the Great Lakes did La Salle sail?

THE FRENCH AND THE INDIANS

French traders often lived with the Indians and learned about their way of life. Some married Indian women and raised families. Indians also learned about the French way of life. For example, missionaries came to Indiana. A missionary is someone who teaches others about his or her religion. Religion is the way people worship the God or gods they believe in.

The Granger Collection

Indians and French **fur traders** met each year to trade. The hat shown above was made by Indians from **trade goods**.

French missionaries hoped to teach Native Americans about Christianity. Some Miami Indians became Christians, but most Indians continued to worship as they had before the missionaries arrived.

It was not long before the Indians began to depend on trade goods instead of making things themselves. They had always hunted with bows and arrows only to meet their daily needs for food and clothing. Now they were hunting with guns and they killed animals to get their furs for trade.

A NEW WAY OF LIFE

You have read why the French explorers and fur traders came to Indiana. The furs that Native Americans traded made the French fur traders rich. As news spread about the fur trade, more French people came to the area. They, too, hoped to become rich in the land that would someday be called Indiana.

 Check Your Reading

1. What is an explorer?
2. Who was the first known European to travel to Indiana? Why did he go there?
3. List three trade goods that the French exchanged for furs with the Indians.
4. **GEOGRAPHY SKILL:** Look at the Atlas map on page 293. Find the rivers, lakes, and portages that you could have used to travel from what is now Indiana to New France.
5. **THINKING SKILL:** Predict how the Indian way of life might have been different if the Indians had not wanted to trade furs with the French.

82

2 Life in a French Fort

READ TO LEARN

Key Vocabulary

stockade

Key Places

Fort Ouiatenon   Vincennes
Lafayette   Fort Miami

Read Aloud

This place is [located] on the Wabash; about 14 French families are living in the Fort, which stands on the north side of the river. This Post has always been a very [large] trading place.

This is how a visitor in the 1700s described an important French fort in Indiana. The fort was near the Wabash River. In this lesson you will read about the way that the French lived in what is now Indiana.

Read for Purpose

1. **WHAT YOU KNOW:** Why was the fur trade important to the French and to the Native Americans?
2. **WHAT YOU WILL LEARN:** How did people live in a French fort?

THREE FRENCH FORTS

In order to protect fur traders, the French built forts throughout the area. These forts made traders safe and gave them homes.

Fort Ouiatenon (wē ot′ ə nōn) was one important French fort. It was built on the Wabash River in 1717. The French named it for the Wea Indians, a part of the Miami Tribe, who lived in the area. Fort Ouiatenon was located near where the town of Lafayette is today.

In addition to Fort Ouiatenon, the French built a fort in Vincennes (vin senz′) and one near Kekionga called Fort Miami. Fort Miami, built in 1715, was located at an important portage between the Wabash and Maumee rivers.

Vincennes was also located on the Wabash River, much farther

AN EARLY FRENCH FORT

Inn

Trading Post

Garden

Stable

Blacksmith

Blockhouse

Stockade

DIAGRAM SKILL: French settlers often received visitors to their forts. Where do you think visitors might have stayed?

south than the other two forts. The river became a major trade route for the French as it was for the Indians. Vincennes became the home of most of the French families that lived in the area. The fort was built in 1732.

Each fort had a large fence, called a stockade, to keep out enemies. Inside the stockade was a blockhouse. A blockhouse was a large, high, square building made of logs. A blockhouse was the best place from which to defend, or protect, a fort. If enemies attacked, soldiers could shoot through small holes in the walls. The walls protected the soldiers when they fought. These forts protected the traders and allowed them to carry on their fur trade for almost 40 years.

LIFE IN A FORT

As years passed and as the fur trade grew, the traders began to think of the forts as their real homes. The forts became almost like small towns once the traders' families were able to live with them.

Many languages were spoken in the forts. French, of course, was spoken by the settlers. But many people also knew Indian languages and used them to speak to the Indians who lived nearby.

The French settlers celebrated holidays and followed their traditions as they had in France. The celebration of the new year was one of their most exciting holidays. People sang and danced.

New Year's Day was also a time to end old disagreements. As one Frenchman remembered, "If anybody was mad at another, they must kiss when they see the other and say *'Mes Etrenne'* (mā′ zā tren)." Those French words mean "my New Year's gift."

Children helped their parents whenever they could. They tended crops, such as corn, that they grew outside the stockade. Boys helped their fathers bundle furs and ship them in canoes down the Wabash River. Girls helped their mothers sew cloth and skins into clothing.

FRENCH HOMES IN INDIANA

By the middle of the 1700s the French had settled in their new

French traders often met with the Indians at French forts to discuss trading.

home. They had learned to live with Native Americans and to trade furs with them. The land that La Salle had explored now contained French forts as well as Indian villages.

 Check Your Reading

1. Why did the French build forts?
2. Why was Fort Miami's location important?
3. What made New Year's Day a special holiday?
4. **GEOGRAPHY SKILL:** Why did the French decide to build forts near the Wabash River?
5. **THINKING SKILL:** Compare the chores children in a fort did with the work you do at home. How are they similar? How are they different?

Using Reference Books

Key Vocabulary

reference book
encyclopedia
guide word
dictionary

When was Robert La Salle born? What are some of the towns that have developed along the Wabash River? Did French children go to school in the early French forts in Indiana? Reference books can be very helpful in answering questions like these. They help you to find facts and other kinds of information about many different subjects. Reference books are found in a special section of the library.

Using an Encyclopedia

One kind of reference book is an encyclopedia. An encyclopedia is a book or set of books that gives information on a number of subjects. If you wanted to find out about a famous person, place, or event, you could look in an encyclopedia.

Encyclopedia articles are arranged in alphabetical order by subject. On the spine of each volume, or book, in an encyclopedia you will find the letters of the alphabet that are covered in that volume.

Some encyclopedias have one volume for each letter of the alphabet. In this kind of encyclopedia, an article about the state of Indiana would be in the *I* volume. In an encyclopedia like this, where would you find an article about Robert La Salle? Remember, encyclopedias list a person with his or her last name first.

Some encyclopedias are divided by guide words instead of letters. The guide words tell which part of the alphabet is covered in each volume. One volume might cover everything from *ship* to *sun*. Would this volume contain information about Spain?

bayou A stream that flows slowly through a swamp or marsh. Bayous are found in the southern United States.
   bay·ou (bī′ü *or* bī′ō) *noun, plural* **bayous.**

bazaar 1. A market made up of rows of small shops or stalls. 2. A sale of different things for some special purpose. We baked a carrot cake for the church *bazaar.*
   ba·zaar (bə zär′) *noun, plural* **bazaars.**

BC Postal abbreviation for *British Columbia.*

B.C. An abbreviation for *before Christ.* It is used in giving dates before the birth of Jesus Christ. 100 *B.C.* means 100 years before the birth of Jesus.

be 1. To have reality; exist. There *is* one apple left. Once there *was* a little child

beagle A small dog with short legs, a smooth coat, and drooping ears. Beagles are kept as pets and also are used to hunt squirrels, rabbits, and other small animals.
   bea·gle (bē′gəl) *noun, plural* **beagles.**

beagle

beak The hard, projecting mouth part of a bird or a turtle. Hawks and eagles have sharp, hooked beaks. Finches have small beaks for eating seeds.

B

Using a Dictionary

Another useful reference book is a dictionary. A dictionary gives the meanings of words. It also shows how to spell and pronounce each word. Some dictionaries include sentences that show how certain words are used.

The entry words in the dictionary are arranged in alphabetical order. Guide words on the top of each page help you to locate the word that you are looking for. The guide words tell you the first and last words that appear on each page.

Look at the dictionary page above. The guide words tell you that *bayou* is the first entry on the page. Find the guide word that shows you the last entry on the page. Would you be able to find the word *beach* on this page? Why or why not?

Reviewing the Skill

1. What kind of reference book would you use to find information about Vincennes, Indiana?

2. What kind of reference book would you use to find out the meaning of the word *missionary*?

3. If the guide words on a dictionary page are **ski/skip**, which of the following words would you find on that page?
   sky   skid   skill   skunk

4. Suppose that you have two volumes of an encyclopedia in front of you. One volume contains everything from *haiku* to *ink.* The other volume has everything from *insect* to *Japan.* Which one would contain an article about Indiana?

5. Why is it important to know how to use reference books?

3 The French and Indian War

READ TO LEARN

Key Vocabulary
French and Indian War
Treaty of Paris
Pontiac's Rebellion
Proclamation of 1763

Key People
George Washington
Pontiac

Key Places
Appalachian
Mountains

Read Aloud

Pontiac is a sensible Indian of few words, [who] commands more respect than any Indian I ever saw.

This was the way a British trader described Pontiac, the Ottawa Indian chief who led a war against the British army.

Read for Purpose

1. **WHAT YOU KNOW:** How would you describe the relations between the French traders and the Native Americans?
2. **WHAT YOU WILL LEARN:** What changes did the French and Indian War bring to the French settlers?

ON THE EDGE OF WAR

As you read at the beginning of this chapter, Britain's colonies were located along the Atlantic Ocean, to the east of what is now Indiana. By the middle of the 1700s these 13 colonies had become successful and were filled with many people.

By the 1750s British fur traders began moving into areas where the French were trading. But most of the Indians in this area preferred to trade with the French. The Indians believed that the French understood their way of life. The British did not live with Native Americans or try to learn their languages.

Some Indians finally decided to trade with the British. They may have decided to do this because they thought that the British offered better goods. When the Indians began to trade with the British, the French got very angry.

France and Britain had been enemies for some time. Throughout the 1700s they fought war after war in Europe. Now the fur trade caused them to fight in North America. The French fur traders and the British colonists both claimed land in what is now the state of Pennsylvania. The French had built a fort there to protect their fur trade. The struggle over the fur trade was about to bring the two countries to war.

WAR BEGINS

In 1754 a young British colonist, George Washington, led an attack on the French army near what is now the city of Pittsburgh. This battle marked the beginning of the French and Indian War.

The French and Indian War lasted from 1754 to 1763. Most of the fighting took place as far away as present-day New York and Canada. The war was given that name because the French and many Indians fought on the same side. On the other side was the British army, helped by the British colonists. The British had a bigger army and better weapons. There were nearly 2 million British colonists living in the eastern part of North America. Only 60,000 French colonists lived in New France.

As a young man, George Washington showed his skill as a leader in the French and Indian War.

In what is now Indiana British troops finally took control of Fort Miami and Fort Ouiatenon. Once the British controlled the Wabash River, they were able to force the French to leave the Wabash Valley and their successful fur trade.

Finally, in 1763 France and Britain signed the Treaty of Paris. A treaty is an agreement between two countries. In this treaty France gave up all its claims to North America. This meant that French forts were now under British rule.

PONTIAC'S REBELLION

But the fighting did not stop. As you read, most Native Americans liked to trade with the French. Many of them were upset when British troops took control of the fur trade. They were also upset because British settlers began using Indian land for farming.

An Indian leader named Pontiac decided to fight the British. Pontiac was an Ottawa war chief who was very well respected by most Native Americans.

Pontiac knew that there were many different groups of Native Americans—the Miami, the Potawatomi, the Ottawa, and others—but he spoke to them as one people.

He told them that they must fight together to make the British leave their home.

Pontiac's plan to unite the various Indian groups worked very well. Many Indians carried war belts through the forests and down the rivers. A war belt was a string of beads and shells that Indians sent to each other as a way of asking for help in war.

The Indians attacked the British in the spring of 1763. Pontiac's Rebellion had begun. When the Indians captured Fort Miami, Fort Ouiatenon, and other forts, the British were surprised. Look at the map on page 91. How many forts did Pontiac capture?

Though Pontiac's plan also depended on help from France,

Native American groups throughout Indiana and surrounding areas listened to Pontiac's message of unity.

The Granger Collection

France had already ended its war with Britain. The war had cost the French too much.

THE REBELLION ENDS

Pontiac's plan failed. As winter came the Indian warriors had to go back to their villages and families to hunt for food.

"All my young men have buried their hatchets," said Pontiac.

Without the support of France, the Indians had to give up the forts they had captured. The British once again took control of the forts. They forced the French to leave their homes. While some French remained at Vincennes, most French colonists left the area.

Today there are not too many signs that the French ever lived here. Some reminders can be seen in Vincennes. In the cemetary at the Old Cathedral, founded in 1749, you can see names of French settlers. Many other towns still have French names like Vincennes such as Terre Haute and Versailles. Can you find another town on the Atlas map on page 295 that has a French name?

THE BRITISH AND THE INDIANS

Even though the Indians lost the war, they were not forced to leave their homes. They stayed in the area and traded with the British.

The British did one thing that pleased the Indians. They promised

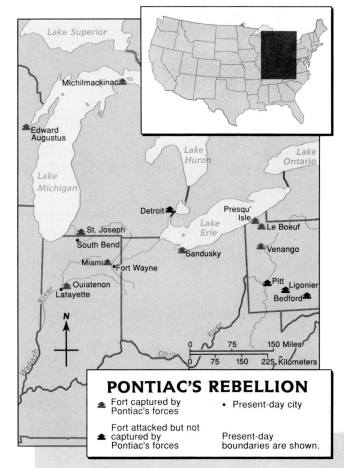

MAP SKILL: How many forts in Indiana did Pontiac capture?

that British colonists would not be allowed to move across the Appalachian Mountains. The Appalachian Mountains are a group of mountains in the eastern part of North America.

This promise was made in the Proclamation of 1763. A proclamation (prok lə mā shən) is something that is officially announced to the public. The proclamation also said that the Indians could keep their homes and land west of the Appalachians.

91

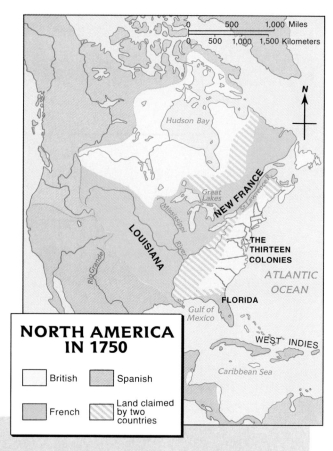

NORTH AMERICA IN 1750

- British
- Spanish
- French
- Land claimed by two countries

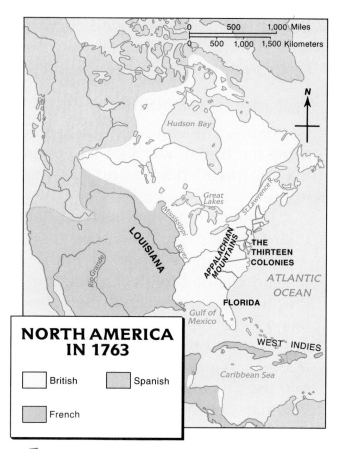

NORTH AMERICA IN 1763

- British
- Spanish
- French

MAP SKILL: Read both map titles. How many years passed between what is shown on each map? Which countries' claims changed the most?

LIVING WITH THE BRITISH

You have read that the friendship between the French and the Indians resulted in a successful fur trade. Their friendship also caused them to fight on the same side in the French and Indian War. They were outnumbered by the British, however, who had more soldiers and more guns. Despite the efforts of the French, and of the Indians who were led by Pontiac, the British took control of what is now Indiana.

Check Your Reading

1. Why did France and Britain fight in North America?

2. Why did most Indians prefer to trade with the French?

3. Describe Pontiac's plan and explain why it failed.

4. **GEOGRAPHY SKILL:** Look at the Atlas map on page 292. Where are the Appalachian Mountains? Why were these mountains used by the British to divide their colonies and Indian lands?

5. **THINKING SKILL:** Why do you think Pontiac decided to fight the British? What else might he have done?

REVIEWING VOCABULARY

Number a sheet of paper from 1 to 3. Beside each number write the letter of the definition that best matches the word or term.

1. *colonies*
   a. A place where people met to exchange goods
   b. A group of mountains in the eastern part of North America
   c. A place that is ruled by another country
2. *missionary*
   a. Someone who travels to unknown lands
   b. Someone who gathers furs to sell
   c. Someone who teaches religion
3. *stockade*
   a. A French fort
   b. A fence around a fort
   c. An English blockhouse

REVIEWING FACTS

1. How did White Beaver help Robert La Salle on his travels?
2. Why was the Wabash River important to the French and the Indians?
3. Name two forts that the French built in present-day Indiana.
4. What changes did the Treaty of Paris bring about in North America?
5. Why did Pontiac work to unite Indian groups against the British?

((≡▷ WRITING ABOUT MAIN IDEAS

1. **Writing a Letter:** Imagine that you are a child living in a French fort before the French and Indian War. Write a letter to a friend in France describing life at the fort.
2. **Writing a Speech:** Imagine that you are Pontiac. Write a speech that you will give to Indian leaders explaining why they should join you in fighting the British.
3. **Writing a Newspaper Story:** Write a newspaper story that describes the end of Pontiac's Rebellion. Be sure to tell how the rebellion ended. Also report what happened to Pontiac's followers.

BUILDING SKILLS: USING REFERENCE BOOKS

1. Name two different kinds of reference books.
2. What kind of reference book would you use to find information about Pontiac?
3. What kind of reference book would you use to find the meaning of the word *treaty*?
4. Why is it important to know how to use reference books?

REVIEWING VOCABULARY

artifact   missionary
colony   prehistoric
explorer

Number a sheet of paper from 1 to 5. Beside each number write the word from the list above that best matches the definition.

1. An object made by people long ago
2. Before the time when people wrote history
3. A territory that is ruled by another country
4. A person who travels to unknown lands
5. A person who teaches others about his or her religion

WRITING ABOUT THE UNIT

1. **Writing a Sales Speech:** Imagine that you are a French fur trader who lives near Fort Ouiatenon. Write a speech that might persuade Indians to trade their goods for yours. Make sure to describe the goods that you are selling and tell why Indians might want to use them.
2. **Writing a Summary:** Write a paragraph summarizing the material that is found in Lesson 4 under the heading "War Begins."

3. **Writing a Comparison:** Write a paragraph in which you compare British fur traders with French fur traders. Compare the goals of these two groups of people. Also compare the way in which each of these groups dealt with Indians.

ACTIVITIES

1. **Making a Diorama:** Make a diorama showing what life was like in a typical Miami village before the French arrived. To get started, re-read the material found in Chapter 3, Lesson 2, about Sweet Breeze and her family. You might also want to do further research in the library.
2. **Researching an Important Person:** Choose one of the Key People mentioned in Unit 2. Use reference books and other library books to learn more about that person. Prepare a report about the person whom you have chosen.
3. **Working Together to Make a Decision:** Work with several classmates to decide on a group project about this unit. The project should help you to review what you have learned. You may wish to prepare a puppet show, draw a comic book, or create a mural.

dug/duplicate

dug Past tense and past participle of **dig.** We *dug* a hole and planted a tree in it. Look up **dig** for more information.
  dug (dug) *verb.*

dugout **1.** A rough shelter that is made by digging a hole in the ground or in the side of a hill. **2.** A long, low shelter in which baseball players sit during a game when they are not playing. Dugouts are built at the side of the field. **3.** A canoe or boat that is made by hollowing out a large log.
  dug·out (dug′out′) *noun, plural* **dugouts.**

duke A nobleman who has the highest rank below a prince.
  duke (dūk *or* dūk) *noun, plural* **dukes.**

dune A mound or ridge of sand that has been piled up by the wind.
  dune (dün *or* dūn) *noun, plural* **dunes.**

dune

D

BUILDING SKILLS: USING REFERENCE BOOKS

1. Would you look in an encyclopedia or a dictionary to find out more about Kekionga?

2. Look at the guide words on the dictionary page above.

   a. Which of the following words would you find on that page?
   duke   dye   desk   dull

   b. Which of the following words might you find on the next page?
   different   duty   cell   dwarf

3. Suppose that you had two volumes of an encyclopedia in front of you. One volume contained everything from *silver* to *Tennessee*. The other volume had everything from *Texas* to *tornado*. Which one would contain an article about Tecumseh?

4. At which times during the course of a school day might you need to use a dictionary? At which times might you need to use an encyclopedia?

 **LINKING PAST, PRESENT AND FUTURE**

French fur traders traveled to parts of North America where few Europeans had ever been. In this unit you read about how they tried to work together with the people whom they met in the new land.
What chances do you think people of today have for similar experiences? What chances might people of the future have?

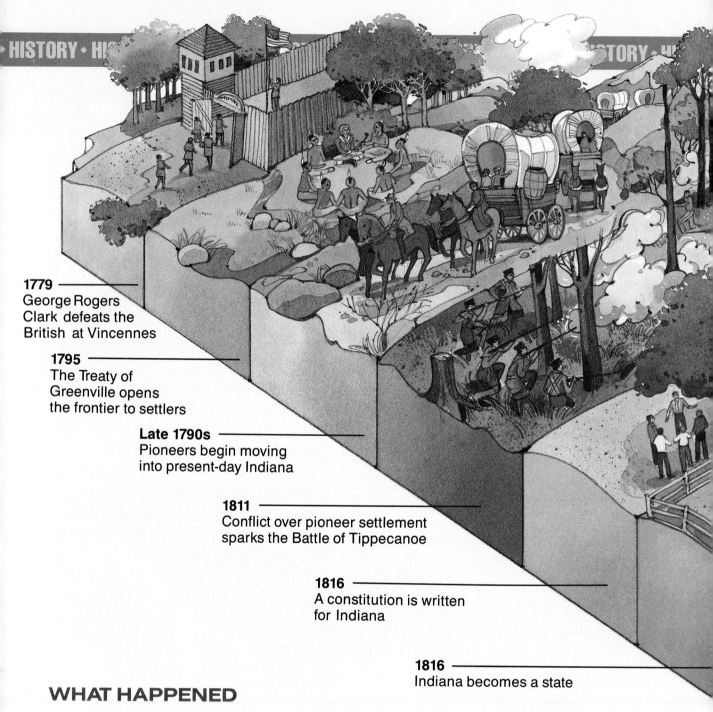

1779
George Rogers
Clark defeats the
British at Vincennes

1795
The Treaty of
Greenville opens
the frontier to settlers

Late 1790s
Pioneers begin moving
into present-day Indiana

1811
Conflict over pioneer settlement
sparks the Battle of Tippecanoe

1816
A constitution is written
for Indiana

1816
Indiana becomes a state

1816-1830
Young
Abraham Lincoln
grows up on the
Indiana frontier

WHAT HAPPENED

You have already read
about some of the people who
helped to build the Indiana territory,
but the whole story has not yet been told.
In this unit you will read about the people and
the struggles that helped Indiana to become
America's nineteenth state.

96

UNIT
3
FROM TERRITORY TO STATEHOOD

CHAPTER 5

AMERICANS COME TO INDIANA

FOCUS

I like the stories I hear at the George Rogers Clark Memorial. I also like to look at the carvings on the bridge near the memorial.

Josh Dobbs lives in Vincennes. He likes learning about the role his town played in the United States' war for independence from Great Britain.

1 The American Revolution

READ TO LEARN

Key Vocabulary

frontier
Declaration of
  Independence
American
  Revolution

Key People

Henry Hamilton
George Rogers Clark

Key Places

Fort Sackville

Read Aloud

We plunged into the water sometimes to the neck. Rain all this day.

This is how one soldier described a secret march through the forests of Indiana in 1779. This march is one of the most famous events in Indiana's history. In this lesson you will read more about the march and why it was so important to the history of our country.

Read for Purpose

1. **WHAT YOU KNOW:** Which country controlled the land west of the Appalachian Mountains after 1763?
2. **WHAT YOU WILL LEARN:** How did George Rogers Clark help Indiana to become part of the United States?

TROUBLE WITH BRITAIN

As you read earlier, Great Britain's Proclamation of 1763 told the colonists that they could not move west of the Appalachians. This pleased the Indians because it protected their land from settlement by British colonists.

The proclamation angered colonists, though, because they wanted to be free to move to the frontier (frun tîr'). The frontier is land at the edge of a settled area. They did not like being told where they could and could not go by the government in faraway Britain.

99

The colonists became even more angry when the British government began to tax them. The tax was to help pay for the cost of the French and Indian War. The colonists thought that they should have some say over the taxes they paid.

WAR BREAKS OUT

In 1776 the 13 colonies broke away from British rule. The settlers named their new country the United States of America, and they called themselves Americans. In a written statement called the Declaration of Independence, they said that they were no longer under Britain's rule. Independence means freedom from rule by others.

Fighting broke out between the British and the Americans as a result of the Declaration of Inde-

pendence. This war, which lasted until 1783, was called the American Revolution. A revolution is a sudden, total change in a government, usually by force.

Most of the battles of the American Revolution were fought in the 13 British colonies. But important battles also took place west of the 13 colonies. These battles helped to decide who would control "the West"—that is, the land west of the Appalachian Mountains.

WAR IN THE WEST

Henry Hamilton commanded the British army in the West. He and other British commanders decided that one way to defeat the Americans would be to get help from the Indians.

Hamilton worked hard to get Indian support. In 1777 he met with leaders of the Miami, Potawatomi, and other Indian groups. He gave them food, guns, and knives. Hamilton also put on war paint and danced a war dance with them. This showed that the British were "on the warpath" against the Americans.

Hamilton told the Indian leaders that the Americans wanted to move west and take over Indian lands. To protect their lands many Indians agreed to fight against the Americans. Bitter fighting broke out between American settlers and the Indians living in the land that is now Kentucky.

Henry Hamilton commanded British forts on the western frontier.

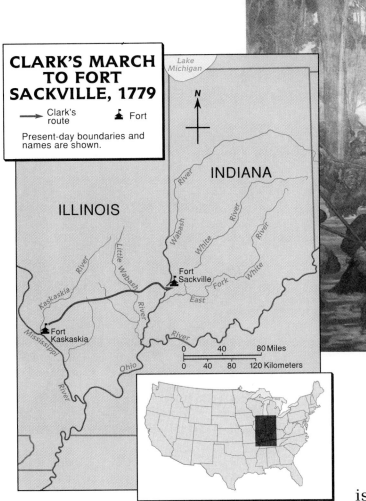

CLARK'S MARCH TO FORT SACKVILLE, 1779

→ Clark's route   ▲ Fort

Present-day boundaries and names are shown.

N

Lake Michigan

INDIANA

ILLINOIS

Wabash River

White River

River

White

East Fork

Fort Sackville

Little Wabash River

Kaskaskia River

Fort Kaskaskia

Mississippi River

Ohio River

0   40   80 Miles

0   40   80   120 Kilometers

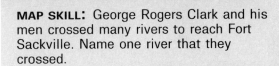

MAP SKILL: George Rogers Clark and his men crossed many rivers to reach Fort Sackville. Name one river that they crossed.

GEORGE ROGERS CLARK

George Rogers Clark, an American who lived on the Kentucky frontier, was 24 years old when the American Revolution began. He was tall and had long, red hair. He dressed in deerskins and was an excellent hunter and fighter. Indians called Clark "long knife."

When war broke out Clark volunteered to help the American side. He got the approval of American leaders in Virginia to fight the British in the West. Then he gathered together 170 volunteers to serve as his army.

Clark already knew that the British had taken over a fort at Vincennes named Fort Sackville. He then learned that Henry Hamilton himself had taken charge of the fort!

Clark reasoned that if he and his men could take Fort Sackville, "we would . . . save the whole American cause." He decided to make a surprise attack on the fort.

CLARK'S MARCH

On February 5, 1779, Clark and his men set off from an American fort at Kaskaskia, in what is today Illinois, and headed east toward Fort Sackville. Look at the map on this page to locate the route that they took.

Clark's capture of Fort Sackville was a great victory for the American cause. A statue at Vincennes honors Clark's memory.

At last, 18 days after they had set out, Clark and his men reached the fort at Vincennes.

CLARK CAPTURES FORT SACKVILLE

Clark sent a messenger ahead to warn the people of Vincennes that an American army was going to attack Fort Sackville. The French townspeople offered to feed the tired and hungry men.

Clark and his men crept up to a small hill that was behind the town. There they could not be seen from the fort. Then the men marched back and forth waving big flags, which were visible over the top of the hill. It looked as if a huge American army was preparing to attack!

Flooded land and overflowing rivers stretched before Clark and his men. The weather was very cold, and very rainy. "Marched all day through rain and water," one of the soldiers wrote in a diary.

Clark's men were getting discouraged. Some wanted to turn back. But Clark kept pushing the men to go on. "Clark encourages his men, which gives them great spirits," the soldier wrote. Their spirits were also lifted when the little drummer boy who was with them used his drum to keep afloat while crossing a cold, deep river.

Just as Clark had planned, the British were unprepared for an attack. Henry Hamilton had not imagined that anyone would cross the flooded plains surrounding Fort Sackville in wintertime.

Clark's men began firing on the fort at night. The frontier fighters were deadly shots. The British soldiers became afraid to stand up to fire their weapons.

The next day Henry Hamilton and his men marched out of Fort Sackville and surrendered. Clark's men then raised the new flag of the United States over the fort.

Today many people visit George Rogers Clark National Historic Park in Vincennes. The park reminds them of Clark's victory at Fort Sackville.

THE RESULTS OF THE WAR

When America won the war in 1783 Britain gave up its rights to the land in the West. This pushed America's borders all the way to the Mississippi River. You can see how much bigger America became by looking at the map on this page.

Now American settlers were free to move west. But the frontier was still home to many groups of Native Americans. The question remained: Who would rule the frontier, the Indians or the Americans? Even though the war with Britain was over, the struggle for the land west of the Appalachians was not.

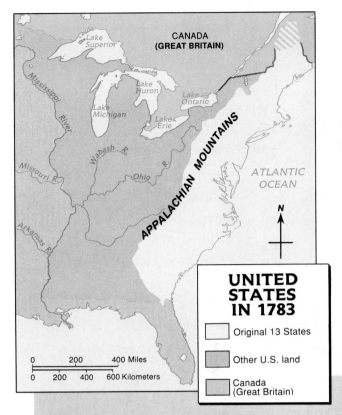

UNITED STATES IN 1783

☐ Original 13 States

☐ Other U.S. land

☐ Canada (Great Britain)

MAP SKILL: Which river marked the western border of the United States in 1783?

 Check Your Reading

1. Why did Indian groups join the British side in the American Revolution?
2. Why was George Rogers Clark's small army able to defeat Henry Hamilton's large army?
3. **GEOGRAPHY SKILL:** Look at the map of Clark's march on page 101. Why do you think Clark believed that taking this route would surprise the British?
4. **THINKING SKILL:** What do you think might have happened if Clark's attack had not caught the British by surprise?

READ TO LEARN

Key Vocabulary

territory
pioneer
Battle of Fallen
    Timbers
Treaty of Greenville

Key People

Little Turtle
Anthony Wayne

Key Places

Northwest
    Territory
Clarksville

Read Aloud

We want peace; restore to us our country and we shall be enemies no longer.

This is what one group of Indians told American settlers who wanted to move west. They would not fight if they were allowed to keep their land. But war broke out as more settlers began moving onto Indian lands.

Read for Purpose

1. **WHAT YOU KNOW:** How do you think the Miami Indians felt about their land?
2. **WHAT YOU WILL LEARN:** How was the Treaty of Greenville a turning point in the history of our state and our country?

THE NORTHWEST TERRITORY

The United States gained control over a huge area of land when it won independence from Great Britain in 1783. As you have read, the land north of the Ohio River was fertile, with many rivers. Native Americans already knew that places such as the Wabash River Valley were excellent places to live.

The American government called this land the Northwest Territory. A territory is land that is owned by a country but is not a state of that country. Locate the Northwest Territory on the map on page 105.

During the 1780s pioneers from Virginia, North Carolina, and other states began to move to the Northwest Territory. Pioneers are the first people of a group to move into an area. They settled in places like Vincennes and Clarksville, a town on the Ohio River named for George Rogers Clark.

THE WAR OVER LAND

The move westward by pioneers disturbed many Native Americans, including the Miami. They feared that pioneers would take their land from them. Indian warriors began to attack pioneers to protect their lands.

The pioneers and the United States Army joined together to fight back. Soldiers burned Indian villages and destroyed their crops. War raged once again on the frontier.

American soldiers attacked the Miami village of Kekionga in 1791. Waiting for them were 1,000 warriors led by the Miami chief Little Turtle. Little Turtle and his warriors defeated the American soldiers. This was a big victory for Native Americans, but it did not end the fighting.

THE BATTLE OF FALLEN TIMBERS

A new commander took charge of the American soldiers—General Anthony Wayne. Wayne was so willing to take risks that his men

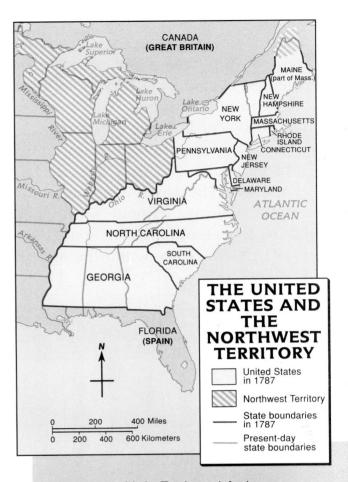

THE UNITED STATES AND THE NORTHWEST TERRITORY

	United States in 1787
	Northwest Territory
——	State boundaries in 1787
----	Present-day state boundaries

MAP SKILL: Little Turtle and Anthony Wayne fought for control over the Northwest Territory. What land was at stake?

The Granger Collection

called him "Mad Anthony." Indians called him "the chief who never sleeps" because he worked so hard to train his soldiers.

Little Turtle warned Miami warriors that Wayne and his army could not be beaten but they did not believe him. The warriors prepared for battle anyway, without Little Turtle's leadership. On August 20, 1794, Wayne's army and the Miami fought at a place in Ohio where a tornado had knocked down many trees. This is the reason that the fight is called the Battle of Fallen Timbers. The battle lasted only one hour before the Indians surrendered. "Mad Anthony" had won.

After the Battle of Fallen Timbers, the Miami listened to Little Turtle. They decided that it was time "to bury the bloody hatchet." This meant that it was time to stop fighting and time to make peace.

To keep watch over the Miami, the Americans built a fort at Kekionga. They called it Fort Wayne, in honor of "the chief who never sleeps."

THE TREATY OF GREENVILLE

In 1795 Little Turtle and other chiefs met with General Wayne at Fort Greenville, in Ohio. They came to an agreement called the Treaty of Greenville. As you have read a treaty is an agreement between nations.

In the treaty the Indians promised to give up land in the eastern part of the Northwest Territory. In return General Wayne promised to let Indians live in the western part. He also promised that the United States would pay the Indians for the land they gave up. Look at the map on this page. Which part of Indiana was opened up to pioneer settlement by the treaty?

MAP SKILL: What land was opened up to pioneer settlement by the Treaty of Greenville?

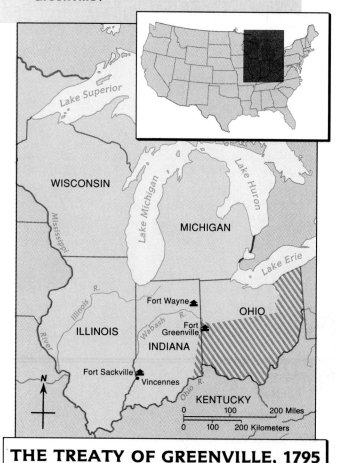

THE TREATY OF GREENVILLE, 1795

Northwest Territory

Land given up by Indians in treaty

Present-day boundaries are shown.

The Treaty of Greenville was signed in present-day Ohio. General Anthony Wayne's signature can be seen at the top of the treaty.

A TURNING POINT

A turning point is the time at which an important change takes place. The Treaty of Greenville was a turning point in American history.

The treaty caused great change in the lives of the Indians. They had to leave their homes behind and move to new land that was already home to other people. Imagine how you would feel if you were forced to move far away from home.

The Treaty of Greenville was also a turning point for the American pioneers. It opened the eastern part of the Northwest Territory to settlement by more Americans. Many pioneers moved there after the treaty was signed.

MAKING WAY FOR SETTLERS

General Wayne's victory and the Indians' signing of the Treaty of Greenville opened up new territory to American settlement. It was not long before pioneers began flocking to the new land.

 Check Your Reading

1. Why did Indians and Americans go to war after the American Revolution?

2. Why is the Battle of Fallen Timbers seen as a turning point in American history?

3. **GEOGRAPHY SKILL:** Which rivers and lakes made up the borders of the Northwest Territory?

4. **THINKING SKILL:** Think about Little Turtle's decision to sign the Treaty of Greenville. Do you think it was the best decision for the Miami people? Explain your answer.

107

Reading Time Lines

Key Vocabulary

time line

As you were reading about the early explorers of our state, you came across a number of phrases that told you when certain important events took place. These phrases may have contained actual dates, such as *in 1776*. Or they may have given you other time clues, such as *one year later* or *a few days later*. To understand the history of our state, you need to know when certain events took place.

Because we do not have a picture of time, we use time lines to help us keep track of events. A time line is a diagram that shows when events took place. It also shows the order in which events happened and the amount of time that passed between them.

Reading a Time Line

The time line below shows some of the important events in the history of the exploration of our state. The name of each event is written beneath the date on which it happened. The earliest event is located at the left end of the time line. The latest event is at the right.

A time line is divided into equal parts. Each part of the time line represents a time period. This time period can be short, such as one month. It can also be long, such as 100 years. Into which time periods is the time line below divided?

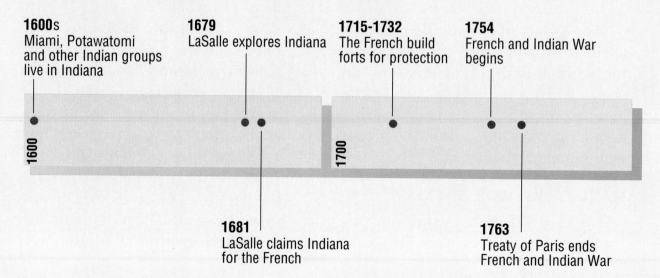

1600s
Miami, Potawatomi and other Indian groups live in Indiana

1679
LaSalle explores Indiana

1715-1732
The French build forts for protection

1754
French and Indian War begins

1600

1700

1681
LaSalle claims Indiana for the French

1763
Treaty of Paris ends French and Indian War

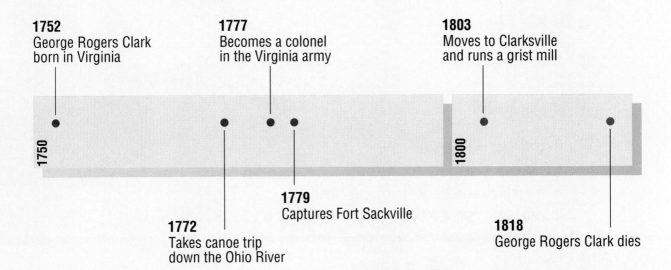

1752
George Rogers Clark
born in Virginia

1777
Becomes a colonel
in the Virginia army

1803
Moves to Clarksville
and runs a grist mill

1750

1800

1779
Captures Fort Sackville

1772
Takes canoe trip
down the Ohio River

1818
George Rogers Clark dies

To read a time line, begin by looking for the earliest and latest events. Which is the first event shown on the time line on page 108? What happened in early Indiana between the years 1650 and 1700?

Look again at the time line on page 108 to see the order in which the events took place. Did the French build forts for protection before or after the French and Indian War began?

Making a Time Line

Time lines can be made for different purposes. The time line above shows the life of George Rogers Clark, about whom you read in Lesson 1. How many years are shown on the time line?

Make a time line of your life. Use the time line above as a guide. Divide the line into two-year periods. Make the year you were born the first date. Then include the year that you started kindergarten or first grade and the year that you entered the fourth grade. Also include at least three other important events in your life.

Reviewing the Skill

Use the information in this lesson and the time lines on page 108 and above to answer the following questions.

1. What is a time line?
2. Between which years did the French and Indian War take place?
3. When did La Salle claim Indiana for the French?
4. In which year did George Rogers Clark capture Fort Sackville?
5. How old was Clark when he became a colonel in the Virginia army?
6. Why is it important to know how to use a time line?

READ TO LEARN

Key Vocabulary

custom
interpreter

Key Places

Deaf Man's Village

Read for Purpose

1. **WHAT YOU KNOW:** What were some reasons that the settlers and the Indians fought?
2. **WHAT YOU WILL LEARN:** How did one person's life change because of this fighting?

THE FRANCES SLOCUM STORY

In Chapter 5 you read about fighting between settlers and the Indians. The following story shows how the fighting greatly changed one woman's life.

MA-CON-A-QUA TELLS A SECRET

In 1835 George Ewing, a trader from Logansport, Indiana, arrived at Deaf Man's Village on the banks of the Mississinewa River. The Deaf Man, after whom the village was named, had been a Miami chief named She-po-ca-nah. Ma-con-a-qua, the widow of Deaf Man, offered the trader lodging and food. Ewing ate supper with Ma-con-a-qua and her family. After dinner the other members of the household excused themselves for the evening. Ma-con-a-qua asked the trader to remain. She wished to speak to him alone.

Ma-con-a-qua looked slightly frightened. She said, "I am old now and afraid I soon may die. I need to give

someone a great secret I have been carrying with me. I do not want to carry this secret to my grave. Please let me give it to you."

Ewing agreed to listen to Ma-con-a-qua's secret. Ma-con-a-qua told him the following story.

"I am not an Indian, even though I look and speak like one. I am the daughter of settlers. I was taken as a child from my home in Pennsylvania by the Delaware Indians. I don't remember when. I don't remember my original name. I don't even remember how to speak English.

"I was adopted by a Delaware chief and his wife, who lived in Ohio. They raised me as if I were their own child. When I was a young woman, my parents and I moved to Indiana to live in the village of Little Turtle, a great war chief of the Miami. Then General Anthony Wayne and his soldiers came to stop the fighting between the settlers and the Indians. General Wayne defeated the Miami. We were forced to give our lands to the settlers.

"My family went back to visit our old home in Ohio. There I met She-po-ca-nah for the very first time. She-po-ca-nah was badly wounded, and I helped him to get well. We married and had four children. As She-po-ca-

nah got older, he became deaf and gave up being chief of the village that we lived in. Finally we moved to the place where you now visit me—Deaf Man's Village.

"I have held this story in my heart for many years. You must not tell this story to anyone. I believe that the settlers have much power. I am afraid that they will make me return to them. I do not wish to leave my children and the land I love. My life here is almost finished. I do not wish to leave this place."

Ewing listened carefully to Ma-con-a-qua's story. He promised Ma-con-a-qua that she would not be forced to go back to her family in Pennsylvania. Then he set out to find them.

THE SEARCH FOR A LOST FAMILY

The trader did not know where to start. He decided to write to the postmaster in Lancaster, Pennsylvania. But the postmaster did not answer his letter. However, two years later a new postmaster in Lancaster found the letter and was fascinated by it. Soon the brothers and sister of Ma-con-a-qua were located. They could hardly wait to meet their long-lost sister, whose name they said was Frances Slocum.

In 1837 Ma-con-a-qua met her brothers and sister. Ma-con-a-qua greeted them politely, but without show-

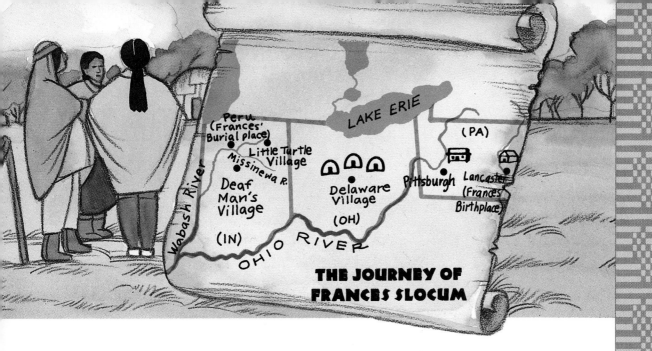

THE JOURNEY OF FRANCES SLOCUM

ing too much emotion, as was the Miami custom. A custom is the usual practice or actions of a group of people. Ma-con-a-qua's brothers and sister, now over 60 years old, recognized her by her reddish-brown hair and by a misshaped finger she had as a child. Ma-con-a-qua could not understand English, and her brothers and sister could not understand the language of the Miami. An interpreter was needed for them to speak to each other. An interpreter is a person who helps people who speak different languages to understand one another. Through the interpreter Ma-con-a-qua's family told her the following story.

THE SEARCH FOR FRANCES

The time was the American Revolution. The Slocum family were Quakers who did not believe in fighting. They were on good terms with the Indians, who respected the ways of the Quakers. However, one of Frances's brothers had fought with the Indians. In revenge a group of Delaware Indians attacked the Slocum home. They kidnapped four-year-old Frances. Mrs. Slocum was filled with sorrow by the disappearance of Frances. She searched for her daughter throughout her lifetime. After Mrs. Slocum died Frances's brothers and sister continued the search.

AT HOME IN INDIANA

Ma-con-a-qua listened calmly to the story. Her brothers and sister had so hoped that they would receive a warm welcome. After a time Ma-con-a-qua did become more friendly toward them. She agreed to visit them at the Bearss Hotel in the town of Peru.

At the hotel Ma-con-a-qua's brothers and sister tried to convince her to go back to Pennsylvania with them. But Ma-con-a-qua would not even go to Pennsylvania for a visit. She was worried that she might die on a visit there. She wanted to die in Indiana. She wanted to be buried near her husband and sons.

Ma-con-a-qua died ten years later. The home and burial place of Frances Slocum, the "White Rose of the Miami," is located outside of Peru, Indiana.

 Check Your Reading

1. Why did Ma-con-a-qua keep the fact that she was a child of settlers a secret?
2. Why did Ma-con-a-qua and the Slocums need an interpreter when they met?
3. Why did Ma-con-a-qua choose to stay in Indiana?
4. **THINKING SKILL:** How might Ma-con-a-qua's life have been different if she had escaped from the Delaware Indians as a child?

REVIEWING VOCABULARY

American Revolution
Declaration of Independence
frontier
territory
Treaty of Greenville

Number a sheet of paper from 1 to 5. Beside each number write the word or term from the list above that best completes each sentence.

1. A _____ is the land that lies at the edge of a settled area.
2. In the _____ the settlers in America stated that they were no longer ruled by Great Britain.
3. The British and Americans fought the _____ for control of the American colonies.
4. A _____ is land that is owned by a country but is not a state.
5. Under the terms of the _____, Indian leaders gave up land in the Northwest Territory.

REVIEWING FACTS

Number a sheet of paper from 1 to 5. Beside each number write **T** if the statement is true. If the statement is false, rewrite it to make it true.

1. Henry Hamilton was an American commander who fought the British during the American Revolution.
2. George Rogers Clark led men through flooded land to attack Fort Sackville.
3. After Henry Hamilton had surrendered, Clark's men raised Indiana's flag over the fort.
4. American soldiers defeated Little Turtle and the Miami at Kekionga in 1791.
5. After the Treaty of Greenville was signed, many Indians had to leave their homes.

✏️ WRITING ABOUT MAIN IDEAS

1. **Writing a Diary Entry:** Imagine that you marched with George Rogers Clark. Write an entry for your diary describing one day of your march.
2. **Writing a Poem:** Imagine that you are an Indian living after the time when the Treaty of Greenville was signed. Write a poem that tells how you feel about what has happened.

BUILDING SKILLS: READING TIME LINES

Read the time line on page 108. Then answer these questions.

1. What does the time line show?
2. When was the Treaty of Paris signed?
3. How many years does the time line cover?
4. What is the latest event shown on the time line?
5. How does a time line help you to understand the order of events?

CHAPTER 6

INDIANA BECOMES A STATE

▼ FOCUS ▼

When I visit the old state capital, it's fun to think about what people did in my town a long time ago.

Living in Indiana's old capital city, Corydon, makes history come alive for Rae Anne Feller. In this chapter you will read about the events that led to Indiana's becoming a state.

1 Shaping the Territory

READ TO LEARN

Key Vocabulary

Ordinance of 1785
Northwest Ordinance
slave
population
census

Key People

William Henry
 Harrison

Key Places

Indiana
 Territory
Grouseland

Read Aloud

The country about this place is, I think, the most beautiful in the world.

The first governor of the Indiana Territory used these words to describe the countryside around Vincennes in 1801. Native Americans and pioneers alike were proud of the land that they called home. In this lesson you will read about the beginnings of American settlement on this beautiful land.

Read for Purpose

1. **WHAT YOU KNOW:** How did the United States gain ownership of the land that included the present-day state of Indiana?
2. **WHAT YOU WILL LEARN:** How did the Ordinances of 1785 and 1787 affect settlement of the Indiana Territory?

A NEW TERRITORY

In Chapter 5 you read that pioneers began moving into the Northwest Territory after the Treaty of Greenville. Because of this treaty, many more pioneers felt safer in moving to the West.

Two important laws shaped life in the Northwest Territory. Both were passed by the United States government in the 1780s.

The Ordinance (ôr′ də nəns) of 1785 organized a system for buying and selling land. It divided the land

117

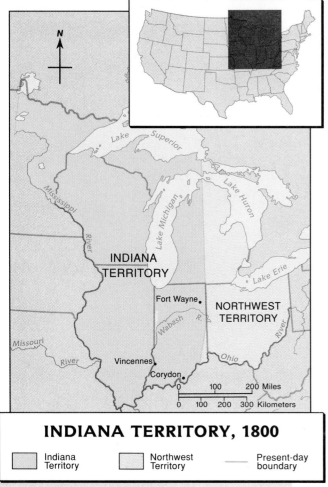

INDIANA TERRITORY, 1800

| | Indiana Territory | | Northwest Territory | | Present-day boundary |

MAP SKILL: What present-day states did the Indiana Territory include?

into townships, or land six miles (10 km) square. Each township was further divided into 36 1-mile (2-km) squares, or sections.

The ordinance set aside one section from each township for a public school. Sections were to be sold for $640 apiece. Although this price was high for most pioneers, the ordinance did provide a system for buying land in the territory.

The second important law, passed in 1787, was called the Northwest Ordinance. It described the rights of Americans living in the new territory. It provided them with a government to help keep order in the land.

The ordinance also stated that people in the territory could not keep slaves. A slave is someone who is owned by another person.

In other parts of the United States, slavery was legal. The first slaves were from Africa. They had been captured there and brought to America in the 1600s.

The Northwest Ordinance was also important because it set up a system for the creation of new states. When more than 60,000 people lived in a territory, they could ask to become a state. Finally, the Northwest Ordinance stated that a territory would be ruled by a governor chosen by the President of the United States.

WILLIAM HENRY HARRISON

In 1800 the Northwest Territory was divided into two parts. The western part was called the Indiana Territory. Look at the map on this page. What was the western border of the Indiana Territory in 1800?

That year a young man, William Henry Harrison, was named the first governor of the Indiana Territory. Harrison had fought with Anthony Wayne at Fallen Timbers. He governed the Indiana Territory for the next 12 years.

Governor Harrison lived in Vincennes, which was the first capital of the Indiana Territory. He built a large brick house there that he called Grouseland.

A CHANGING TERRITORY

While Harrison was governor, the borders of the Indiana Territory changed several times. In 1805 Congress broke off land from the Indiana Territory to create the Michigan Territory. In 1809 the Indiana Territory was divided again to create the Illinois Territory. This left the Indiana Territory with the borders that our state has today.

Governor Harrison and the pioneers wanted the new Indiana Territory to grow. But, as you read in Chapter 5, the Treaty of Greenville promised Native Americans that most of the land in the Indiana Territory was theirs, not the pioneers'.

To open up the land to pioneer settlement, Harrison signed treaties with several Native American leaders between 1803 and 1809. Under the terms of the treaties, Native Americans gave up their rights to land in the southern part of the territory in exchange for money.

Soon afterwards, thousands of pioneers began to settle on this land. The Indians who lived there had no choice but to look elsewhere for places to live.

THE TERRITORY GROWS

By 1809 the Indiana Territory was smaller in size than it was in 1800. However, the population in

William Henry Harrison's beautiful home was named Grouseland.

The Granger Collection

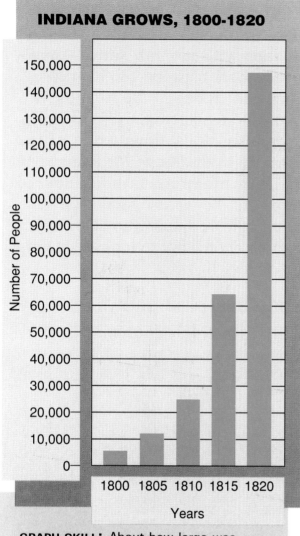

INDIANA GROWS, 1800-1820

Number of People

150,000
140,000
130,000
120,000
110,000
100,000
90,000
80,000
70,000
60,000
50,000
40,000
30,000
20,000
10,000
0

1800 1805 1810 1815 1820

Years

GRAPH SKILL: About how large was Indiana's population in 1820? How many more Hoosiers were there in 1820 than in 1810?

there were only 5,641 pioneers in the territory. In 1812, however, the number had grown to over 30,000 people. By 1815 a census showed that the count was up to 63,897! As the graph on this page shows, the next five years brought even greater changes.

A TIME OF CHANGE

The Indiana Territory's early years were busy ones. The territory's borders changed twice. Treaties with Native Americans opened up new land to thousands of pioneers.

Governor Harrison was pleased with these changes. The territory was growing. Soon it would reach statehood. Native Americans were angry, however. These changes were destroying their way of life. In the next lesson you will read about their fight to save their lands.

 Check Your Reading

1. How did the Ordinance of 1785 organize the land in the Indiana Territory?
2. What were three important parts of the Northwest Ordinance?
3. **GEOGRAPHY SKILL:** Name two territories that were created from land that was part of the Indiana Territory.
4. **THINKING SKILL:** Compare and contrast the Indiana Territory in 1800 with the Indiana Territory in 1815.

the territory was growing. Population is the number of people who live in a place. The graph on this page shows how quickly the territory's population was increasing.

In 1800 a census was taken in the Indiana Territory. A census is a count of the number of people who live in a certain area. It showed that

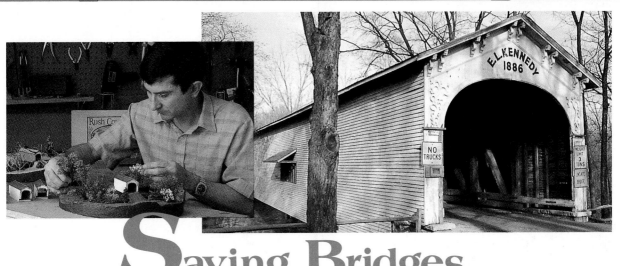

Saving Bridges

Jim Irvine lives in Rush County on the land his grandfather farmed years ago. Down the hill from Jim's house is the Offutt's Ford Covered Bridge. In Jim's yard there is a half-scale model of an entrance to the bridge. The model is mounted on wheels so that it can be towed in parades to remind people of the wonderful old bridges.

Years ago there were hundreds of covered bridges in Indiana. But over time many of the bridges have been destroyed. Some were damaged by heavy traffic. Others were replaced with wider and stronger bridges.

Irvine was concerned that soon all of the historic covered bridges in Rush County would be gone. He decided to build models of the covered bridges to help persuade people that they should try to save them.

Irvine made detailed sketches of the bridges. "I need exact drawings so that I can make the models to scale—1 inch equals 20 feet," he explained. Irvine works on his models whenever he has free time.

Several of Irvine's friends also became interested in preserving the old bridges. Together they formed the Rush County Heritage Corporation. The group reminded government officials of the need to repair and maintain the existing covered bridges.

The Heritage group also started the Moscow Covered Bridge Festival. Each June the festival is held in Moscow, Indiana. Irvine sells his covered bridge models there. He gives all the money he makes from the models to the Rush County Heritage Corporation. "I know the money will be used to take care of the old bridges," Irvine says.

Irvine's talents and unselfish efforts help to preserve an important part of his county's history. His efforts have helped Indiana to retain a glimpse of its past.

Understanding Cause and Effect

Key Vocabulary

cause   effect

Amy forgot to set her alarm clock before going to bed. The next morning she overslept. Forgetting to set her alarm clock was the cause of her oversleeping. A cause is something that makes something else happen. Oversleeping was the effect of forgetting to set the alarm. An effect is what happens as a result of something else.

Read the two sentences below.

- Mark won the spelling bee.
- For weeks Mark studied lists of spelling words every evening.

The first sentence states an event that happened. The second sentence states the cause, or reason that the event happened. Mark won the spelling bee *because* he studied lists of words every evening.

Identifying cause and effect will help you to understand how events are related. You will see how one event leads to another.

Trying the Skill

Read each sentence below. Then tell which sentence states a cause and which sentence states an effect.

- William Henry Harrison and Tecumseh met to discuss the trouble between the pioneers and the Indians.
- Fighting broke out throughout the Indiana Territory between the pioneers and the Indians.

HELPING YOURSELF

The steps on the left can help you to identify causes and effects. The example on the right shows one way to apply these steps to the two sentences on page 122.

One Way to Find Cause and Effect	Example
1. Look at the events being described.	Indians and pioneers fought; Harrison and Tecumseh met.
2. In each sentence look for words that signal causes, such as *because*, *since*, and *as a result of*. If you do not find any word clues, ask yourself if one event is the reason that something else happened.	Did the fighting cause the two leaders to meet?
3. If the answer is yes, you have found a cause.	The trouble between the two groups was the reason the two leaders met.
4. Look for words that signal effects, such as *so*, *therefore*, and *as a result*. If you do not find any word clues signaling effects, ask yourself what happened as a result of the cause. What happened is an effect.	As a result of trouble between the two groups, the two leaders met.

How were you able to tell which sentence stated a cause and which sentence stated an effect?

Applying the Skill

Now apply what you have learned. Read each pair of sentences below. Tell which sentence states the cause and which sentence states the effect.

- The Eagles practice hard each day.
- The Eagles win almost every game.
- Karen's grades are always high.
- Karen listens very carefully in class.

Now check yourself by answering the following questions.

1. What is the first thing you should do to identify cause and effect?

    a. Find the cause.
    b. Look at the events being described.
    c. Ask what happened.

2. What is one effect of practicing hard?

3. What is one effect of careful listening in class?

Reviewing the Skill

1. What is the difference between a cause and an effect?

2. What are the four steps you could follow to find cause and effect?

3. Why is it important to be able to tell the difference between causes and effects?

2 Indians Fight For Their Land

READ TO LEARN

Key Vocabulary

Battle of Tippecanoe
War of 1812
Battle of the Thames

Key People

Tecumseh
Tenskwatawa

Key Place

Prophetstown

Read Aloud

He is a bold, active, sensible man, daring in the extreme and capable of any undertaking.

This is how William Henry Harrison described an Indian leader. Although the two men were enemies, they had a great deal of respect for each other. In this lesson you will read about the final struggle between Native Americans and pioneers in the Indiana Territory.

Read for Purpose

1. **WHAT YOU KNOW:** What were some reasons for the struggles between the Indians and the pioneers?
2. **WHAT YOU WILL LEARN:** Which events led to the end of fighting between the Indians and the pioneers?

TECUMSEH AND THE PROPHET

In the last lesson you read about the treaties that Harrison signed with Indian leaders. Many Indians felt that Harrison's land purchases were wrong. One of their leaders was named Tecumseh (tə kum′ sə). Tecumseh was a strong and intelligent man who was respected by Indians and pioneers alike.

Tecumseh said that land purchases by Harrison and the pioneers must stop. If necessary, Tecumseh believed, all Native Americans should unite and fight together against the pioneers to defend their lands.

Another well-known leader was Tenskwatawa (ten skwät′ ə wä), Tecumseh's younger brother. Because many Indians believed that Tenskwatawa could see into the future, they called him "the Prophet."

Harrison told the Indians that the Prophet had no special powers. In 1806 he said, "If he really is a prophet, let him cause the sun to stand still." The Prophet said that he could do this, for he knew that an eclipse was coming. An eclipse of the sun happens when the sun is hidden by the moon for a time.

Before long the sun appeared to stand still, just as the Prophet had predicted. Now even more Indians believed that the Prophet had special powers. Tecumseh and the Prophet told them that they should not allow pioneers to take away their lands.

But Indians continued to lose their lands in the southern part of the territory. In 1810 Tecumseh met with Harrison at a place near Grouseland. He told Harrison that the land belonged to all Indians. No one leader or group of Indians could sell land unless all Indians agreed to it. Tecumseh showed Harrison how Indians felt about losing their lands by crowding him off a bench on which they both were sitting. This angered Harrison.

Bad feelings grew at the meeting. At one point Harrison pulled out his sword and Tecumseh his tomahawk. Later the two leaders put their weapons away, but they knew that their meeting was a failure.

The meeting between Tecumseh (*above*) and William Henry Harrison lasted for days, but it did not solve the two leaders' disagreements.

THE BATTLE OF TIPPECANOE

After his meeting with Harrison, Tecumseh worked even harder to unite all Indians against pioneer settlements. Harrison believed that Tecumseh and his followers were preparing for war. He decided to attack them first.

Tecumseh and the Prophet lived in a village along the Tippecanoe River called Prophetstown. Harrison chose to attack when Tecumseh was away, knowing that the Indians depended on him for leadership. Before dawn on November 7, 1811, the Battle of Tippecanoe began.

The Indians believed a promise made by the Prophet that bullets could not kill them. But this time the Prophet was wrong. Many warriors were killed. Soon after dawn the Indians retreated. The Battle of Tippecanoe was over.

THE WAR OF 1812

Harrison's victory at the Battle of Tippecanoe did not bring peace to the Indiana Territory. Instead, it helped to start more fighting. The struggle between the Indians and the pioneers continued.

The Indians began to receive help from British soldiers in Canada. The pioneers became angry at the British for helping Indians to attack frontier settlements. The British were also attacking American ships at sea. For these reasons the United States went to war with Britain. This war was called the War of 1812 because it began in 1812.

MAP SKILL: The Battle of Tippecanoe lasted only a few hours. In which direction was the battle from Vincennes?

The Granger Collection

One important battle in the War of 1812 involved William Henry Harrison and Tecumseh. Harrison was now a general in the American army, and Tecumseh was a general in the British army. The Battle of the Thames (temz) took place in Canada in 1813. Locate the battle site on the map on this page.

Harrison defeated the British and the Indians. Tecumseh was killed in the battle. This was the last major battle between Native Americans and pioneers in the Indiana Territory.

INDIAN LOSSES, PIONEER GAINS

It is easy to understand how the Indians must have felt about losing battles. But what pained them even more was the loss of their lands.

In 1818 the Miami and other Indian groups signed a treaty. It stated that they would leave their homes in the central part of Indiana by 1821. Later they joined the trail of Indians moving West, beyond the Mississippi River, where they hoped to live in peace.

As the Indians' moved, all of Indiana became open to settlement by pioneers. In the next lesson you will read about how the territory became a state.

SHOWDOWNS BETWEEN HARRISON AND INDIANS: 1810–1813

Indiana Territory   ✗ Battle   ♠ Fort

Lake Superior
CANADA
(GREAT BRITAIN)
N
Lake Michigan
Lake Huron
MICHIGAN TERRITORY
Thames ✗
Lake Erie
ILLINOIS TERRITORY
Fort Wayne ♠
PA
Tippecanoe ✗
Wabash R.
OHIO
Meeting near Grouseland, 1810
INDIANA TERRITORY
Ohio River
Vincennes
VIRGINIA

0 50 100 Miles
0 50 100 Kilometers

Check Your Reading

1. What did Tecumseh tell William Henry Harrison about the Indians' lands?
2. Was the Battle of Tippecanoe a turning point in Indiana history? Explain your answer.
3. **GEOGRAPHY SKILL:** Study the map on this page. Why do you think Ohio was the first state made from land in the Northwest Territory?
4. **THINKING SKILL:** List three questions that you could ask to find out more about Tecumseh and his fight to save Indian lands.

Do Settlers Have the Right to Buy Indian Land?

Around the time that Indiana became a state, groups of Potawatomi and Miami lived and hunted for food on land north of the Wabash River. But as more and more settlers came to Indiana, they began to claim the Indians' land for their own farms. They asked the United States government to make treaties with the Indians for their land. The government offered money and land west of the Mississippi River to the Indians in exchange for their land in Indiana. The government tried to convince them that they would find plenty of hunting land west of the Mississippi.

Many Native Americans needed money to pay their debts to traders. Some Potawatomi and Miami also needed money to buy food because much of their wild game had been driven away.

However, several Potawatomi and Miami leaders refused to sign treaties or to sell their land. Like Tecumseh, they believed that land should be shared by everyone and could not be bought or sold.

Did the settlers have the right to buy Indian land?

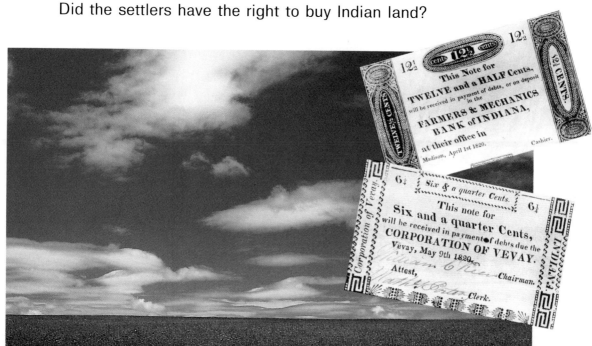

POINT ☆\☞

Land Should Not Be Sold

In the 1820s and 1830s government leaders tried to convince the Miami and the Potawatomi of northern Indiana that they should sell the land they used for hunting.

Chief Menominee, a Potawatomi leader, refused to sell his land to the United States government. Menominee said:

> I have not sold my lands. I will not sell them. I am not going to leave my lands and I do not want to hear any more about it. I do not believe that the President of the United States will by force drive me away from my home, the graves of my people, and my children who have gone to the Great Spirit.

- Why did Chief Menominee believe that he would be able to remain on his land?

COUNTERPOINT ☜\☆

Land Can Be Bought and Sold

As time went on, the government put more and more pressure on the Indian leaders to sell their land. New settlers were arriving each day and were impatient to purchase land. Government leaders told the Indians: "The government is willing to give for your land much more money than all the game upon it would sell for."

Government leaders also told the Indians that life in the West would be better for them. They also promised that the new western lands would belong to the Indians forever.

One leader wrote:

> You will then have a country filled with game, and you will also [be paid for] the land you have left. This [new] land will be reserved for you alone. It will be yours as long as the sun shines and the rain falls.

- What did government leaders offer to the Indians in return for their land?

UNDERSTANDING THE POINT/COUNTERPOINT

1. Why did some Potawatomi and Miami refuse to sell the land on which they lived and hunted?
2. Why did the United States government want the Indians to sell the land?
3. Which side do you think made the stronger case? Why?

3 Statehood

READMAP TO LEARN

Key Vocabulary
constitution
delegate

Key People
Jonathan Jennings

Key Places
Corydon
Indianapolis

Read Aloud

It is one of the most important duties that free men were ever called on to [do].

One of Indiana's first newspapers used these words to describe the steps taken to make Indiana a state.

Read for Purpose

1. **WHAT YOU KNOW:** Have there always been 50 states in the United States? How do you know?
2. **WHAT YOU WILL LEARN:** Why was the writing of a constitution important to our state?

THE MEETING AT CORYDON

June 10, 1816, was a hot and humid day in Corydon, the capital of the Indiana Territory since 1813. There was nothing unusual about the day's weather, but people were excited. A meeting was about to begin that would prepare the territory for statehood.

In order to become a state, a territory had to have a constitution (kon sti tü' shən). A constitution is a plan of government written by delegates, or people who speak for the voters who elected them.

Forty-three delegates gathered at the capital to write Indiana's constitution. Sometimes they met under the shade of a large elm tree because it was so hot indoors. Later this tree became known as the "Constitutional Elm." You can visit the Corydon Capitol State Historic site today.

DISCUSSIONS AND DECISIONS

The first thing the delegates did was to elect Jonathan Jennings as president of the meeting. This choice was no surprise. The young

Jonathan Jennings helped to write the constitution under this tree. The capitol building was completed later.

lawyer had represented the Indiana Territory in Congress since 1809. He was a popular and hard-working leader among the pioneers.

Under Jennings's leadership, the constitution took shape. It provided for the founding of free schools and a university. It stated that people would have the freedom to worship, speak, and write as they wished.

Perhaps most important, the delegates wrote that "all power is inherent in [belongs to] the people." By this they meant that the people of Indiana would control their own government. They would vote to make their own laws. Not everyone could vote, however. Women, Indians, and African-Americans were not allowed to vote at this time.

Jennings and the delegates ran into problems when they discussed slavery. The Northwest Ordinance had outlawed slavery in the Northwest Territory. Even so, some delegates thought that slavery should be allowed in the new state.

Jennings disagreed with these delegates. He said it was wrong for one person to own another person.

131

Lake Michigan

MICHIGAN TERRITORY

Fort Wayne 🛡

N

ILLINOIS
TERRITORY

KNOX

OHIO

WAYNE

FRANKLIN

DEARBORN

ORANGE

JEFFERSON

JACKSON

SWITZERLAND

Vincennes

WASHINGTON

CLARK

GIBSON

HARRISON

KENTUCKY

Corydon ★

PERRY

POSEY

WARRICK

0   20   40 Miles

0 20 40 60 Kilometers

INDIANA IN 1816:
A Frontier State

Counties
County line

★ State capital

Unorganized land

🛡 Fort

MAP SKILL: Was most of Indiana made up of counties or of unorganized land in 1816?

Most of the delegates agreed with Jennings that slavery should not be allowed in Indiana.

THE BIRTH OF A STATE

After weeks of hard work, the constitution was completed. Then it was sent to Washington, D.C., for approval by the nation's leaders. At last, on December 11, 1816, President James Madison signed a law that made Indiana the nineteenth state in the nation.

Jonathan Jennings was elected the first governor of Indiana. In 1820 he helped to pick out a new location for Indiana's capital in the center of the state. Most pioneers lived near the Ohio River at this time, as you can see from the map on this page. However, Jennings knew that soon people would live in every part of Indiana.

In 1825 the state government moved to its new location. Some people wanted to call the new capital "Tecumseh." In the end it was named Indianapolis, which means "the city of Indiana."

A FRONTIER STATE

December 11, 1816, was a very special day for the people of Indiana. Pioneers all across the new state celebrated Indiana's statehood. In the next chapter you will read about the difficult but exciting life of the Indiana pioneers.

 Check Your Reading

1. Name two types of rights that were written into the constitution of Indiana.
2. How did slavery divide the delegates at Corydon?
3. **GEOGRAPHY SKILL:** Why was Indianapolis chosen as the new state capital?
4. **THINKING SKILL:** Write a list of the events, in order, that led to Indiana's becoming a state.

REVIEWING VOCABULARY

census   population
constitution   slave
delegate

Number a sheet of paper from 1 to 5. Beside each number write the word from the list above that best matches the definition.

1. A person who is owned by another person
2. The number of people living in an area
3. A count of the people who live in a country or an area
4. A plan of government
5. A person who is given the right to speak for others

REVIEWING FACTS

1. What did the Northwest Ordinance state about slavery?
2. Why was Tecumseh an enemy of William Henry Harrison?
3. What caused central Indiana to be opened up to settlement by pioneers?
4. Name three things provided for in the Indiana Constitution of 1816.
5. What was the difference between the way William Henry Harrison became governor and the way Jonathan Jennings became governor?

WRITING ABOUT MAIN IDEAS

1. **Writing a Letter:** Imagine that you have lived in Indiana for 16 years. It is now 1816. Write a letter to a friend in Kentucky in which you describe how Indiana has changed since the days when it first became a territory in 1800.
2. **Writing a Conversation:** Imagine that you were present at the meeting between William Henry Harrison and Tecumseh in 1810. Describe the conversation that took place between the two men.

BUILDING SKILLS: UNDERSTANDING CAUSE AND EFFECT

Answer the questions listed below.

1. What steps should you follow in order to understand cause and effect?
2. Read the following two sentences and tell which states a cause and which states an effect: (a) Many pioneers moved to the frontier in Indiana. (b) Indians signed treaties which stated that they must give up their lands.
3. In this chapter you have read that Indiana became a state. Write one cause and one effect of this event.
4. Why is it important to know the difference between cause and effect?

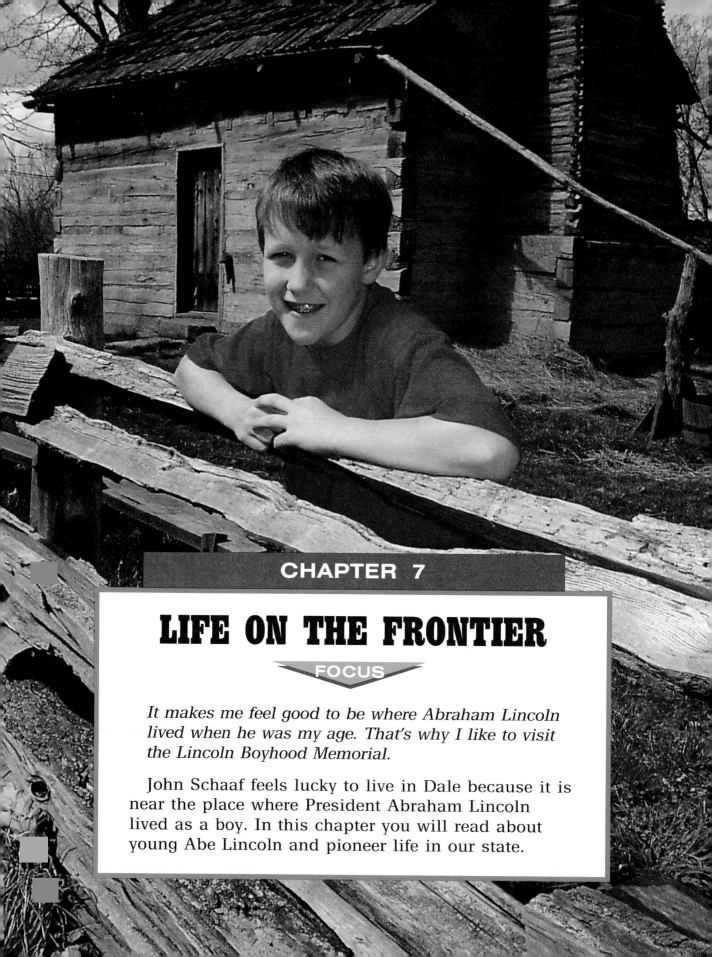

CHAPTER 7

LIFE ON THE FRONTIER

FOCUS

It makes me feel good to be where Abraham Lincoln lived when he was my age. That's why I like to visit the Lincoln Boyhood Memorial.

John Schaaf feels lucky to live in Dale because it is near the place where President Abraham Lincoln lived as a boy. In this chapter you will read about young Abe Lincoln and pioneer life in our state.

READ TO LEARN

■ **Key Vocabulary**

ferry
lean-to
log cabin

Key People

Abraham Lincoln

Key Places

Little Pigeon Creek

■ **Read Aloud**

[My father moved] from Kentucky to what is now Spencer County, Indiana, in my eighth year. We reached our new home about the time the State came into the Union. It was a wild region, with many bears and other wild animals still in the woods.

These words were written by Abraham Lincoln. He was describing Indiana as it looked when he was a young boy.

■ **Read for Purpose**

1. **WHAT YOU KNOW:** What does the word *frontier* mean?
2. **WHAT YOU WILL LEARN:** What are some ways in which pioneers worked together?

A LONG JOURNEY

When Indiana became a state in 1816, it seemed as if everyone was moving to the frontier. Although pioneers came to Indiana from all over the United States, most of them came from nearby Pennsylvania, Virginia, North Carolina, and Kentucky. The pioneers hoped that life would turn out to be better in the new state of Indiana.

Abraham Lincoln is probably Indiana's most famous pioneer. He was later elected President of the United States. In 1816 when Lincoln was a young boy, he and his parents, Thomas and Nancy, and his sister, Sarah, left their home in Knob Creek, Kentucky, and moved to Indiana. Thomas Lincoln was able to buy land in Indiana because of the Ordinance of 1785.

The Lincoln family traveled from Kentucky by horse and wagon. It was a difficult way to travel because there were no roads. Many other pioneer families traveled on rivers, such as the Ohio River. Most pioneers walked if they were not lucky enough to ride in a wagon. To cross the Ohio River from Kentucky to Indiana the Lincolns had to hire a **ferry**. A ferry is a boat that carries people and things across a river or a lake. There were no bridges on the Ohio River, but there were many ferries to carry the pioneers across it. Imagine how exciting it must have been for Abraham and Sarah to cross the wide Ohio River! Most pioneers never learned to swim, so it must have been a little scary, too.

Abraham Lincoln and his family traveled by **ferry** across the Ohio River. Like most pioneers, young Lincoln worked hard on the frontier.

Once the Lincoln family reached the Indiana shore, they had to make their way through forests of oak, shagbark hickory, and tulip trees. The forests were so thick that Thomas Lincoln had to use his ax to cut a path for the family to follow. When young Abe grew up he was an excellent woodsman, too.

BUILDING A HOME

Once pioneers reached the piece of land that they had bought, they would build a house. In order to stay warm and dry before their new home was ready, they would build a **lean-to**. A lean-to is a shelter with three sides made of branches and twigs. The fourth side of a lean-to is completely, or fully, open.

Once they had built a lean-to, the pioneers usually began building a **log cabin**. They cut down big trees

and stacked them to make the walls of the log cabin. The Lincoln family built their log cabin near **Little Pigeon Creek** in what is now Spencer County. You can see a log cabin like the one they built at the Lincoln Boyhood National Memorial.

Most log cabins had only one room, which the family used as a kitchen, bedroom, and living room. Usually there was an attic, or loft, where the children slept and where food was stored. Cold air, rain, and snow came in through cracks in the roof and walls. One pioneer who remembered sleeping in the loft as a child said:

When you got up in the morning, you shook the snow off the covers, grabbed your shirt and britches [pants,] and hopped down the ladder to the fireplace, where it was good and warm.

LIVING OFF THE LAND

The pioneers had to work hard to make or grow the things they needed. One way they got food was by hunting animals. During Abraham and Sarah's first year in Indiana they ate almost nothing but deer, rabbit, and wild turkey that their father hunted. A gun was one of the most important tools that a pioneer owned.

The pioneers were farmers as well as hunters. Before they could farm, however, they had to cut down the big trees that covered the land.

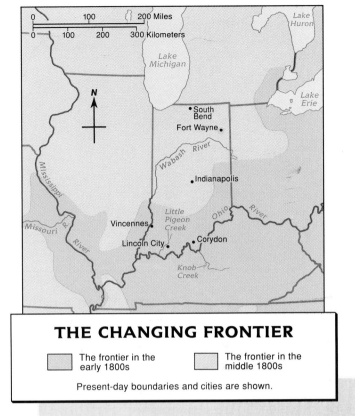

THE CHANGING FRONTIER

☐ The frontier in the early 1800s   ☐ The frontier in the middle 1800s

Present-day boundaries and cities are shown.

MAP SKILL: Which major rivers were located at the heart of the frontier in the early 1800s?

An ax was as important as a gun to the pioneers. Abraham learned to use an ax soon after he came to Indiana. He helped his father to cut down trees and split logs to make fences. Abraham grew very strong from this hard work.

After the pioneers cleared their land, they planted crops. Corn was their most important crop, as it had been for the Miami Indians, about whom you read in Chapter 3. Pioneers ate a lot of corn, usually in the form of corn bread. They also fed corn to their animals. Before winter came, a pioneer family might kill

Building **log cabins** was one of many ways that pioneers worked together on the frontier.

one of its hogs so that there would be enough meat for those months when it was too cold to go hunting.

The pioneers also made their own furniture and clothing. Many dressed in deerskins at first, but later they wore homemade cloth dresses, shirts, and pants. Pioneers rarely wore shoes when the weather was warm. One pioneer recalled, "Shoes for us boys came last. Sometimes Pap didn't get to us bigger boys until pretty late in the fall."

WORKING TOGETHER

Pioneers did not work alone. Sarah Lincoln helped her mother cook, sew, and make soap. She picked beans in the garden and sometimes helped Abraham plant corn.

Pioneer families also helped each other. Often many families would gather for a house-raising or a barn-raising. They built, or raised, the walls of a house or barn by working together. It took many men

to lift the heavy logs for the walls. Hard work was easier when it was shared by many people.

Pioneers also shared the work of logrolling. Logrolling was the gathering of cut trees into large piles for burning. Governor Jonathan Jennings was well liked by the pioneers because he often came to logrollings to help out.

Pioneers also shared work and fun at husking bees. The husk, or the covering on an ear of corn, had to be pulled off each ear after it was picked. Everyone gathered in a circle and sang, played games, or told jokes as they husked the golden ears of corn. The words to one of the songs they sang went like this:

There's every kind of game, my boys, also the buck and doe, When we settle on the banks of the lovely Ohio.

Afterward, the pioneers might eat a big supper of ham, corn bread,

green beans, and fruit pie. Then they would dance and play more games such as leapfrog and hide-and-seek. They also had foot races and tug-of-war contests.

SORROW ON THE FRONTIER

Life on the frontier was not only fun and hard work. There was sadness, too. Some pioneers were killed by wild animals. Though the forest was usually the pioneers' friend, it could also be their enemy.

Pioneers also died from diseases. Abraham Lincoln's mother, Nancy, died of "milk sickness." She had drunk milk from a cow that had eaten the poisonous white snakeroot plant. Thomas Lincoln made his wife's coffin out of wood from the forest and young Abraham carved the pegs that held it together. With great sadness, the family buried her coffin on a hill near their cabin.

PIONEER FAMILIES

Indiana's pioneers had to clear their own land in order to build their homes and to plant crops. Fathers, mothers, children, and neighbors had to depend on each other. Working together made the work easier and more fun. In the next lesson you will read about two groups of pioneers who built special communities in Indiana.

 Check Your Reading

1. What were two of the pioneers' most important tools? Why were they important?
2. Which pioneer tasks required teamwork?
3. **GEOGRAPHY SKILL:** Look at the map on page 137. How far was the Lincolns' pioneer journey?
4. **THINKING SKILL:** What are three questions you could ask to find out more about pioneer life?

Identifying Fact and Opinion

Key Vocabulary

fact   opinion

Imagine that you and a friend are reviewing some of the material you learned in the previous lesson in preparation for a quiz. Your friend tells you that Abraham Lincoln lived in Indiana from 1816 until 1830. This statement is a **fact**. You can check it in an encyclopedia or a history book to see if it is true. A fact is a statement that can be proved true.

Your friend then tells you that Abraham Lincoln loved Indiana more than any other place he ever lived. This statement cannot be proved. It is your friend's **opinion**. An opinion is a belief or feeling that a person has about something. A person may have the opinion that Abraham Lincoln loved Illinois or Kentucky more than Indiana. Another may have the opinion that he loved Indiana the most.

It is important to be able to tell the difference between fact and opinion. Otherwise, you may accept someone's opinion as fact.

Trying the Skill

Tell whether each of the following statements is a fact or an opinion.

1. Abraham Lincoln lived in Indiana.

HELPING YOURSELF

The steps on the left are one way to tell the difference between facts and opinions. The example on the right shows how to use these steps to recognize which statements about Abraham Lincoln are facts and which are opinions.

One Way to Recognize Fact and Opinion	Example
1. Ask yourself if the statement can be proved true.	Could you prove that the Lincolns moved to Indiana?
2. If the answer is yes, ask yourself how it could be proved true.	How could you check to see if they moved? You could look up this information in a history book or in an encyclopedia.
3. If you do not think a statement can be proved true, ask yourself if it gives someone's beliefs or feelings. Look for clue words such as *the best*, *should*, or *I think*.	Is the statement that the Lincolns should not have moved someone's belief? The word *should* is a clue that the statement is an opinion.

2. The Lincolns should not have left Kentucky.

3. Abraham's mother, Nancy Lincoln, died in Indiana.

Applying the Skill

Now apply what you have learned. Tell whether each statement below about the events in Abraham Lincoln's early life is a fact or an opinion.

1. Abraham Lincoln was born in 1809.

2. The Lincoln family made the best decision when they moved to Indiana.

3. I think Abraham Lincoln always helped his father on the farm.

4. The Lincoln family crossed the Ohio River to get to Indiana from Kentucky.

Now check yourself by answering the following questions.

1. How do you know that Statement 1 is a fact?
   a. It is someone's belief or feeling.
   b. It has word clues.
   c. It can be proved true.

2. How do you know that Statement 2 is an opinion?
   a. It can be proved true.
   b. It uses word clues that tell you that the writer is giving his or her personal beliefs.
   c. Everyone would agree with it.

Reviewing the Skill

1. What is a fact? What is an opinion?

2. How can you tell the difference between a fact and an opinion?

3. When would it be helpful to be able to tell the difference between facts and opinions?

READ TO LEARN

Key Vocabulary
preacher
Harmonist
Owenite

Key People
George Rapp
Robert Owen

Key Places
Harmonie
New Harmony

Read Aloud

Here the members kindly assist each other in difficulty and danger, and share with each other the enjoyments and misfortunes of life.

This is a description of a special place in Indiana. The pioneers who came to this part of Indiana hoped to find the freedom to live and practice their own beliefs.

Read for Purpose

1. **WHAT YOU KNOW:** Why is the right to think or say what you believe an important freedom?
2. **WHAT YOU WILL LEARN:** Who were the Harmonists and the Owenites, and what was special about their way of life?

THE HARMONISTS

As you have read, some Hoosier pioneers had been born in America and were hoping to start over and build a better life for their families. Other pioneers came from other countries looking for freedom. They knew that Indiana's constitution would give them freedom of religion and freedom to follow their beliefs and to say what they thought.

George Rapp was a preacher who had lived in Germany. A preacher is a person who speaks on a religious subject. In the early 1800s not all Germans were free to preach their beliefs. Rapp moved to America because he knew that he could have religious freedom here. Many other Germans followed Rapp to America.

Rapp and his followers are often called Harmonists (här' mo nists), because they wanted to live in harmony. They even called their new home Harmonie. The word *harmony* means "good feelings or peace among people." The Harmonists wanted to spend their life on earth in peace.

In 1814 Rapp and his followers moved from Pennsylvania to the Indiana frontier. At a place along the Wabash River they built Harmonie, which was their home for the next ten years.

The Harmonists believed in hard work. They shared work as well as property with each other. The Harmonists believed that money, too, should be shared equally. They planted many different crops, including grapes and fruit trees as well as corn. These crops were sold to local people. These sales helped the Harmonists become quite wealthy. They built a large town of 160 brick and wood houses. Many of these houses still stand today.

You can see them if you visit the town of New Harmony near Evansville.

THE OWENITES

When the Harmonists left Indiana in 1824 they sold their land and buildings to Robert Owen, a wealthy man from Scotland. Owen believed that people could be taught to overcome selfish feelings and behave as good, or honest, people.

Many people in Scotland thought that Owen's ideas were foolish. Owen decided to come to America in order to have the freedom to speak his beliefs. Owen changed

This model shows the community of Harmonie, which George Rapp and his followers built in 1814.

The Granger Collection

Robert Owen bought Harmonie and renamed it New Harmony in 1824.

the name of Harmonie to New Harmony because he wanted the town to be a place for new ideas.

People from Europe and other parts of America came to New Harmony with Owen. They are often called Owenites (ō′ ən īts). Famous teachers and scientists from Europe helped Owen to set up schools and a library and to print books. The Owenites started the first preschool in the United States.

Most Owenites, however, did not want to spend their time farming. They wanted to study new ideas. Once the Owenites ran out of food, Owen had to spend his own money to feed them. Soon he and most of the Owenites left Indiana.

A LIFE OF FREEDOM

The Harmonists and the Owenites had not known what would happen to them in America. They were special pioneers who had the courage to move to a new country in order to have a chance for freedom.

You have read that many different people came to live in Indiana. Pioneers such as the Lincoln family, the Harmonists, and the Owenites shared the same hope for freedom and a better life. In Chapter 9 you will read about another group's hope for freedom.

 Check Your Reading

1. Why did George Rapp come to Indiana?
2. Why did most of the Owenites leave Indiana?
3. GEOGRAPHY SKILL: Which natural resources did the Harmonists use in Harmonie?
4. THINKING SKILL: Compare the Harmonists' views about farming with the Owenites' views.

144

REVIEWING VOCABULARY

Number a sheet of paper from 1 to 3. Beside each number write the letter of the choice that best completes each sentence.

1. A ferry is a boat that
   a. crosses an ocean.
   b. carries people across a river.
   c. has sails and an engine.
2. A lean-to is
   a. a shelter that has an open side.
   b. a house that has four walls.
   c. a roof that is held up by poles.
3. A log cabin is
   a. a house with many rooms.
   b. a shelter made of twigs.
   c. a house made of logs.

REVIEWING FACTS

Number a sheet of paper from 1 to 5. Beside each number write **T** if the statement is true. If the statement is false, rewrite it to make it true.

1. Abraham Lincoln was born in Indiana.
2. Pioneers like the Lincolns grew all of their own food.
3. At a husking bee people shared the work of raising a barn.
4. George Rapp bought land and buildings from the Harmonists.
5. The Owenites began the first preschool in the United States.

WRITING ABOUT MAIN IDEAS

1. **Writing a Letter:** Imagine that you are a Hoosier pioneer. Write a letter inviting your neighbors to a group gathering, such as a barn-raising, a logrolling, or a husking bee. Be sure to tell the date, time, place, and purpose.
2. **Writing About Freedom:** Some people came to America in order to be free to worship and speak as they chose. Write a paragraph about one of these freedoms and tell why you think that it is important.

BUILDING SKILLS: IDENTIFYING FACT AND OPINION

1. What steps should you follow to figure out whether a statement is a fact or an opinion?
2. Tell whether each of the following statements is a fact or an opinion.
   a. Abraham Lincoln was born in Kentucky.
   b. Mrs. Lincoln should not have drunk the poisoned milk.
   c. George Rapp moved to the Indiana Territory in 1814.
   d. Sharing property is a good idea.
3. Why is it important to be able to tell the difference between a fact and an opinion?

REVIEWING VOCABULARY

constitution   population
frontier   territory
pioneer

Number a sheet of paper from 1 to 5. Beside each number write the word from the list above that best completes the sentence.

1. Near the edge of a settled area is land known as a ____.
2. A ____ is land that is not a state but is governed by another country.
3. A ____ is among the first people of a group to settle new land.
4. In 1812 the Indiana Territory had a ____ of 30,000 people.
5. In 1816 people met to write a ____ that stated how Indiana would be governed.

◀ WRITING ABOUT THE UNIT

1. **Writing About Cause and Effect:** William Henry Harrison's signing of treaties with Indians was to have many effects on the Indiana Territory. List three effects that resulted from his actions.
2. **Conducting an Interview:** Imagine that you are interviewing Tecumseh after his meeting with William Henry Harrison in 1810. Write four questions that you would like to ask him. Then write the answers that you think he might have given.
3. **Writing a Comparison:** Write a paragraph comparing the leadership skills of Tecumseh with those of William Henry Harrison. Compare the goals that the men had for their people, and the methods that each of them used to try to reach those goals.

ACTIVITIES

1. **Researching a Historical Person:** Use the library to learn more about William Henry Harrison. Find out when and where he was born, what he is famous for, and how and when he died. Then present your findings in an oral or a written report.
2. **Studying Place Names:** Many places in our state were named after people. Clarksville is one example. Make a list of several places in Indiana. Use the library to find out how each one got its name.
3. **Working Together to Make a Time Line:** Work with several classmates to make a time line of the major events described in this unit. Draw a picture for each event listed on your time line.

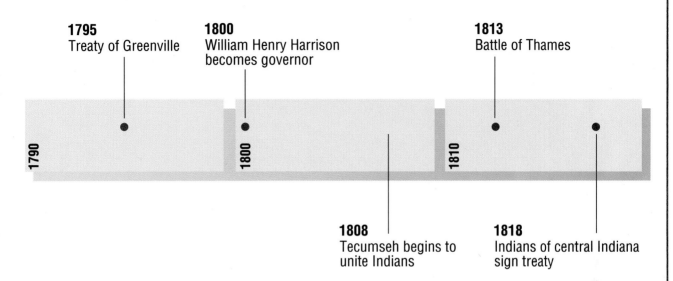

1795
Treaty of Greenville

1800
William Henry Harrison
becomes governor

1813
Battle of Thames

1790

1800

1810

1808
Tecumseh begins to
unite Indians

1818
Indians of central Indiana
sign treaty

BUILDING SKILLS: READING TIME LINES

Study the time line above to answer the following questions.

1. How many years are shown on the time line? Into which time periods is the time line divided?

2. In what year did Tecumseh begin to unite the Indians?

3. Which event on the time line above took place first? Which event took place last?

4. Which event shown on the time line above happened first?
   a. Battle of the Thames
   b. William Henry Harrison becomes territorial governor

5. Where would you place each of the following events on the time line shown above?
   a. 1805—census shows that 12,000 pioneers live in the territory
   b. 1811—the Battle of Tippecanoe

LINKING PAST, PRESENT, AND FUTURE

You have read that people fought over the ownership of American land in the 1800s. People today still fight over the control of land. Can you think of regions today in which different groups are fighting over land? Can you think of ways in which such fights could be avoided in the future?

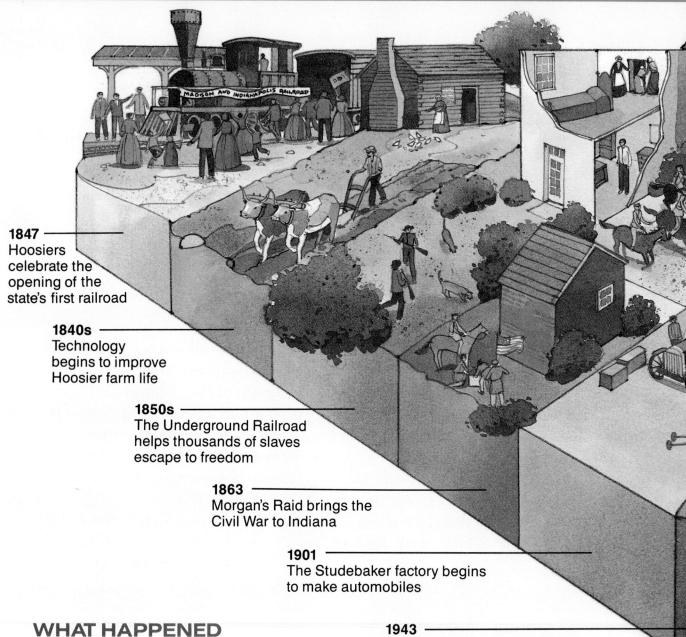

1847
Hoosiers celebrate the opening of the state's first railroad

1840s
Technology begins to improve Hoosier farm life

1850s
The Underground Railroad helps thousands of slaves escape to freedom

1863
Morgan's Raid brings the Civil War to Indiana

1901
The Studebaker factory begins to make automobiles

1943
Hoosier Ernie Pyle reports on World War II to Indiana and the world

1990s
Progress in education helps students throughout the state

WHAT HAPPENED

Indiana was a young and growing state in a young and growing country. But there were still problems to work out. Hoosiers went to fight in a terrible war that tore America apart. You will learn about that war, and about how Indiana moved on afterwards to build a stronger state.

UNIT
4

INDIANA GROWS

CHAPTER 8

INDIANA ON THE MOVE

FOCUS

I live in Connersville near where the old canal used to be. Part of the canal has been restored, and there are a lot of fun things to do there.

Andy Sidell likes to go to Metamora, where he can visit the old Whitewater Canal. In this chapter you will read about the role canals, roads, and railroads played in Indiana's growth as a state.

1 The Crossroads of America

READ TO LEARN

▪ Key Vocabulary

transportation   flatboat
trace   steamboat
corduroy road   navigable
plank road   canal

Key Places

Michigan Road
National Road
Wabash and Erie Canal
Madison

▪ Read Aloud

There weren't many roads leading out of Indianapolis. For the Ohio River towns you had your choice of two roads. . . . They were roads in name only. . . . A wagon would go thump, thump, thump over them, shaking the daylights out of you.

This is how one farmer described traveling on the state's earliest roads. In this lesson you will read about how travel changed in the 1800s. You will also read about how these changes improved life in our state.

▪ Read for Purpose

1. **WHAT YOU KNOW:** What are some of the important roads that people use in your community?
2. **WHAT YOU WILL LEARN:** How did Indiana's rivers, canals, and railroads help the state to grow?

ROADS LEADING WEST

"Old America seems to be breaking up and moving westward," wrote one man who was traveling west in the early 1800s. "We are seldom out of sight, as we travel towards the Ohio, of family groups before and behind us."

Many pioneers traveled westward in covered wagons. Wagons were one form of transportation (trans pər tā′ shən) that settlers used to come to Indiana. Transportation is a way of moving goods and people. Indiana grew as its transportation improved.

151

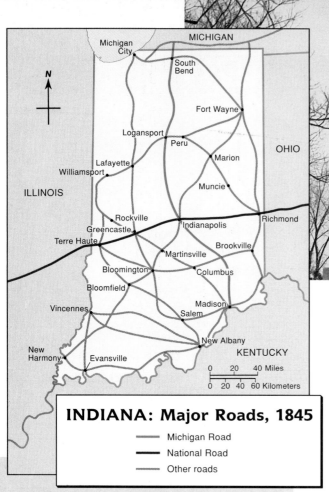

INDIANA: Major Roads, 1845

— Michigan Road
— National Road
— Other roads

MAP SKILL: This monument and marker are found along Indiana's National Road. In which city did this road meet the Michigan Road?

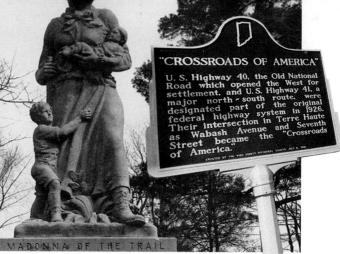

"CROSSROADS OF AMERICA"

U.S. Highway 40, the Old National Road which opened the West for settlement, and U.S. Highway 41, a major north-south route, were designated part of the original federal highway system in 1926. Their intersection in Terre Haute as Wabash Avenue and Seventh Street became the "Crossroads of America."

MADONNA OF THE TRAIL

TRAVEL BY LAND

Most early pioneers traveled to Indiana on foot or horseback. They followed trails called **traces** that animals had made in the forest. One of the most famous was named the Buffalo Trace. It ran across the state from near New Albany to Vincennes on the Wabash River.

Traces were too narrow for wagons to travel along, so pioneers began to widen them. In the 1820s Hoosiers began building a large road for wagons. They called it the **Michigan Road**. As you can see from the map on this page, it connected the northern and southern parts of the state. Today much of this road is called U.S. Route 421.

In the 1830s Hoosiers worked with Americans in other states to build an even longer road called the **National Road**. This road started in Maryland, traveled all the way across Indiana, and ended in Illinois. It was an important route for pioneers moving westward. Today this route is called U.S. Route 40. Look at the map on this page. Which cities in Indiana were located along the National Road?

These roads were not like the roads of today. Imagine bumping along a dirt path with tree stumps sticking out in many places. If it rained you would get stuck in mud as thick as molasses. Then you would have to step down into the mess to help free your wagon and your horses.

Many of these early roads were called corduroy roads. These bumpy, uncomfortable roads were made from logs laid across the trails. Soon the pioneers began to split the logs into flat planks to make the roads smoother. These were called plank roads. Although better than corduroy roads, plank roads rotted easily and became very slippery when it rained. Even though it was difficult, travel increased throughout the state with these new roads. As the number of roads grew, Indiana grew.

TRAVEL BY WATER

As you know, the rivers of Indiana had been used for transportation ever since the days of the Miami. Travel by water became especially important to farmers since shipping was cheaper and faster than carting goods over land.

Each spring, as the rivers filled with melting snow, farmers built flatboats to take their goods to market. A flatboat was a large, wooden boat with a flat bottom and square ends. Flatboats could only travel downstream with the river's current. When farmers set off for ports like New Orleans, they knew they would have to find another way home.

INDIANA: Canals and River Routes, 1850s

.... Wabash and Erie Canal

~ River navigable by steamboat

------- Whitewater Canal

MAP SKILL: Canals and railroads could be found throughout the state. Where did the Wabash and Erie Canal join the Ohio River?

153

As a young man in 1828 Abraham Lincoln helped to pilot a flatboat from Little Pigeon Creek to New Orleans. After Lincoln and his partner sold their goods, they rode home on a new steamboat. Steamboats are boats that are powered by steam engines, so they can go either up or down rivers.

Steamboats became the fastest way to travel in America during the 1820s. Farm goods could get to market in days rather than weeks. Steamboats stopped at towns like Terre Haute and Lafayette to pick up and drop off passengers and goods. Business boomed in towns where steamboats stopped.

Steamboats, however, could only travel on rivers that were navigable (nav′ i gə bəl). Navigable rivers are wide and deep enough for boats to use. Although Indiana has many rivers, only a few are navigable by steamboat, as you can see on the map on page 153.

Many farmers lived far away from navigable rivers. They, too, wanted to ship their goods to market. So in the 1830s Hoosiers began to dig canals. A canal is a waterway for boats that is dug across the land.

In 1853 the Wabash and Erie Canal, America's longest, was completed. As you can see on the map on page 153, it began on the shores of Lake Erie at Toledo, Ohio. The canal followed the Wabash River until it reached Terre Haute. Then it continued south as far as Evansville, where it ended its 468-mile (749-km) journey. Now many farmers in northern Indiana could ship their corn to markets along Lake Erie.

Other canals were built in Indiana, including the Whitewater Canal. You can visit the Whitewater Canal State Historic Site at Metamora to learn more about our state's canals.

Steamboats traveled up and down rivers carrying people and products.

The Granger Collection

The canals helped to increase trade and travel in the state. But there were also many problems. The canals often froze in winter. In summer they were often too shallow for boats. By 1874 the Wabash and Erie Canal had closed. One reason was that an even better form of transportation had arrived in Indiana. Can you guess what it was?

AN IRON WEB

Indiana's first steam railroad was completed in 1847. It connected Indianapolis to Madison, on the Ohio River. Other railroads were built after that. As you can see on the map on this page, by the 1880s it seemed as though an iron web connected many of Indiana's towns and cities.

Trains could travel in almost any weather, and iron tracks could be laid almost anywhere. Indiana's railroads connected the state with other parts of America. Many travelers passed through Indianapolis because it was a center of America's transportation routes. This gave Indiana the nickname "The Crossroads of America."

TRAVEL BRINGS CHANGE

Improvements in transportation helped Indiana to grow and change. Some of the most important growth and changes took place on the state's farms. You will read about these changes in the next lesson.

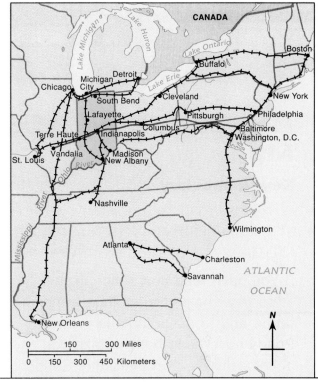

CROSSROADS OF AMERICA, 1860

├─┼─┤ Major railroad route   ── State border

── National Road   ── National border

MAP SKILL: Railroads linked the growing nation. How many railroad lines went through Indianapolis?

Check Your Reading

1. How were pioneers helped by the building of the National Road?
2. What were some of the problems with river transportation?
3. **GEOGRAPHY SKILL:** Look at the map on this page. Which transportation routes passed through Terre Haute?
4. **THINKING SKILL:** How did changes in transportation help Indianapolis to grow?

155

Reading Road Maps

Key Vocabulary
road map
interstate highway
bypass

You have read how roads in this state have helped to change transportation and to make Indiana grow. Roads have been built to take you almost anywhere in the state. Suppose that you wanted to visit the Indiana Dunes State Park. How would you know how to get there? One way would be to use a road map.

Road Maps

A road map of Indiana shows you its cities and towns and the roads that connect them. Road maps show travelers how to get from one place to another. Look at the road map on page 157. The purple lines show interstate highways. The word *interstate* (in′ tər stāt) means "between or among two or more states." Interstate highways, or routes, are wide, with two or more lanes in each direction. Some of the interstate highways in Indiana are I-65, I-70, and I-74.

The red lines show U.S. routes. U.S. Routes 36, 52, and 231 are in Indiana.

State highways stop at a state's borders. Routes 3, 10, and 64 are state highways. State routes on the road map are shown in black. Which state highways are located near you?

Numbers and Symbols

Most roads are marked with numbers that are printed inside special symbols. Some roads have more than one number because they are part of more than one highway. For example, U.S. Routes 27 and 33 run together near Fort Wayne.

Notice that odd-numbered roads on the road map usually run north and south. Even-numbered roads usually run east and west. Interstate highways with three-digit numbers usually bypass, or go around, cities and then rejoin the main interstate highway. What is the number of the interstate highway that connects Indianapolis and Gary? What is the number of the highway that connects Kokomo and Indianapolis? Is it an interstate highway, a U.S. route, or a state highway?

Planning a Route

Suppose that you lived in Indianapolis and you wanted to visit a friend in Greencastle. One way to get to Greencastle would be to travel west on U.S.

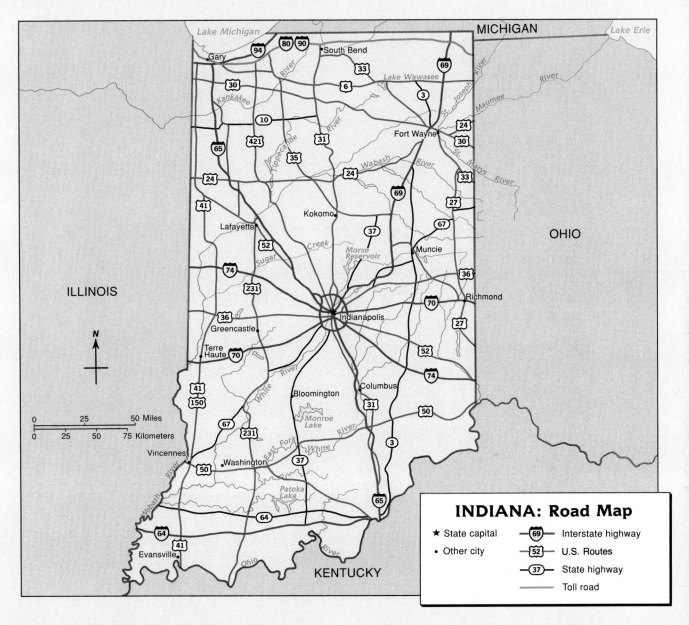

INDIANA: Road Map

★ State capital — Interstate highway (69)
• Other city — U.S. Routes (52)
— State highway (37)
— Toll road

36. Then go south on U.S. 231, which leads directly to Greencastle. Can you find another route from Indianapolis to Greencastle?

Reviewing the Skill
1. What is a road map?
2. What kind of road is Route 421?

3. Plan two routes from Greencastle to Gary. For the first route use interstate highways as much as possible. For the second route try to use only state or U.S. routes.

4. Why is it important to be able to read a road map?

2 Farm Life Improves

READ TO LEARN

Key Vocabulary

self-sufficient   interdependent
technology   Grange
reaper

Key People

James Oliver

Read Aloud

Pop was the first to start. Faster and faster [he and his horse] went until the judges could hardly keep up. Everybody was hollering and cheering like it was a horse race. Uncle Israel didn't even have a [chance] with his old wooden plow.

This is how one man described a plowing race at the Marion County Fair in the 1830s. The man's father won because he used a metal plow. In this lesson you will read about the new plows and other new machines and tools that helped to make farm life in Indiana easier.

Read for Purpose

1. **WHAT YOU KNOW:** What do your dinner table, grocery store, and local farm stand all have in common?
2. **WHAT YOU WILL LEARN:** How did Hoosier farm life improve in the 1800s?

A STATE OF FARMERS

Most Hoosiers lived on farms in the 1800s. As you read in Chapter 7, farm life in the early 1800s was filled with hard work. Settlers had to be self-sufficient. Self-sufficient means that you can provide for all your own needs.

Settlers needed corn in order to live. To one man it "seemed like an everlasting job" to raise each corn crop. The settlers needed good weather to grow their crops. If there was not enough rain, or if there were too many storms, they suffered a great deal. Settlers also had to make

158

The Granger Collection

Difficult chores filled many hours of pioneer life.

everything else they needed. That meant shoes, furniture, soap, candles, and clothing. All of these tasks took a great deal of time, too.

Imagine that you are a pioneer child helping your mother to make soap. For what seems like hours you stir a big, steaming pot filled with animal fat and lye, which was made by pouring water through the ashes from the fire. By the time your turn is finished, your arms hurt and your head pounds. The pot cools. But it will have to be stirred again—and again and again—until the mixture turns into soap.

Farm work became easier as the 1800s progressed. New transportation allowed farmers to sell their goods in new places. New machines helped to make farm work easier. As farming changed, life in Indiana changed.

TECHNOLOGY BRINGS CHANGE

The farmers' lives were changed and made easier by technology (tek nol′ ə jē), which made new ways of farming possible. Technology means using new ideas and tools to meet people's needs.

In 1831 the reaper was invented. A reaper was a horse-drawn machine that could cut grain. Before farmers started using reapers, they had to cut grain in the fields by hand. With a reaper, though, a farmer's horse did most of the work. You can see how the reaper worked by looking at the chart on page 160. By 1850 many farmers in America used reapers in their fields.

Hoosier James Oliver invented a new steel plow and began making it in South Bend in the 1870s. Oliver's plow, called a chilled plow, was much stronger and easier to use than the old wooden or iron ones. Better still, steel plows did not rust very much, and soil did not stick to them as it did to wooden and iron plows. By the 1880s Oliver's plow

CHANGES IN TECHNOLOGY

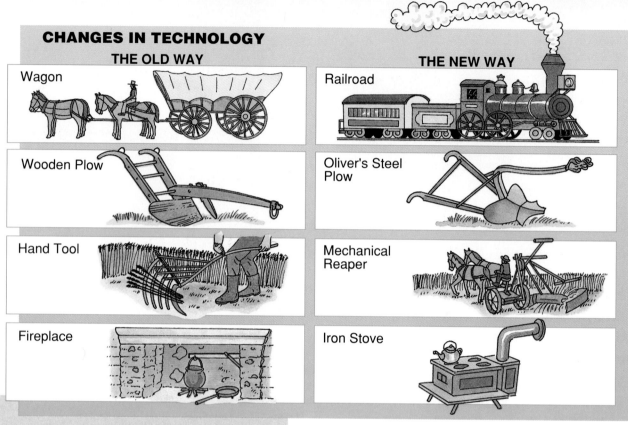

THE OLD WAY

Wagon

Wooden Plow

Hand Tool

Fireplace

THE NEW WAY

Railroad

Oliver's Steel Plow

Mechanical Reaper

Iron Stove

CHART SKILL: Which of these new advances in technology was invented in Indiana?

was the most popular plow in the world. Look at the chart above to understand these changes.

CORN AND HOGS

As farm work became easier, farmers began to plant more corn than ever before. By 1860 only three states grew more corn than Indiana. Now farmers grew more corn than their own families could eat or use. This meant that they had extra corn to sell.

Early settlers had a hard time getting their crops to towns where merchants bought corn. Wagon travel was very difficult. Farmers in the north lived far from navigable rivers. Even when they got their corn to town, however, farmers did not get a high price for it. Corn sold cheaply because so many farmers were selling it.

One product that sold for a good price was hogs. Hoosier farmers had always raised hogs. These ran wild in the forests and found their own food. But now farmers began to feed them corn. This made the hogs fatter and worth more money.

Farmers began to raise more hogs than ever before. By 1860 Hoosiers raised more hogs than any other state in the nation. Because of its importance as a hog market, Madison became known as "Porkopolis."

160

MONEY FOR SHOPPING

With the money that they made from corn and hogs, farmers could buy new tools and other things that were made in other parts of the country. Families could now buy cloth and shoes instead of having to make them. They could have iron stoves instead of using fireplaces.

Imagine how happy you would have been if your mother came home with bars of soap from the general store. Now you and she would no longer have to spend hours making soap!

All of this buying and selling made Hoosiers and other Americans interdependent. This means that people in one region depend on people in other regions to help them meet their needs and wants.

HOOSIERS TOGETHER

As you have read, pioneers liked to get together for events such as log rollings and husking bees. As time passed, though, farmers found other reasons to meet.

One special treat for farm families was a trip to town. Often on Saturday afternoons, a family would hitch up their wagon and drive to town. In town they could talk with neighbors and also buy the supplies that they needed.

Often the children would run to the candy store the minute the wagon came to a stop. Their father might stop to talk with other men about a new railroad, James Oliver's new plow, or the price of hogs.

Meanwhile, their mother might walk over to the general store. There she could buy anything from sugar and tea to flypaper and iron pots. She could also buy cloth to make clothes for the family.

Farm families also got together at county and state fairs. The first Indiana State Fair was held in 1852. Its purpose was to encourage Hoosiers to take pride in the work they did as farm families. Have you ever gone to the State Fair? It is still held today in Indianapolis.

The steel plow and new hog markets both helped Indiana to grow.

Since 1852 Hoosiers from across the state have come to Indianapolis each year for the State Fair.

As at fairs today, prizes were given for the biggest hogs and the best homemade foods. There were exhibits of new machines that showed farmers how they could improve their farming. There was also plenty of food to eat and friends to see.

Hoosiers also met at meetings of the Grange. The Grange was the name of a club for farmers. Grange meetings were get-togethers where people could visit and enjoy good food. But they also gave Hoosiers a chance to exchange stories and new ideas about farm life.

INDIANA FEEDS AMERICA

Farm life changed greatly in the 1800s. Farm families no longer had to work all day to make what they needed. Thanks to new machines, they could sell the extra farm goods that they didn't need. With the money that they made, they could buy some of the things they needed to live. Now they had more time to relax and enjoy themselves.

Indiana's hogs and corn fed people all over America. By shipping hogs and corn across the nation by rail and water, Indiana's farmers helped America to grow.

 Check Your Reading

1. Why was James Oliver's steel plow better than wooden plows?
2. Why were trips to town important to farm families?
3. What was the purpose of the first Indiana State Fair?
4. **GEOGRAPHY SKILL:** Look at the map on page 152. Which route might a farmer have taken to get his hogs from Indianapolis to Madison?
5. **THINKING SKILL:** How did the steel plow and the reaper help farmers to raise more hogs?

162

REVIEWING VOCABULARY

flatboat   steamboat
navigable   technology
self-sufficient

Number a sheet of paper from 1 to 5. Beside each number write the word or term from the list above that best completes the sentence.

1. A _____ could travel up or down rivers.
2. Although Indiana has many rivers, only a few are _____ by boat.
3. A _____ could carry goods downstream but not upstream.
4. A _____ farm family made all the things it needed to live.
5. New _____, such as trains and farm machines, improved farm life.

REVIEWING FACTS

Number a sheet of paper from 1 to 5. Beside each number write **T** if the statement is true. If the statement is false, rewrite it to make it true.

1. Most early pioneers reached Indiana by railroad.
2. The Michigan Road connected eastern and western Indiana.
3. A corduroy road was made of logs laid side by side across the road.
4. James Oliver's reaper helped to make farm life easier.
5. The State Fair helped farmers to be proud of the work they did.

WRITING ABOUT MAIN IDEAS

1. **Making a Poster:** Prepare a poster that displays some of the inventions that improved Indiana's transportation in the 1800s. Add labels that explain how they improved transportation in the state.
2. **Writing a Newspaper Advertisement:** Imagine that the year is 1847. Write a newspaper advertisement for the Madison and Indianapolis Railroad. In it describe how railroads are helpful to people. Draw a picture to include in your advertisement.
3. **Writing a Letter:** Imagine that an invention mentioned in Chapter 8 has improved your life. Write a letter to the inventor. In it tell how the invention has improved your life.

BUILDING SKILLS: READING ROAD MAPS

Look at the road map on page 295. Then answer these questions.

1. How many different kinds of roads are shown on the map?
2. Which color is used for interstate highways?
3. What highway would you take to get from Gary to Indianapolis?
4. Describe two situations in which people might need to use a road map.

CHAPTER 9

A DIVIDED NATION

FOCUS

What I like best about the Coffin House is the upstairs bedroom, where they hid people who were escaping from slavery. The room has a secret little door that was hidden by putting a bed in front of it.

Anna Hess sometimes works as a guide at the Coffin House in Fountain City. In this chapter you will read about the people who owned this house, slavery, and the terrible war that tore our country apart.

1 The Underground Railroad

READ TO LEARN

Key Vocabulary

slave state
free state
Underground Railroad

Key People

Chapman Harris
Catherine Coffin
Levi Coffin

Read Aloud

When the sun comes back and the first quail calls,
Follow the Drinking Gourd.
Then the Old Man is awaitin' for to carry you to
freedom,
Follow the Drinking Gourd.

This is a song about slaves escaping to freedom. The Drinking Gourd is what slaves called the Big Dipper, a group of stars that guided them on their journey. You are about to read how Hoosiers helped many slaves to escape.

Read for Purpose

1. **WHAT YOU KNOW:** What did Indiana's constitution say about slavery?
2. **WHAT YOU WILL LEARN:** How did some Hoosiers help some slaves to gain their freedom?

SLAVERY IN THE UNITED STATES

In the middle 1800s the United States was divided over the issue of slavery. In the South almost 4 million African-Americans worked as slaves for white owners. The states in which slavery was practiced were known as slave states. The North, where slavery was not allowed, was made up of free states. Indiana was a free state.

Slaves had no rights. They were treated as property. Slave families were often split up when family members were bought and sold by different owners. They worked long

165

and difficult hours. "As soon as it is light in the morning . . . until it is too dark to see" is how one slave described his working day.

FREEDOM TRAIN

Some slaves risked their lives by running away from their owners to Canada, where they could live in freedom. Thousands of slaves traveled through Indiana on their journey north. In order to escape, slaves slipped away from plantations at night and ran as far away as possible before morning. They hid during the day, sleeping in fields and in woods. When night returned slaves continued their journey, staying away from the main roads. If they were caught they would be returned to their owners and beaten.

The Underground Railroad helped many escaping slaves. The Underground Railroad was not a railroad, nor was it underground. It was a name for the system of secret routes that escaping slaves followed to freedom. The routes were secret because it was against the law to help a slave escape. People who led slaves on this dangerous journey were known as "conductors." The houses in which slaves hid were called "stations," and the route from one station to another was called "the line."

INDIANA'S CONDUCTORS

Three main lines of the Underground Railroad ran through Indiana. Look at the map on this page to find the routes in Indiana used by many slaves to escape to freedom. How many Hoosier cities on the map were linked to the Underground Railroad?

Many African-Americans who were former slaves helped run the railroad. One Hoosier conductor was an African-American named Chapman Harris, who lived near the Ohio River. He kept a rowboat on the bank of the river in order to carry runaway slaves across. After dark Harris would strike an iron anvil that he had placed in a large

MAP SKILL: How many major escape routes passed through Indiana?

THE UNDERGROUND RAILROAD: Indiana and its Neighbors

→ Underground Railroad route

Present-day names and boundaries are shown.

Free state

Canada

Slave state

Escaping slaves were helped by the Coffins and many other Hoosiers in the Underground Railroad.

tree. An anvil is an iron or steel block on which metals are hammered into shapes. To the slaves who waited for his signal from across the river, the anvil's sound was the sound of freedom.

Catherine Coffin and her husband, Levi Coffin, were Indiana's most famous Underground Railroad conductors. Many escaping slaves came to "Aunt Katy," as Mrs. Coffin was known, needing a warm bed and a hot meal. The Coffins hid many slaves in a secret upstairs room. Levi Coffin later wrote, "We found it necessary to always be prepared to receive such company." From 1827 to 1847 Catherine and Levi Coffin helped more than 3,000 slaves to escape to freedom.

SLAVERY CONTINUES

The Underground Railroad helped some slaves to gain their freedom, but it did not end slavery or the troubles between the North and the South. As you will read in the next lesson, these troubles would soon explode into war.

✔ Check Your Reading

1. What was the main difference between slave states and free states?
2. Which job did Harris and the Coffins perform in the Underground Railroad?
3. **GEOGRAPHY SKILL:** Why do you think that so many Underground Railroad lines began at rivers?
4. **THINKING SKILL:** Explain how the Underground Railroad could be described as an effect of slavery.

167

Recognizing Point of View

Key Vocabulary

point of view

Read what Tom and David have to say about their school football teams.

Tom: Football is fun for both players and fans.
David: Football is a dangerous sport. Players can get hurt.

Tom and David have opposite points of view about football. Point of view is the way that a person looks at something. People often look at the same subject from different points of view. Being able to identify a person's point of view allows you to make up your own mind about the subject.

Trying the Skill

Below are two statements by speakers with different points of view about the conductors in the Underground Railroad. Read them both carefully.

The risks involved in the Underground Railroad were too great. Those Hoosiers should not have risked their lives to help the escaping slaves.

The Hoosier conductors were brave people. They knew the risks involved with helping escaping slaves, but acted anyway.

How would you describe the two points of view?

HELPING YOURSELF

The steps on the left will help you to recognize a person's point of view. The example on the right shows one way to apply these steps to the statements on page 168.

One Way to Determine Point of View	Example
1. Identify the subject.	The subject is the risks of involvement with the Underground Railroad.
2. Identify the information included.	The statements discuss the danger and risks involved with being part of the Underground Railroad.
3. Identify words that are expressions of opinion. They tell how a person feels about something.	One speaker says "should not have risked their lives." That tells you that the speaker is giving an opinion.
4. Tell the point of view expressed.	The first speaker does not think that people should have risked their lives.

Applying the Skill

Now apply what you have learned. Identify the points of view expressed by the two speakers below.

The Underground Railroad was a good effort but it really didn't make that much difference. Slavery still existed throughout the South.

The people who worked in the Underground Railroad made a huge difference in the lives of thousands. Over 2,000 escaping slaves were led to freedom.

To check yourself, answer the following questions.

1. What topic are the speakers talking about?
   a. the risks of the Underground Railroad
   b. whether or not the Underground Railroad made a difference
   c. famous people in the railroad
2. Which phrases helped you to determine the first point of view?
   a. *really didn't make that much difference*
   b. *slavery still existed*
   c. *was a good effort*
3. The second point of view is shown by
   a. the subject identified.
   b. the words *made a huge difference*.

Reviewing the Skill

1. Define *point of view*.
2. What are some steps you should take to identify point of view?
3. Why is it important to understand a person's point of view?

169

2 The Civil War

READ TO LEARN

Key Vocabulary

secede   Iron Brigade
Confederacy Emancipation
Union   Proclamation
Civil War

Key People

Oliver P. Morton
John Hunt Morgan

Read Aloud

The roar of both cannon and musketry [guns] *was terrible and unceasing* [did not stop]. *The fight was mostly in the woods, and the twigs and limbs and splinters were flying in every direction.*

This is how one Indiana soldier, in a letter home, described a battle in which he had fought. Many soldiers, including the author of this letter, died in one of our nation's most bitter wars.

Read for Purpose

1. **WHAT YOU KNOW:** In what ways did Northerners and Southerners have different ideas about slavery?
2. **WHAT YOU WILL LEARN:** What role did Hoosiers play in the Civil War?

LINCOLN IS PRESIDENT

Abraham Lincoln, whose early years you read about in Chapter 7, became a lawyer and an important national leader. In 1860 he became President of the United States. At this time when the country was growing, slavery was an issue on everyone's mind.

As Americans pushed farther west new territories were settled. The people of these new territories began asking for statehood, just as Hoosiers had done years before. Most Southerners hoped that the new western territories would become slave states. Most Northerners wanted them to be free states.

170

Both President Abraham Lincoln (*left*) and Governor Oliver P. Morton (*right*) worked hard to keep the Union together.

Lincoln was strongly against the spread of slavery. Although he did not say that slavery should be ended in the South, many Southerners believed that Lincoln would try to free the slaves. The slave states decided to secede (si sēd′), or to break away, from the United States. They formed a new country called the Confederate (kən fed′ ər it) States of America, also called the Confederacy (kən fed′ ər ə sē).

Lincoln did not think that the slave states had the right to secede. The United States was a Union of states, he said, that could not be broken. He was ready to fight a war, if necessary, to "save the Union."

Many agreed with Lincoln. One important Hoosier, Indiana's new governor, Oliver P. Morton, said, "If it was worth a bloody struggle to establish this nation, it is worth one to preserve it."

THE CIVIL WAR

On April 12, 1861, Confederate troops fired on Fort Sumter in South Carolina. This was the beginning of the American Civil War. A civil war is a war between people from the same country. The Civil War lasted from 1861 to 1865. Find the Union and the Confederate states on the map on page 172.

Indiana gave strong support to the Union cause. Nearly 200,000 Hoosiers fought for the Union. Some of these soldiers were African-Americans, many of whom were former slaves. Perhaps the most famous Indiana soldiers were those who fought in the Iron Brigade. The Iron Brigade was a group of soldiers who came from Indiana and other neighboring states. These brave

171

men showed such strength that people said they were as strong as iron.

Over 25,000 Hoosier soldiers were killed in the Civil War. That is more than the number of people living in Clay County today. But more soldiers died from sickness than were killed in battle. "It is very cold and we are suffering severely [very badly]," one Indiana soldier wrote in his diary. Many other soldiers on both sides were wounded.

THE WAR AT HOME

Hoosiers who were not soldiers, mostly women and children, took over the work on the farms. Women also raised money and collected food, books, and bandages for the soldiers. Many others served as nurses. There were also women who worked in Indianapolis in the Union arsenal. An arsenal is a place where guns and other war materials are made or stored.

On July 8, 1863, almost 2,500 Confederate soldiers on horseback attacked southern Indiana. Led by John Hunt Morgan, a Confederate general, they had crossed the Ohio River from Kentucky. Morgan's men, known as "Morgan's Raiders," set fire to buildings and took goods and money.

Hoosiers were frightened by Morgan's Raiders. But they were

MAP SKILL: Which of Indiana's neighbors was a slave state?

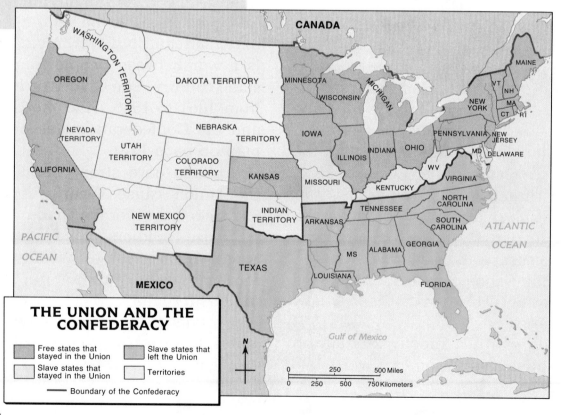

THE UNION AND THE CONFEDERACY

- Free states that stayed in the Union
- Slave states that stayed in the Union
- Slave states that left the Union
- Territories
- Boundary of the Confederacy

In the summer of 1863, Morgan's Raid brought the Civil War to Indiana's soil.

more afraid that his soldiers would try to capture the arsenal in Indianapolis. The raiders were finally slowed down by an armed group of Hoosiers in Corydon. This gave Governor Morton time to send more soldiers to Indianapolis to protect the arsenal. Morgan probably heard about the soldiers at the capital and headed instead towards Salem and Versailles. "Morgan's Raiders" were finally captured in Ohio.

THE END OF SLAVERY

President Lincoln issued the Emancipation (i man sə pā′ shən) Proclamation, which became law on January 1, 1863. This public statement said that slaves in every Confederate state held by the Union army were now free. Many Hoosiers were very pleased when Lincoln finally made his statement about freeing the slaves.

Some men in the Union army were also glad to hear the news. Very few African-American men had been allowed to fight for the Union. Soon many freed slaves would take part in the Union's struggle to remain one nation. One African-American regiment, the Indiana 28th, fought bravely in the war.

173

Soldiers of the Iron Brigade fought bravely during the Civil War.

SOLDIERS GO HOME

*The men will cheer, the boys
    will shout,
The ladies they will all turn
    out,
And we'll all feel [great] when
    Johnny comes marching home.*

This song was written by a soldier in a Union army marching band. Many people like him hoped that the war would soon end.

The Civil War finally ended on April 9, 1865, when the Confederate army surrendered in Virginia. But President Lincoln, who had done everything he could to keep the Union together, did not live to help the nation heal. Five days after the South's surrender, an angry man who blamed Lincoln for the South's trouble shot and killed him.

The nation mourned the death of one of our greatest Presidents. His body was carried across the country on a funeral train. Many Hoosiers cried when the train made its stop in Indianapolis. They remembered the boy who had grown up in the hills of southern Indiana.

THE FUTURE OF THE UNION

After a long and bloody fight, the Civil War was over. The Union was once again whole, and slavery was ended. But the struggle of African-Americans was not yet finished. They were no longer slaves, but they were still not treated as equals. In the next chapter you will read how Hoosiers, and all Americans, struggled with the problems of equality, or justice, for African-Americans in the years to come.

Check Your Reading

1. Why did Indiana fight on the side of the Union?
2. How did Hoosiers who stayed at home help the Union in the war?
3. **GEOGRAPHY SKILL:** Look at the map on page 172. Which slave states did not join the Confederacy? Were there any free states that sided with the Confederacy in the war?
4. **THINKING SKILL:** Read Governor Morton's words on page 171. What was his point of view about war against the South?

174

REVIEWING VOCABULARY

Number a sheet of paper from 1 to 3. Beside each number write the letter of the definition that best matches the word or term.

1. *Underground Railroad*
   a. A railroad line used by escaping slaves
   b. A set of tunnels used by escaping slaves
   c. A set of secret routes for escaping slaves
2. *secede*
   a. To break away from a country
   b. To form a new country
   c. To fight a war against your own country
3. *Confederate States of America*
   a. The new name for the United States of America
   b. A group of states that wanted to end slavery
   c. The states that withdrew from the United States to form their own country

REVIEWING FACTS

1. How did Chapman Harris help the Underground Railroad?
2. Why did western settlement help to start the Civil War?
3. How did Hoosiers help the Union's war effort?

WRITING ABOUT MAIN IDEAS

1. **Writing a Journal Entry:** Imagine that you are a "conductor" on the Underground Railroad. Use your imagination to write a journal entry about one incident in which you were involved.
2. **Writing an Opinion Paragraph:** Look at Governor Morton's statement on page 171. Do you agree or disagree with him? Write a paragraph giving your opinion and your reasons for it.
3. **Writing a Letter:** Imagine that you are a former slave who has joined Indiana's 28th Regiment to fight in the Civil War. Write a letter to a friend explaining why you joined the regiment to fight for the Union.

BUILDING SKILLS: RECOGNIZING POINT OF VIEW

1. What are some steps you could take to identify the point of view of a writer?
2. Write two sentences about the Underground Railroad from the points of view of Chapman Harris and a slave owner.
3. When is it important to try to recognize point of view in a statement?

CHAPTER 10

OUR GROWING HERITAGE

FOCUS

Some of the old Studebaker cars look funny because they're so different from the cars we have today. But I think it would have been neat to ride around in one of them.

Terrence Ford used these words to describe his visit to the Studebaker Museum in South Bend. In many ways the museum tells the story of how South Bend, and the rest of Indiana, grew and changed during the 1900s.

1 The Growth of Cities

READ TO LEARN

Key Vocabulary

manufacturing
immigrant

Key People

Henry and Clem
 Studebaker
Elwood Haynes

Key Places

Gary

Read Aloud

I, Henry Studebaker, agree to sell all the wagons my brother Clem can make. [Signed] Henry Studebaker
I agree to make all he can sell. [Signed] Clem Studebaker

This agreement between brothers was the beginning of a small wagon shop in South Bend. Later the brothers' company became Indiana's largest automaker. South Bend became a big city thanks in part to the business of Henry and Clem Studebaker.

Read for Purpose

1. **WHAT YOU KNOW:** Which part of Indiana was settled first by pioneers?
2. **WHAT YOU WILL LEARN:** How did the building of factories help Indiana to grow?

INDIANA GROWS WITH AMERICA

Americans worked hard to build up their country after the Civil War. They used iron to make new railroads and steel to make new buildings. Indiana helped America by manufacturing the iron, steel, and other products that the country needed in order to grow. Manufacturing is the making of large num-bers of products in factories. As manufacturing increased, Indiana grew and changed.

SOUTH BEND GROWS

South Bend is a good example of how manufacturing helped Hoosier cities to grow. In 1850 there were 1,700 people living in South Bend. The towns along the busy Ohio

177

River were much bigger than this. Almost twice as many people lived in Madison, the "Porkopolis" you read about in Chapter 8.

Then people began to build factories in South Bend. James Oliver started his plow factory. The Singer Company began making cabinets for its sewing machines there.

In 1852 two brothers named Henry and Clem Studebaker opened a wagon shop in South Bend. You read their agreement in the lesson opener. The brothers advertised their wagons with this poem.

> The Studebaker won't wear out
> No matter how you drive about.
> Pile on your rocks, this is
> no joke,
> This wagon is as stout as oak.

By 1873 the Studebakers claimed that they were the world's largest wagon manufacturer.

Thousands of people moved to South Bend to find jobs in the new factories. Some of the people were immigrants. An immigrant is a person who comes to another country to live. Immigrants came to South Bend from countries such as Germany, Ireland, and Poland.

By 1920 South Bend was almost 11 times bigger than Madison! There were 71,000 people in South Bend, compared with 6,700 in Madison. Immigrants and people from farms had moved to other northern cities as well. By 1900 more Hoosiers lived in cities than on farms. The northern part of the state was more crowded and had more cities than did the southern part.

The Studebaker factory first made wagons, then cars. The Studebaker brothers sit in one of their first cars.

New steel and automobile factories sprang up in the early 1900s.

STEEL AND CARS

Other Hoosier cities grew as new factories were built. In 1909 the United States Steel Company built a steel mill on the shores of Lake Michigan. Soon many people lived there. The new town was named Gary, after the steel company's chairman. Gary's steel mill became the largest in the world.

Automobile manufacturing also helped Hoosier cities to grow. One of the first automobiles was made by Elwood Haynes of Kokomo. He drove his car for the first time on the Pumpkinvine Pike in 1894. His speed was 8 miles (13 km) per hour.

Several auto companies built factories in Indiana. They made world-famous cars such as the Duesenberg, Stutz, and Cord. The most successful, however, was the Studebaker factory in South Bend. Clem and Henry's company switched from making wagons to making automobiles in 1902.

FROM FARMS TO CITIES

In the 1850s Indiana was a state of small farms and villages. By 1900 Indiana was becoming a state of towns and cities thanks in part to Hoosier manufacturing. In the next lesson you will read about the many ways in which Hoosier life changed in the 1900s.

 Check Your Reading

1. Name three Hoosier products that helped America to grow.
2. Why did South Bend grow so quickly in the late 1800s?
3. GEOGRAPHY SKILL: Look at the map on page 152. Why was South Bend a good place in which to start a wagon shop?
4. THINKING SKILL: What effect did the Studebakers' wagon shop have on South Bend?

1⁻

READ TO LEARN

Key Vocabulary

centennial
World War I
Great Depression
World War II
recycling

Key People

Franklin D. Roosevelt
Paul V. McNutt
Ernie Pyle

Key Places

Ernie Pyle State
Historic Site

Read Aloud

Our Centennial Celebration [included] over 3,000 school children, floats, wagons, vehicles of all kinds, log cabins on wagons—all more than two miles in length.

Thousands of Hoosiers lined the streets in Daviess County to watch this parade. It was 1916—the year of Indiana's one-hundredth birthday. People proudly remembered the history of their state and looked ahead to what the coming years would bring.

Read for Purpose

1. **WHAT YOU KNOW:** What are two important events that took place during Indiana's first 100 years of being a state?
2. **WHAT YOU WILL LEARN:** How did life change for most Hoosiers during the twentieth century?

A BIRTHDAY CELEBRATION

In 1916 Hoosiers all over the state celebrated Indiana's centennial (sen ten′ ē əl). *Centennial* means "a hundredth anniversary." There were big parades, like the one in Daviess County. Children performed plays about George Rogers Clark and the pioneers.

Remembering the state's past made Hoosiers want to preserve, or protect, parts of their heritage. They created a museum at Corydon. They set aside land for state parks and

In the early 1900s Hoosiers celebrated the **centennial** of our state and prepared for **World War I**.

forests. Turkey Run, in Parke County, was one of the first state parks to be opened.

THE FIRST WORLD WAR

As Hoosiers were celebrating Indiana's centennial, a bitter war was being fought in Europe. **World War I** started in 1914. France, Great Britain, and Russia were fighting against Germany, Austria-Hungary, and Turkey.

New weapons such as machine guns and nerve gas made this war especially deadly. Airplanes were also used for the first time in war. Hoosier Wilbur Wright and his brother Orville had flown the first successful airplane in 1903.

At first many Americans said that the war was none of their business. But then German submarines began attacking American ships. In the spring of 1917 the United States went to war.

Over 130,000 Hoosiers fought in the war. That is greater than the population of Evansville today! More than 3,000 Hoosiers died.

The war ended when Germany surrendered in November 1918. Hoosier soldiers came home to a big celebration in Indianapolis. All Americans hoped that this had been "the war to end all wars."

HARD TIMES

After the war business boomed in Indiana. In 1929, however, the **Great Depression** began. This was a time when businesses failed all over the country and many people lost their jobs. For the next ten years the United States struggled through a time of terrible poverty.

Many Hoosiers lost their jobs during the Great Depression. Some people could not afford to buy food for their families. Others made clothes out of whatever material they could find, such as feed bags.

People began to look to the government for help. In 1932 Franklin D. Roosevelt was elected President of the United States. He put many people back to work building roads and highways. Hoosier workers also built a wall in Evansville to protect the city from flooding.

Like Roosevelt, Governor Paul V. McNutt tried his best to help needy Hoosiers. For example, he provided money for elderly people who had very little savings. Roosevelt's and McNutt's actions helped many people, but they did not end the Great Depression.

WORLD WAR II

Hard times and unrest throughout the world caused war to break out again in Europe and Asia in 1939. On December 7, 1941, Japanese planes attacked American ships docked at Pearl Harbor, Hawaii. This action brought the United States into World War II.

Once again many Hoosiers helped their country to fight in a fierce and bloody war. This time 300,000 Hoosiers went to fight overseas. More than 10,000 were killed.

Hoosier factories operated around the clock to make supplies for the war effort. Hoosier steel was used to make tanks and ships. The Studebaker factory began making army trucks instead of cars. The Great Depression ended as America geared up for war.

Many women went to work in factories. Children helped the war effort, too. They collected paper and tin cans for recycling. To recycle means to use something again.

The **Great Depression** was a difficult time for Hoosiers throughout Indiana.

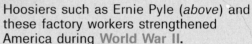

Hoosiers such as Ernie Pyle (*above*) and these factory workers strengthened America during World War II.

THE FRONT LINES

Many Americans read newspaper articles by Ernie Pyle to learn about what the war was like for ordinary soldiers and sailors. Pyle was a Hoosier from Dana. In one article he wrote about a boy whom soldiers met in Italy.

The soldiers' favorite was a stocky little fellow of about eight. . . . He had on a blue Navy sweater and the biggest pair of British tropical shorts I ever saw. They came clear below his knees.

Pyle had the gift of being able to describe war as seen through the eyes of ordinary people. You can visit the Ernie Pyle State Historic Site in Dana.

In 1945 Pyle went to Asia to cover the fighting there. In April he was killed in battle. One month later Germany surrendered. In August Japan also surrendered, bringing an end to World War II.

PEACE AT LAST

The war's end brought great joy to Hoosiers. "Bells and whistles blew like crazy," one woman remembered. People wanted to put their lives back together after 16 years of hard times and war.

 Check Your Reading

1. How did Hoosiers celebrate Indiana's centennial?
2. Why was the Great Depression a time of hardship?
3. How did Hoosier factories help the United States's war effort during World War II?
4. **THINKING SKILL:** Beginning with Indiana's centennial and ending with the end of World War II, list all the events mentioned in this lesson in the order in which they occurred.

Reading Circle and Line Graphs

Key Vocabulary
graph
line graph
circle graph

In this chapter you read about the growth of cities in Indiana. As manufacturing developed and the number of railroads grew, the population of Indiana also increased. A graph can show you the population growth of Indiana over a period of many years. A graph is a diagram that allows you to compare different facts and figures. Graphs can show a lot of information with the use of very few words.

Reading a Line Graph

One kind of graph is a line graph. A line graph shows changes that took place over a period of time. The line graph on this page shows the population of Indiana from 1900 to 1980.

To read a line graph, first look at its title. Next read the label on the bottom of the graph. What information does this label give? Find the label on the left side of the graph. What information does this label give?

Now locate the year 1900 at the bottom of the graph. To find out the population of Indiana in the year 1900, look at the dot above 1900. The dot is between the numbers 2 and 3 on the left side of the graph. Since the 2 and

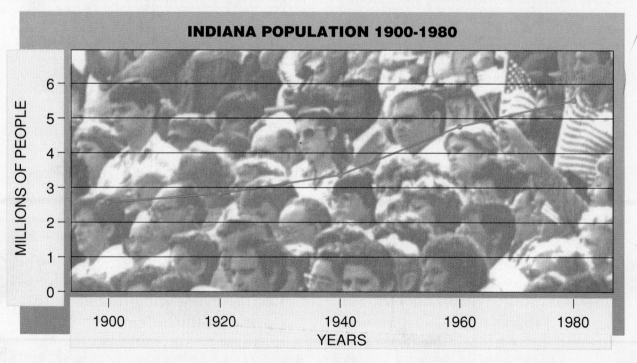

INDIANA POPULATION 1900-1980

MILLIONS OF PEOPLE
6 —
5 —
4 —
3 —
2 —
1 —
0 —

1900   1920   1940   1960   1980
YEARS

the 3 stand for millions of people, the population of Indiana in 1900 was between 2 and 3 million. Notice that the dots for each year are joined to make a line that rises on the graph as the population increases.

Reading a Circle Graph

Another kind of graph is a **circle graph**. This kind of graph shows how something can be divided into parts.

Together, all the parts make up the whole. A circle graph is often called a pie graph because the parts look like slices of a pie.

The circle graph on this page shows how the land in Indiana is used. Some of the land is covered with forests. Suppose that you want to compare the amount of forest land with the amount of land used for growing corn. The circle graph can help you.

First read the title of the graph. The circle represents the total amount of land in Indiana. Each part of the circle represents a different way in which the land is used. Which occupies more land in Indiana, forest land or cornfields?

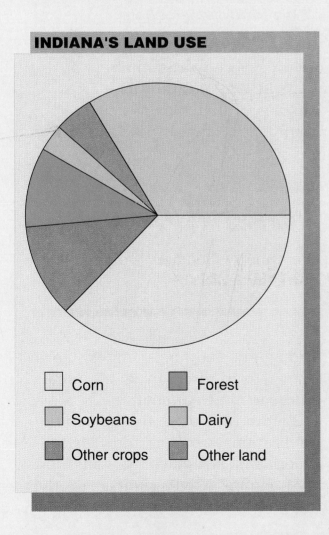

INDIANA'S LAND USE

- ☐ Corn
- ☐ Soybeans
- ☐ Other crops
- ☐ Forest
- ☐ Dairy
- ☐ Other land

Reviewing the Skill

Use the information and the graphs in this lesson to answer the following questions.

1. What is a graph? Name two kinds of graphs.
2. At which time did the population of Indiana reach 4 million?
3. Between which two years did the population of Indiana show the greatest increase?
4. Which use of land occupies the smallest number of acres in Indiana?
5. Why is it useful to understand how to read graphs?

185

3 A Time of Change

READ TO LEARN

Key Vocabulary

discrimination
civil rights
segregation
Ku Klux Klan
integration

Key People

Ida H. Harper
D. C. Stephenson
Henry J. Richardson, Jr.
Robert L. Brokenburr
Richard Hatcher

Read Aloud

We have any number of places [that] display signs in their windows, "white only." . . . We need some action out here. . . . I want justice for all.

A woman from East Chicago wrote these words to an African-American leader during World War II. She was tired of being treated unjustly because of the color of her skin. In the coming years she would see Hoosiers take action to improve life in our state.

Read for Purpose

1. **WHAT YOU KNOW:** What does the word *equality* mean to you?
2. **WHAT YOU WILL LEARN:** Why were many Hoosiers working for equal rights in the twentieth century?

THE FIGHT FOR RIGHTS

In the last lesson you read about Indiana's centennial celebration in 1916. There was much to be proud of in Hoosier history. But there were problems, too. One large problem was that women and African-Americans had faced discrimination throughout Indiana's history as a state. Discrimination is an unfair difference in treatment.

Before and after the centennial celebration, women and African-Americans struggled to win their civil rights. Civil rights are the rights of all people to be treated

Ida H. Harper (*right*) helped women to gain their voting rights.

equally under the law. You will read about their struggles and their victories in this lesson.

THE RIGHT TO VOTE

For many years women in the United States and Indiana were not allowed to vote. After the Civil War women began to fight for this right. One leader in the struggle was Ida H. Harper. Harper was born in 1851 in Fairfield. She became a writer for a newspaper in Terre Haute. Later on she used her writing skills in Indianapolis and Washington, D.C. to win rights for women.

In 1920 Harper saw her dream come true. The United States Constitution was changed in order to grant women the right to vote. Soon the Indiana state constitution was also changed. American women had gained this very important civil right at last.

LIVES OF HARDSHIP

African-Americans suffered even more from discrimination than did Hoosier women. They were faced with segregation, or forced separation, from other Hoosiers. Factory owners often refused to hire them. They could not go to certain restaurants or parks. They could only live in separate neighborhoods.

Segregation was a painful part of daily life for many African-American Hoosiers. "I went into a restaurant today and asked for a sandwich," wrote one woman. "The waitress told me she could not serve me." Imagine being in this woman's place. How would you feel?

Even schools were segregated. African-American students had to go to their own schools, which were

187

often in poor condition. Students shivered through classes each winter because the schoolrooms had no heat. Segregation was as real to children as it was to their parents.

THE KU KLUX KLAN

In the early 1920s thousands of Hoosiers joined the Ku Klux Klan. This was a secret group that hated people who members felt were different from themselves. Klan members marched through streets and burned crosses to frighten people. In some other states they beat and even killed people.

By the early 1900s many African-Americans and immigrants had moved to Indiana. Many immigrant families were Roman Catholic or Jewish—people who were considered "different" by the Ku Klux Klan. Klan members refused to accept the fact that life in Indiana was changing. With angry words and violence they tried to drive away Hoosier neighbors who they felt were different from them.

The Ku Klux Klan became an important force in Indiana's state government. Several government officials were known to be members of the Klan. But in 1924 the Klan's leader in Indiana, D. C. Stephenson, was arrested and jailed for murder. This caused most members to leave the Klan. Few Hoosiers belong to the Klan today. Even so, Indiana's involvement with the Ku Klux Klan is one of the most painful memories in our state's history.

Ku Klux Klan members used threats and violence against fellow Americans.

THE BEGINNINGS OF CHANGE

In the 1930s African-Americans, like almost all Hoosiers, suffered from the hard times of the Great Depression. People struggled to survive after losing their jobs.

But things began to change after World War II began. Factories, badly in need of workers, began to hire African-Americans and women. Henry J. Richardson, Jr., an African-American lawyer, led the fight against school segregation. In 1949 the state government passed a law that made school segregation illegal.

However, many other forms of segregation still existed. For example, in 1960 the famous baseball player Jackie Robinson came to visit Indianapolis. He was refused a motel room because he was an African-American.

Many people in the southern United States began to fight segregation during the 1950s. Their fight for civil rights soon spread to Indiana. The civil rights movement continued throughout the 1960s. It brought great change to Indiana and to the rest of the United States.

THE CIVIL RIGHTS MOVEMENT

In 1961 State Senator Robert L. Brokenburr fought for and won the passage of a civil rights law. It outlawed discrimination in restaurants, hotels, and hiring for jobs.

Brokenburr's civil rights law was a turning point in our state's history. It furthered integration in our state. Integration means "making something open to all people."

The people of Gary led the Hoosier movement for civil rights. In 1967 Richard Hatcher was elected mayor of Gary. He was one of the first African-Americans to become

Richard Hatcher, elected mayor of Gary in 1967, worked to end the pain of segregation in Indiana.

Young Hoosiers of all races play together. The 1972 meeting in Gary helped make this dream come true.

mayor of a large American city. Hatcher was elected five times and served in office for 20 years.

In March 1972 Gary hosted the nation's first meeting of African-American leaders. Mayor Hatcher welcomed the 8,000 people who had come to the meeting. Years later he said:

It was probably one of the most glorious moments of my life when I walked out and saw all of [the] people. . . . There was this . . . warm feeling of brotherhood and sisterhood.

The meeting at Gary was one of the high points of the American civil rights movement.

PROGRESS FOR ALL

Much has changed since Indiana's centennial in 1916. African-Americans and women have won civil rights that were once denied them. Women have voted since 1920. Segregated restaurants and hotels no longer exist. These victories have helped to protect the civil rights of all Hoosiers.

These changes have made Indiana a better place to live. There is still room for more progress to be made in our state. But when Indiana turns 200 in 2016, there will be much to celebrate.

 Check Your Reading

1. What is the difference between segregation and integration?
2. Why did the Ku Klux Klan become so powerful in Indiana?
3. How did Gary lead the civil rights movement in Indiana?
4. **THINKING SKILL:** What was Richard Hatcher's point of view about the meeting of African-American leaders in Gary?

READ TO LEARN

Key Vocabulary

publicity

Read for Purpose

1. **WHAT YOU KNOW:** What was life like for African-Americans in the South before the Civil War?
2. **WHAT YOU WILL LEARN:** What was life like for African-American women after the Civil War?

Madam C. J. Walker

You read about slavery in Lesson 1 of Chapter 9. After the Civil War ended all slaves were free. But even though African-Americans were no longer slaves, they did not have the same opportunities as whites did. It was not easy for them to get jobs. For women it was especially difficult. Women, including African-American women, still did not have the right to vote. This is the story of one woman's struggle to make a better life for herself.

SARAH'S STRUGGLE

Sarah Breedlove, an African-American woman, was born in Louisiana on December 23, 1867, after the Civil War had ended. As a child she saw how hard African-Americans had to struggle to earn a living.

Sarah's life was not easy. When she was young both of her parents died and she went to live with her sister. When she was only 14 years old, Sarah married Moses McWilliams. They had one daughter, Lelia, in 1885. Two years later Moses was killed, and the young mother was left a widow.

After her husband died, Sarah moved to St. Louis, Missouri, hoping for a better life. She decided that she needed to go to school in order to improve her life. Sarah went to night school. During the day she washed clothes in order to support herself.

Sarah thought that it was important to look her best. She believed this because, as an African-American woman, she had very few opportunities for improving her life. She knew that a person was often judged by his or her appearance. Sarah believed that if she did not look good she might not be given the chances she needed to get ahead.

Sarah's strong desire to look her best led her to make her own hair-care products. She soon began selling her products door-to-door to other African-Americans in St. Louis.

MADAM WALKER OF INDIANAPOLIS

In 1905 Sarah married Charles J. Walker in Denver. She then began to use the name Madam C. J. Walker on her products. Sarah's business began to expand. She opened an office in Pittsburgh, Pennsylvania, where her daughter was living at the time. In 1910 Sarah opened a laboratory and a beauty school in Indianapolis.

Sarah's factory in Indianapolis had about 15 employees. At the factory Sarah created other hair-care and beauty products.

Sarah opened beauty schools in other cities. She employed thousands of salespeople all over the country. The railroads that passed through Indianapolis made it easy to ship products all over the United States.

Sarah's company provided new job opportunities for African-American women. African-American women could now work in her beauty shops or they could sell Madam C. J. Walker products. Until this time many African-American women could not get jobs in business. They usually worked doing household tasks such as cleaning or sewing.

Sarah encouraged African-American women to go into business. She also encouraged them to attend school and to be proud of their heritage.

As Sarah became wealthy, she bought much land. In Indianapolis she bought land that included the block on which the Walker Building now stands on Indiana Avenue. She also bought land in Gary and in other cities across the country. In New York she bought many houses, including two in Harlem that were converted into a beauty parlor and school. The fronts of these two houses were remodeled with Indiana limestone.

Sarah donated a great deal of money to African-American groups. In Indianapolis she gave money to Bethel AME Church, Flanner House, and the Senate Avenue YMCA. Every year she gave 50 Christmas baskets to poor families. She helped to pay the bills of orphanages and senior citizens' homes. She also gave money to other groups, such as the National Association for the Advancement of Colored People (NAACP).

A GROWING COMPANY

As her company grew, Sarah spent most of her time traveling and speaking. Sarah's trips provided excellent publicity for her products. Publicity is the means that are used to bring a person or thing to the attention of the public. On some trips Sarah spoke not only of her products but also of her pride in being an African-

American and a woman. Occasionally she spoke out against issues that she felt were wrong.

In 1916 Sarah moved to Harlem in New York City. The stress of traveling and speaking began to wear her down. While on a trip to St. Louis in April 1919, she became very ill. She returned to New York and died the next month at the age of 51.

After her death Sarah's company continued to operate. In 1927 the Walker Company built a new building in Indianapolis. This building included a factory, offices, a theater, a casino, a drugstore, and a coffee shop. Over the years the company developed other products, including toothpaste, bath oil, and perfume.

A HELPING HAND

Sarah Breedlove Walker worked hard to create a better life for herself. She became one of the most successful African-American businesswomen of her day. Because of her hard work she helped to create opportunities for other African-American women to lead better lives.

Check Your Reading

1. What was Sarah's dream?
2. What did Sarah make and sell?
3. What new types of jobs did Sarah create for African-American women?
4. **THINKING SKILL:** What was Sarah's life like before she went to night school? How was Sarah's life different after she went to night school?

4 Education for All

Key Vocabulary

public university
private university

Key Places

Bloomington
Lafayette
Muncie

Read Aloud

Indiana, Indiana, Indiana we're all for you!
We will fight for the cream and crimson
For the glory of old IU
Indiana, Indiana, Indiana we're all for you!

This is a song known to thousands of students at Indiana University in Bloomington. Indiana University is one of our state's many excellent universities. In this lesson you will read about education in Indiana's past, present, and future.

Read for Purpose

1. **WHAT YOU KNOW:** How many universities in Indiana can you name?
2. **WHAT YOU WILL LEARN:** How have Hoosiers shown their commitment to good education through the years?

EDUCATION AND OUR STATE

The right to an education has a long history in Indiana. The pioneers knew that education would help Indiana to develop as a state. They provided for the founding of many schools. Hoosiers today continue the tradition of working for excellence in education.

The Ordinance of 1785, which you read about in Chapter 6, set aside Hoosier land for schools. In 1806 the first Hoosier college was created at Vincennes. That college still exists today. It is called Vincennes University.

When the state constitution was written in 1816, it provided for the creation of a state college. Eight years later Indiana College opened in Bloomington, which was then a tiny frontier village. In 1838 the state college was renamed Indiana University.

For several years only a few students attended the university because it was hard to reach from other parts of the state. Indiana University grew quickly after the Civil War, however. Hoosiers built a railroad connecting Bloomington to the rest of the state. Today over 33,000 students attend Indiana University at Bloomington. They study subjects such as history, music, and law.

PUBLIC AND PRIVATE UNIVERSITIES

In 1874 the state opened a college for the study of agriculture. Purdue University was named after John Purdue, a merchant from Lafayette. Today Purdue is famous throughout the nation for its agricultural and engineering schools.

Vincennes, Indiana University, and Purdue are public universities, or schools that operate using money from taxes. You can see from the map on this page that Indiana has many other fine public universities.

Two of Indiana's public universities began as places where people learned how to be teachers. One is Indiana State University in Terre Haute. Another is Ball State University in Muncie. Today people can still learn about teaching at these schools, but other subjects are taught there as well.

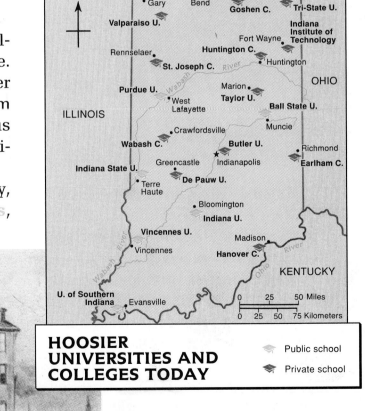

MAP SKILL: Vincennes University's oldest building is shown below. Is it a public or private school?

HOOSIER UNIVERSITIES AND COLLEGES TODAY

Public school
Private school

What kinds of educational possibilities do you hope for in the future?

Hoosiers also have their choice of attending fine private universities. A private university is a school that does not receive money from the state. Locate a private university on the map of Indiana on page 197.

The University of Notre Dame, in South Bend, is perhaps Indiana's best-known private university. Like many other private universities, Notre Dame was founded by a church. The university was founded by the Roman Catholic Church in 1842. Today over 9,000 students attend Notre Dame.

EDUCATION FOR THE FUTURE

Colleges and universities are only one part of education in our state. The other part includes elementary schools and high schools.

In the 1980s Indiana began new programs to improve these schools. As a result, computers are being used more often in classrooms. One program provides students with computers to use at home. The state government is working to pass laws that will improve Hoosier schools in other ways. Its "Project 2000" hopes to make Indiana's schools even better by the year 2000.

 Check Your Reading

1. Why did few students attend Indiana University before the Civil War?
2. Name one public university and one private university that are located in Indiana.
3. GEOGRAPHY SKILL: Find two colleges or universities on the map on page 197 that are close to your home.
4. THINKING SKILL: In what ways are Indiana University and the University of Notre Dame similar to each other? In what ways are they different?

198

REVIEWING VOCABULARY

Number a sheet of paper from 1 to 5. Beside each number write **T** if the statement is true. If the statement is false, rewrite it to make it true.

1. *Manufacturing* means making a great many products in factories.
2. *Immigrants* enter a country in which they were not born and make it their new home.
3. *World War I* came after the Great Depression.
4. *Civil rights* are the rights of all people to be treated equally under the law.
5. *Integration* forces people to be separate from one another.

REVIEWING FACTS

1. Why did South Bend grow in the late 1800s?
2. Identify one Hoosier who fought for voting rights for women.
3. Why was the Great Depression hard for most Hoosiers?
4. How did Hoosiers add to America's war effort during World War II?
5. List the names of two African-American Hoosiers who fought against segregation.

WRITING ABOUT MAIN IDEAS

1. **Writing a Postcard:** Imagine that you are an immigrant who has moved to South Bend in the 1880s. Write a postcard to your family in Europe telling about your new life in Indiana.
2. **Writing from a Point of View:** Write about how each of these people might have felt about Indiana's centennial celebration: the governor of Indiana; an African-American Hoosier; a young woman.
3. **Writing an Interview:** Imagine that the year is 1967 and you are in Gary. Write five questions that you would ask Richard Hatcher, who has just been elected mayor.

BUILDING SKILLS: READING LINE AND CIRCLE GRAPHS

Study the graphs on pages 184–185. Then answer these questions.

1. What is the difference between a line graph and a circle graph?
2. What was Indiana's population in 1950?
3. Which use of land occupies the largest number of acres in Indiana?
4. Why are graphs useful?

REVIEWING VOCABULARY

centennial

discrimination

Emancipation
    Proclamation

integration

interdependent

Iron Brigade

Ku Klux Klan

recycling

secede

transportation

Number a sheet of paper from 1 to 10. Beside each number write the word or term from the list above that best matches the definition.

1. Ways of moving people and goods
2. Depending on one another to help meet needs and wants
3. To withdraw from a group
4. A group of soldiers who fought in the Civil War
5. The announcement that slaves in the Confederate states were free
6. A one-hundredth anniversary
7. To use again
8. An unfair difference in treatment
9. A group of people that hates people different from themselves
10. The act of making something open to people of all races

◖▭▶WRITING ABOUT THE UNIT

1. **Writing About Change:** Think about the ways in which life in Indiana changed between the 1800s and the 1960s. Write a paragraph that describes one such change.

2. **Writing About a Person:** Pick one person from Unit 4 whom you admire. Write a paragraph explaining why you admire that person. End with a sentence telling what you would like to say if you ever met him or her.

3. **Writing a Song:** Choose a piece of music that you like. Then choose an event that took place in our state's history during the 1900s. Write your own words to the music you have chosen that describes this event.

ACTIVITIES

1. **Making a Poster:** Choose a few events about which you read in Unit 4. Make a poster using art and words that ties these events together.

2. **Researching Education:** Find out more about education in Indiana. Use the library to learn about the history of one college or university in your area. If possible, ask questions of people who have attended this school. Make a list of the facts that you discover.

3. **Working Together to Make a Book:** Work with a small group of classmates to create your own book about Indiana. Include information from this textbook as well as other information you find in newspapers, magazines, and other sources.

BUILDING SKILLS:
RECOGNIZING POINT OF VIEW

Read the following points of view and answer the questions below.

We seceded because the Northern states went too far in ordering us around. They have no right to tell us what we can and cannot do.

I believe that slavery is wrong. This war is about human rights, not just states' rights.

1. What topic are the speakers talking about?
2. Which words helped you to determine the first point of view?
3. Describe two situations in which it would be useful to understand another person's point of view.

LINKING PAST, PRESENT AND FUTURE

Rivers were very important transportation routes in the early history of our state. Today travel by boat is only one form of transportation used by Hoosiers. What are some others? What other forms of transportation might be in use when you grow up?

State quilt

State tree:
Tulip tree

UNIT

5

State bird:
Cardinal

INDIANA TODAY

LIFE IN OUR STATE

On these pages you see some of the symbols of Indiana. These are all things found in our state that make it different from any other. In the last three units you read the story of our state's past. Now let's find out what Indiana is like today.

State seal

State flower:
Peony

CHAPTER 11

THE PEOPLE OF INDIANA

FOCUS

I like to write poetry. That's why my favorite Hoosier author is James Whitcomb Riley.

Ebony Utley recently visited the house in Indianapolis where Indiana's most famous poet lived. In this chapter you will read about the people in our state and how they enjoy and express themselves.

1 Hoosiers: A Proud People

READ TO LEARN

■ Key Vocabulary

rural

■ Read Aloud

For here we know no sections, east or west,
Or north or south. Here are the people bound
By many sacred ties to all the rest.
Here is the heartbeat of the nation sound.

Max Ehrmann, a poet from Terre Haute, wrote these words in a poem called "Indiana." The poem says that people from many different places have come to Indiana—from Africa, Asia, Europe and the Americas. Even so, they are united as Hoosiers and Americans. In this lesson you will find out about the many different people who call Indiana home.

■ Read for Purpose

1. **WHAT YOU KNOW:** How do people in your community work together?
2. **WHAT YOU WILL LEARN:** What are some things that make Hoosiers special?

HOOSIERS TODAY

Our state name means "land of Indians," but Indiana is now home to many different people. People have come from all over the nation and the world to live in the cities and towns of our state.

Today more than 5.5 million people live in Indiana. Only 13 states in the United States have more people. Indiana is known as a farm state, but today most Hoosiers—about 6 out of 10—live in cities. Until the early 1900s most Hoosiers lived in rural areas, or the country.

Look at the bar graph on page 206. It shows the population of the

GRAPH SKILL: Indiana's population is centered in its cities. About how many more people live in Evansville than in South Bend?

THE FIVE LARGEST CITIES IN INDIANA

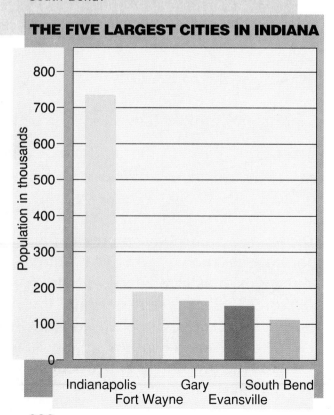

five largest cities in Indiana. Indianapolis is our largest city. What is our second-largest city?

RELIGION IN INDIANA

Jacob Miller and his family own a farm in Lagrange County. The Miller farm, however, is very different from most farms in Indiana.

Like the pioneers of long ago, Jacob and his brothers prepare the land for planting with a horse-drawn plow. His family drives to town in a buggy, not a car. They never watch television—the Miller family has never owned one.

Jacob and his family are Amish (ä´ mish). The Amish are members of a religious group that believes in living simple lives. Jacob's father tells people that the Amish like to live "close to the land." For this reason they farm the land without tractors. It is also the reason that they wear simple clothing and do not own televisions or cars.

For Jacob and many other Hoosiers, religion is an important part of everyday life. The Amish are one of many religious groups in Indiana. There are many other religious groups in our state, including Roman Catholics, Baptists, Lutherans, Methodists, and Jews.

Religion is an important part of many people's traditions. Of course, not every Hoosier is a member of a religious group. And not all religious groups in our state have the

The Amish (*left*) live a special way of life. The festival shown above honors the early pioneers.

same beliefs. Religious beliefs in Indiana are varied, just like our state's land and its people.

HOOSIER HOLIDAYS

Hoosiers live varied lives, but they have one thing in common— they all love holidays! Almost every week of the year you can find a festival going on somewhere in our state. A festival is a special celebration, like a fair. You can find out more about Hoosier festivals in the Almanac on page 320. Which is your favorite Hoosier festival?

Many festivals honor the pioneer heritage of our state. In October you can go to the Feast of the Hunters' Moon. It is held at Fort Ouiatenon, which you read about in Chapter 4. There you can feel what it was like to be an early pioneer. You can listen to pioneer music, watch folk dancing, and hear stories that were first told long ago by Indiana's early settlers and Indian groups.

HOOSIERS ALL

Our state's people are as different as Indiana's Dune Country is from the Ohio River. But no matter where or how Hoosiers live, they all help to make Indiana a special place. In the next lesson you will read about how the arts add to life in our state.

 Check Your Reading

1. Why don't Amish people use machines on their farms?
2. Name two reasons that Hoosiers have festivals.
3. **GEOGRAPHY SKILL:** Where in Indiana do most Hoosiers live?
4. **THINKING SKILL:** List three questions that you could ask to learn more about the people who live in our state.

Comparing Maps

Key Vocabulary
population map
land-use map

Throughout this book you have been using maps to help you to understand the history and geography of Indiana. Each of the different maps helped you to learn something different about our state.

As you have seen, maps show information in a special way. Each map, however, usually shows only one kind of information. By comparing maps that show different kinds of information, you can learn even more about Indiana.

The maps on page 209 both show Indiana. Each map presents different information about the state. Read the title of each map. What kind of information is shown on each map?

Different Kinds of Maps

Map A is a population map. It shows the number of people per square mile (per square kilometer) in different areas of our state. You can use it to discover in which areas of Indiana many people live and in which areas few people live.

Map B is a land-use map. It shows some of the different ways people in Indiana use the land to earn a living.

You already know that many people in our state work on farms. The land-use map shows the areas in Indiana which are covered by farmland. The land-use map also shows how much land is used for coal mining, manufacturing, and various other kinds of land use.

Study the key for each map to make sure that you understand what the colors used on the map stand for. Find the key for **Map A**. It uses different colors to show how many people live in a particular area. Which color is used to show areas where there are fewer than 50 people per square mile (fewer than 20 people per square kilometer)?

Look again at **Map B**. The key on **Map B** uses different colors to show how people use the land. Which color is used to show areas used mainly for mining coal? Which kind of land use covers the largest area of the map?

You can use both the population map and the land-use map to make comparisons. Together these maps will show you how population and land use affect one another. For example, find the two most heavily populated areas in the state. Now look at the manufacturing areas on the land-use map. Are the areas that are used for manufacturing heavily populated?

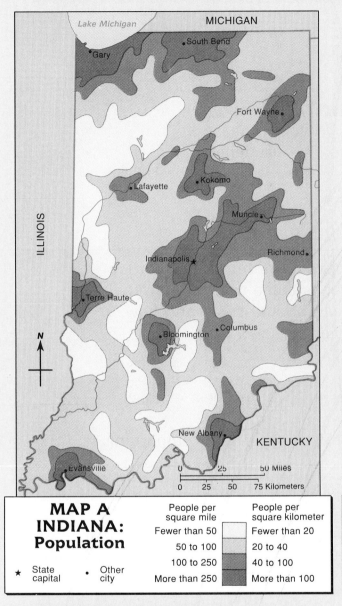

MAP A
INDIANA:
Population

People per square mile	People per square kilometer
Fewer than 50	Fewer than 20
50 to 100	20 to 40
100 to 250	40 to 100
More than 250	More than 100

★ State capital   • Other city

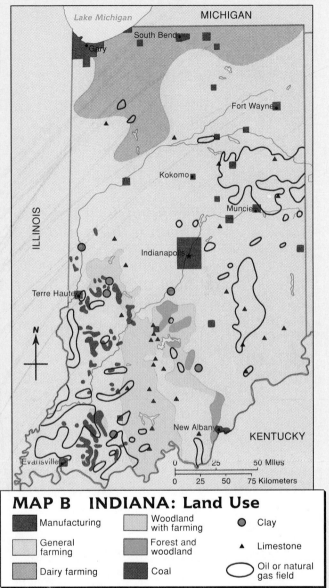

MAP B   INDIANA: Land Use

- Manufacturing
- General farming
- Dairy farming
- Woodland with farming
- Forest and woodland
- Coal
- ⬤ Clay
- ▲ Limestone
- ⬭ Oil or natural gas field

Reviewing the Skill

Use the maps on this page to answer the questions below.

1. How many people per square mile (per square kilometer) would you find in Terre Haute?

2. Which economic activity occupies most of the land in Indiana?

3. Which city is located in the more heavily populated area—Richmond or New Albany?

4. Compare the two maps on this page. Are the areas labeled "woodland" heavily populated?

5. Why is it helpful to compare different kinds of maps of the same place?

209

2 Hoosier Artists

READ TO LEARN

▣ Key People

James Whitcomb Riley   Gene Stratton Porter
Booth Tarkington   Cole Porter
Theodore Dreiser   Hoagy Carmichael

▣ Read Aloud

We make our own reality—
We dream a thing and it is so.

A famous Hoosier poet wrote these lines about artists and how they make their dreams come true through their art. In this lesson you will read about artists and how they have added to our Hoosier heritage.

▣ Read for Purpose

1. **WHAT YOU KNOW:** In what ways do you best express your feelings?
2. **WHAT YOU WILL LEARN:** Why are the arts an important part of Hoosier culture?

ART IN OUR STATE

Mrs. Jefferson asked her class what kind of art they liked. "I like to read books," said Nicholas Hayes. "Stories about pioneers are some of my favorites."

"I like playing music," said Karen Baker. "I'm learning to play 'On the Banks of the Wabash' on the piano now."

Nicholas and Karen described two different art forms that can be found in Indiana. When you think of art, you might think of paintings and sculpture. But writing and music are forms of art, too. You will read about some of Indiana's writers and musicians in this lesson.

"THE HOOSIER POET"

The early 1900s have been called Indiana's "Golden Age" of writing. During that time more writers of best-selling books came from Indiana than from any other state except New York. One of the most famous was James Whitcomb Riley, who was nicknamed "the Hoosier Poet." You read some of his words at the beginning of this lesson.

Riley was born in the town of Greenfield in 1849. Greenfield's main street was the busy National Road. Riley watched many travelers pass by on the road as they headed west. Seeing them made him want to travel, too. As a child, Riley "traveled" by reading many books at the town library.

When Riley was a teenager, he joined a traveling show that toured the state. Then he wrote stories for a newspaper. These experiences gave Riley plenty to write about in his poems.

Riley wrote many of his poems for children. "Little Orphant Annie" is one of his most popular poems. Today Hoosiers of all ages still like to say these lines:

> *An' the Gobble-uns 'll git you*
> *Ef you*
> *Don't*
> *Watch*
> *Out!*

OTHER GOLDEN AGE WRITERS

Booth Tarkington was another writer who was a part of Indiana's Golden Age. Tarkington was born in Indianapolis in 1869.

When he was young, Tarkington loved to play tricks on people. Sometimes this got him into trouble at school. In his books about a boy named Penrod, Tarkington wrote

James Whitcomb Riley, shown below surrounded by children, lived in this house in Greenfield.

WRITERS OF INDIANA'S "GOLDEN AGE"

JAMES WHITCOMB RILEY
1849-1916
Popular Writings:
"When the Frost Is on the Punkin,"
"Raggedy Man"

BOOTH TARKINGTON
1869-1946
Popular Writings:
Penrod,
The Gentleman From Indiana

THEODORE DREISER
1871-1945
Popular Writings:
Sister Carrie, An American Tragedy

GENE STRATTON PORTER
1868-1924
Popular Writings:
A Girl of the Limberlost,
Friends in Feathers

CHART SKILL: Which writers were born within two years of each other?

about someone just like himself. Americans have enjoyed reading about Penrod's funny adventures.

Another famous Hoosier writer was Theodore Dreiser. Dreiser was born in Terre Haute in 1871. His older brother, Paul Dresser, wrote Indiana's state song, "On the Banks of the Wabash." Dresser changed his name from Dreiser when he became an actor.

The Dreiser family was very poor. Theodore was able to go to Indiana University only because a high school teacher helped to pay his way. The hardships that Dreiser experienced color each of his books. Unlike most authors of his time,

Dreiser wrote honestly about the issues of greed and lack of honesty in America. Two of his best-known books are *Sister Carrie* and *An American Tragedy*.

The writings of Gene Stratton Porter also added much to Indiana's Golden Age. She was born in 1868 on a small farm in the Wabash River Valley. Her real name was Geneva, but she was nicknamed "Gene."

Porter was raised by her father because her mother was often sick. He taught her and her brothers many things about plants and animals. From him Gene and her brothers learned to love the outdoors. Porter's love of the outdoors can be seen in all of her books. Among the most famous are *Freckles* and *A Girl of the Limberlost*.

Cole Porter (*left*) and Hoagy Carmichael wrote songs that became popular all over America.

HOOSIER SONGWRITERS

Indiana has given America some of its finest songwriters. The most famous is Cole Porter.

Porter was born in the town of Peru in 1891. He began taking piano lessons when he was eight years old. When he was only 11 years old Porter published his first song, "The Bobolink Waltz." He later went to New York and became a songwriter for many hit shows and movies. Today musicians all over the world still love to perform "Night and Day," "You're the Top," and other Porter songs.

Hoagy Carmichael was another popular Hoosier musician. Carmichael was born in Bloomington in 1899. He studied law at Indiana University, but music was his first love. In 1927 Carmichael wrote the song that made him famous—"Star Dust." Today you can still hear "Star Dust" on the radio.

ART FOR EVERYONE

As you have read, art is not limited to just painting and sculpture. Writing and music are important forms of art, too. Hoosier artists have added a great deal to our Hoosier heritage—and to America's heritage as well.

 Check Your Reading

1. What and when was Indiana's Golden Age?
2. Who is "the Hoosier Poet"?
3. **GEOGRAPHY SKILL:** How did growing up in Terre Haute help Paul Dresser to write the song for which he is famous?
4. **THINKING SKILL:** Sort the following list of artists into two groups: writers and songwriters. Hoagy Carmichael, Gene Stratton Porter, Booth Tarkington, Cole Porter, Theodore Dreiser.

3 Hoosier Athletes

Key Vocabulary

recreation

Key People

Ray Harroun   Larry Bird
Bobby Knight   Knute Rockne
Oscar Robertson   Wilma Rudolph

Read Aloud

Gentlemen, start your engines. . . .

These words start off the famous Indianapolis 500 automobile race each year. People come from all over the world to watch this sporting event. You will read about the Indianapolis 500 and other Hoosier sports events in this lesson.

Read for Purpose

1. **WHAT YOU KNOW:** What kinds of sports teams does your community have?
2. **WHAT YOU WILL LEARN:** How do sports bring Hoosiers together?

HAVING FUN

What do you like to do for fun? Read a book? Go to the movies? Play basketball? All of these activities are different kinds of recreation (rek rē ā′ shən). Recreation is what people do in order to relax and enjoy themselves. For many Hoosiers going to sports events is a favorite form of recreation. You will read about sports that Hoosiers love in this lesson.

THE INDY 500

Which sports event draws more than 250,000 people to Indianapolis each Memorial Day weekend? It is, of course, the 500-mile (800-km) automobile race called the Indianapolis 500. This race is nicknamed the "Indy 500."

How did this race get started? In 1909 a group of Hoosier automobile makers began testing their cars on a dirt track in Indianapolis. They wanted to see how fast their cars could go safely. In May 1911 they held their first race.

The first Indy 500 lasted more than six hours. The first winner was Ray Harroun of Indianapolis. He went around the track 200 times to win, just as racers do today. But unlike today's racers, Harroun's top speed was only about 75 miles (120 km) per hour.

Today's racing cars reach speeds of over 220 miles (352 km) per hour! This makes the Indy 500 very exciting. Racing fans will always remember when Gordon Johncock beat Rick Mears by less than one second in the 1982 Indy 500.

THE "LITTLE 500"

The Indy 500 is not the only big race in Indiana. Every spring students at Indiana University get together to race in the Little 500 Bicycle Race. Teams of students bike 200 times around a track—a total distance of 50 miles (80 km).

This Hoosier tradition began in the 1950s. It has become one of the most popular events in Bloomington. Today more than 30,000 people gather to cheer the Little 500 racers.

"HOOSIER HYSTERIA"

Hoosiers enjoy many kinds of sports. Basketball, however, causes a special kind of excitement. Every basketball season "Hoosier Hysteria" (hi ster′ ē ə) takes over the state. This means that people root hard for their basketball teams, whether they are school teams or professional teams.

The cars that race around the Speedway have changed since Ray Harroun drove this one in 1911.

Hoosiers of all ages love to watch high school, college, and professional basketball.

Anderson High

1989 Girls State Champs

Larry Bird

Bobby Knight, Oscar Robertson

It is a cold Friday night in Anderson. Outside the night is still. Snow falls softly. Inside Anderson's high school gym, though, it is hot. Screams, cheers, and the smell of popcorn fill the air.

Anderson is playing Highland—an important game for both teams. Some 9,000 people have crowded themselves into the gym. Even more watch the game on television. This is one example of Hoosier Hysteria.

Hoosier Hysteria fills school gyms during both girls' and boys' basketball games. Girls' basketball has become popular since the 1970s, when girls' teams were first started in schools.

People all over the state get especially excited when the Indiana University basketball season begins. The Hoosiers, coached by Bobby Knight, are one of the best college basketball teams in the nation. They have won the National Collegiate Athletic Association (NCAA) Championship five times. Indiana University's gym, which seats 17,000 people, is always full when the Hoosiers are playing!

FAMOUS HOOSIER PLAYERS

Some of America's finest basketball players have played in Indiana. One example is Oscar Robertson. Robertson was the first Hoosier named Most Valuable Player in the National Basketball Association. He was also the first Hoosier to score 25,000 points in his career.

Robertson was born in Indianapolis and began his outstanding career on the Crispus Attucks High School team. Robertson then played college basketball and broke many records. He broke even more records as a member of the Cincinnati Royals. Robertson was named to both the National Basketball Hall of Fame and the Indiana Hall of Fame in 1982.

Another member of the Indiana Hall of Fame is Larry Bird, who was born in French Lick. In high school Bird was named to Indiana's high school All-Star team. Then he played for Indiana State University in Terre Haute. Bird has gone on to become a superstar with the Boston Celtics.

Football, track, and bicycle racing are some of the other sports that Hoosiers love.

The Granger Collection

Knute Rockne

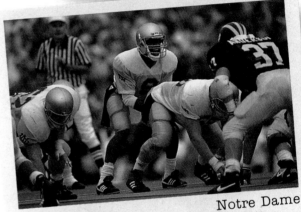

Notre Dame

Wilma Rudolph

The Little 500

217

"Hoosier Hysteria" fills gyms throughout our state every winter.

Hoosiers also enjoy watching Indiana's professional basketball team, the Indiana Pacers. The Pacers' home court is at the Market Square Arena in Indianapolis. Like Bloomington's, this arena seats 17,000 people.

MORE CHAMPIONS

Other Hoosier sports have produced great champions. Knute Rockne is one. Rockne coached the University of Notre Dame's football team in the early 1900s. During his 13 years as coach, Notre Dame won 105 games and lost only 12. Today Notre Dame continues to be one of the best college football teams in the country.

Our state has also been called home by many Olympic champions. One is Wilma Rudolph. Rudolph was born in Tennessee but now lives in Indianapolis. When she was younger, Wilma had polio, a disease that once crippled many children, and other serious illnesses. However, she overcame her illnesses and won three gold medals in track and field at the 1960 Olympics. You can read about other Olympic champions in the Almanac on page 325.

COMMUNITY SPIRIT

Hoosiers are proud of their many fine athletes, whether they are local players or world champions. They gather at sports events to show their community spirit—and to enjoy some Hoosier Hysteria as well!

 Check Your Reading

1. How did the Indy 500 begin?
2. Who was the first Hoosier to be honored as Most Valuable Player in the National Basketball Association?
3. What is Knute Rockne famous for?
4. **THINKING SKILL:** Find three facts stated in this lesson. How do you know they are facts and not opinions?

REVIEWING VOCABULARY

land-use map   recreation
population map   rural

Number a sheet of paper from 1 to 5. Beside each number write the word or term from the list above that best completes the sentence. One of the words or terms is used twice.

1. The farm was located in a beautiful ____ area.
2. The park's ____ area had four basketball courts and a baseball field.
3. Mrs. Jackson's students used a ____ to see how many people lived in their county.
4. Mr. Lee's students looked at a ____ to see how people use the land in Indiana to earn a living.
5. Many people enjoy ____ because it is relaxing and fun.

REVIEWING FACTS

Number a sheet of paper from 1 to 5. Beside each number write **T** if the statement is true. If the statement is false, rewrite it to make it true.

1. Indiana's "Golden Age" was a time when many best-selling books were written by Hoosier authors.
2. Theodore Dreiser wrote funny stories about boys growing up in Indianapolis.
3. Cole Porter is best known for his song "Star Dust."
4. Oscar Robertson was the first Hoosier basketball player to score 25,000 points in his career.
5. Wilma Rudolph began to win races when she was a young child.

WRITING ABOUT MAIN IDEAS

1. **Writing a Report:** Read a poem by James Whitcomb Riley. Then write a report describing: (a) what the poem was about, (b) what kind of language Riley used in the poem, and (c) why his special use of language made the poem more interesting.
2. **Writing a Descriptive Paragraph:** Write about your favorite festival in Indiana. Explain what the festival celebrates and what people do at the festival. In the last sentence, tell why it is your favorite festival.

BUILDING SKILLS: COMPARING MAPS

Use Map A and Map B on page 209 to answer the questions below.

1. Name two cities in which there are 100 to 250 people per square mile.
2. Where does dairy farming take place in Indiana?
3. Compare the two maps. How many people per square mile live in manufacturing areas?
4. When might you want to compare different maps of the same place?

219

CHAPTER 12

HOOSIERS AT WORK

FOCUS

For my chores I feed the pigs, clean out pens, and help when the sows have baby pigs. I also help when it comes time to harvest the corn and soybeans.

This is how Eric Field describes his life on the Field's farm in Decatur County. In this chapter you will read about farming and other ways in which Hoosiers earn their livings.

READ TO LEARN

Key Vocabulary

agriculture   livestock
economy

Key People

Orville Redenbacher

Read Aloud

The workday may stretch to 14 hours or more, but I would not want to leave our farm and live in the city.

This is how Donna Hibschman feels about working on her family's farm. In this lesson you will read about why farming is more than a way to earn a living for Donna and her family. It is also a way of life.

Read for Purpose

1. **WHAT YOU KNOW:** How did the Miami Indians raise corn?
2. **WHAT YOU WILL LEARN:** How is Hoosier farming today different from Hoosier farming in the past?

NEW WAYS OF LIFE

A long time has passed since the early days of Indiana, when people lived off the food they grew on their own land. Now most people buy their food in supermarkets.

However, farming is still a way of life for some Hoosiers today. These farmers earn a living from agriculture (ag' ri kul chər). Agriculture is the business of growing crops and raising animals.

Agriculture is an important part of our state's economy. Economy is the way a state or country uses its resources to meet people's needs and wants. You have read about how important corn has been to Indiana ever since the days of the Miami Indians.

Today corn is still Indiana's most important farm product. Other products include soybeans, wheat, and livestock. Livestock are animals raised on a farm for money. Hoosier farmers work hard to raise these products for people across the nation and around the world.

22

Raising **livestock** and growing corn are two jobs of many Hoosier farmers.

A FARMER'S DAY

"Bzzz!" Donna Hibschman sighs, then leans out of bed and turns off her alarm clock. It is 4:30 A.M.—the start of a new day for Donna and her husband Joe.

The Hibschmans are farmers who live in northern Indiana, near Syracuse. They begin each day by feeding their herd of cows. Next they milk the cows with milking machines. Later on a large truck comes to take the milk to a dairy.

After milking the cows, Joe moves on to work in the fields. Like most farmers, Joe plants fields with corn one year and with soybeans the next year.

"We plant soybeans because they are good for the soil," Donna says. "A crop like corn may use up the minerals in the soil," she ex-

plains. Planting soybeans helps to put minerals back into the soil.

Today Joe plows a field using a tractor. Hoosiers have used tractors instead of horses since the 1920s. Using a tractor makes a farmer's job much easier. Other machines help farmers to plant and harvest crops.

Because of these machines, one farmer can now grow enough food to feed 54 people each year! Think about the ways farming has changed since the days of the pioneers. Pioneer farmers, you remember, worked hard just to raise enough food for their own families.

Donna spends most of the morning working with her computer. It helps her to keep records of the farm's bills. More and more Hoosiers are using computers to help them run their farms.

Late in the afternoon Joe and Donna check on their cows to make sure that they are all right. After dinner they milk the cows for the second time. At last they go to bed. They must rest before the alarm wakes them up again at 4:30 A.M.!

A CORN BELT STATE

Indiana is part of the Corn Belt. The Corn Belt is a region in the United States that has just the right climate for growing corn. The Corn Belt produces more corn than any other area in the world. Look at the map on this page. How many states are part of the Corn Belt?

Hoosier corn is used in many different ways. Most is grown as food for livestock. Some is grown for people to eat. For example, Indiana is the biggest producer of popcorn in the country. Hoosier Orville Redenbacher began one of the biggest popcorn companies in America in 1952. The company is based in Valparaiso.

Did you know that corn is also used to make automobile fuel? Ethanol (eth′ ə nôl) is a fuel made from

THE CORN BELT

CANADA

ND, MN, SD, WI, MI, NE, IA, IL, IN, OH, KS, MO

L. Superior, L. Michigan, L. Huron, L. Erie

Missouri R., Mississippi, Ohio R.

N

Areas where corn is grown

MAP SKILL: Which section of Indiana is part of the Corn Belt?

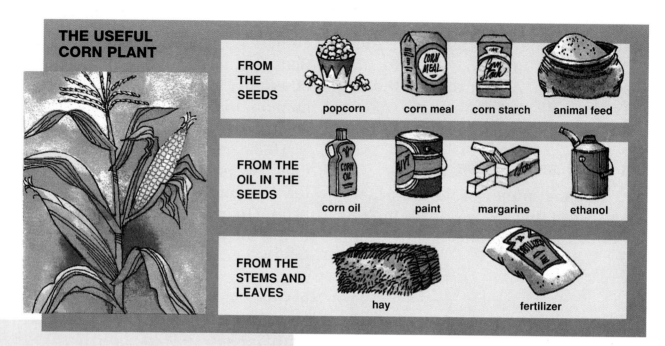

THE USEFUL CORN PLANT

FROM THE SEEDS
popcorn   corn meal   corn starch   animal feed

FROM THE OIL IN THE SEEDS
corn oil   paint   margarine   ethanol

FROM THE STEMS AND LEAVES
hay   fertilizer

CHART SKILL: Which part of the corn plant is used to make fuel for use in automobiles and trucks?

corn. It is added to gasoline to help it to burn more cleanly. American automakers are now making more cars and trucks that burn ethanol. The use of ethanol in gasoline helps to keep our air cleaner.

Look at the chart on this page. What other products are made from Hoosier corn?

Corn and other farm products are a major part of Indiana's economy. However, the number of small family farms in our state is shrinking. The cost of running a farm today is high, but farm goods are selling at low prices. Many families can no longer afford to stay in the farming business. Most farming in our state is now done on large farms owned by companies.

FARMING HELPS OUR ECONOMY

These company-owned farms, as well as family-run farms like the Hibschmans', help to make Indiana's economy strong. In the next lesson you will read about other jobs that add to our state's economy.

 Check Your Reading

1. What are three major crops that are grown in Indiana?
2. Why do farmers grow corn one year and soybeans the next?
3. Name three corn products.
4. **GEOGRAPHY SKILL:** Look at the map on page 223. Which states to the west of Indiana are part of the Corn Belt?
5. **THINKING SKILL:** Look at Donna Hibschman's words in the Read Aloud on page 221. Do they state a fact or an opinion? Explain your answer.

2 Manufacturing and Mining

READ TO LEARN

Key Vocabulary

industry
pharmaceutical
strip mining
environment
pollution

Key People

C. G. Conn
Eli Lilly

Read Aloud

Indiana is a composite of steel mills and country clubs, factories and colleges . . . , cornfields and campuses.

This is how one Hoosier writer described Indiana. He saw that farming makes up only one part of life in our state. "Steel mills" and "factories" are an important part as well.

Read for Purpose

1. **WHAT YOU KNOW:** What kinds of products are made in the area in which you live?
2. **WHAT YOU WILL LEARN:** How are manufacturing and mining an important part of Indiana's economy?

JOBS IN MANUFACTURING

What do a television set, a bar of steel, and a school bus have in common? For one thing, all of these things are made in Indiana.

In Chapter 10 you read that manufacturing grew up in our state during the late 1800s. For many years manufacturing was Indiana's biggest industry. An industry is all of the businesses that make one kind of product.

At present only eight states produce more manufactured goods than Indiana. For every one Hoosier who works in farming, there are six who work in manufacturing. In this lesson you will read about the many different manufactured goods that our state produces.

DIAGRAM SKILL: Several steps are involved in steelmaking. What happens during the second step?

METALWORKING

Making steel and other metals is Indiana's top manufacturing industry. Hoosier steel is used to make cars and other products. What are some other things that are made with steel?

Steel manufacturers need iron, a coal product named coke, and limestone to make steel. Iron comes to

HOW STEEL IS MADE

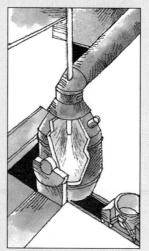

1. Burnt limestone and scrap metal are added to furnace.

2. Melted iron is poured into furnace.

3. Oxygen is blown into furnace.

4. Steel is poured and taken away to be cooled and shaped.

the northern mills from other states by rail or ship. Coal and limestone come from southern Indiana.

Iron, coke, and limestone are melted in blazing-hot furnaces. The temperature inside the furnaces can reach 2,000°F (1,100°C)—or about 10 times the temperature of boiling water! Workers take samples often to see when good, strong steel has formed out of the mixture.

Imagine that you are at a mill watching this process. You stand behind a thick door with a tiny window. First, though, you are given special glasses to wear. This is because the ingredients are so hot that they shine like the sun. If you were to look at them without glasses, you would hurt your eyes.

Huge buckets pour the white-hot liquid metal into molds to cool. Later the steel is shaped into bars, slabs, or rods at a finishing mill. The diagram on page 226 tells you more about how steel is made.

During the early 1900s metal making became Indiana's most important manufacturing industry. In Chapter 10 you read about the birth of the steel industry in Gary. Today our state is one of America's leading producers of steel.

CHANGES IN INDUSTRY

Steel is no longer made the way it was during the early 1900s. Production methods have improved. Computers now control machines that perform many of the tasks people once did. As a result, far fewer workers are needed to make steel. Steel can also be made more cheaply in other countries. This has cut down on the demand for Hoosier steel.

These changes have affected many people who live in cities in northern Indiana. For many steel workers it has been difficult to find new jobs. Others have received job training and have found new work in other industries.

Other Hoosier industries have also undergone great changes since the early 1900s. The automobile industry was once strong in our state, as you read in Chapter 10.

MAP SKILL: In which cities are electronic products manufactured?

INDIANA: Manufacturing

Electronics   Machinery   Steel
Food products   Metal products   Transportation equipment

Indiana still manufactures buses, trucks, and some cars. Mostly, though, Hoosiers today make parts for car makers in Michigan.

In recent years the high-technology, or "high-tech," industry has grown in Indiana. Companies in Kokomo and Fort Wayne make computer chips for use in cars, motorcycles, and fighter planes.

Some high-tech manufacturers use robots to make products. One automobile company in Lafayette uses more than 120 robots to manufacture its cars and trucks.

TELEVISIONS TO TUBAS

Indiana is home to many other industries besides the steel and high-tech industries. It is also America's largest producer of televisions, stereos, buses, and recreational vehicles (RVs).

Elkhart is known as the "Band Instrument Capital of the World" because over half of America's band instruments are made there. The musical instrument industry began just after the Civil War, when C. G. Conn started a company in Elkhart. Since then other businesses have begun making musical instruments in that city.

Another very important Indiana industry is the pharmaceutical (fär mə sü′ ti kəl) industry. Pharmaceuticals are medicines sold in drugstores. Indiana is home to several of the world's largest pharmaceutical companies.

"Colonel" Eli Lilly started his pharmaceutical company in Indianapolis in 1876. It was a big success. Today the company that he began sells its products all over the world.

Robots (*below*) manufacture trucks in Lafayette. Band instruments and pharmaceuticals are also made in Indiana.

MINING

Many Hoosiers work in mining, another important industry. You read about limestone in the Traditions lesson beginning on page 50. Did you know that Hoosiers mine two thirds of all the limestone used in America's buildings?

Coal is another important part of Indiana's mining industry. Most Hoosier coal is found near the earth's surface. Miners use huge machines to strip away the earth covering the coal. This process is called strip mining.

Strip mining is an easy and inexpensive way to take coal out of the earth. However, it damages the environment (en vī' rən mənt). An environment is the conditions in which people, plants, or animals live. Strip mining leaves the ground bare. Very few plants can grow on strip-mined land.

Today mining companies are required by law to repair the land after they have finished mining. They fill in the huge holes left by mining with rocks and soil. They plant trees and grass to help the land to recover.

Coal is a good source of energy. Power companies burn coal to produce electricity. Burning coal, however, causes air pollution. Pollution is what makes the air, soil, or water dirty. You will read about one kind of air pollution in the Point/Counterpoint on pages 230–231.

Unless it is controlled, strip mining hurts our state's environment.

A STATE OF MANY INDUSTRIES

Today Indiana is one of America's most important manufacturing states. Many different products are made within our state's borders. This is what helps to make Indiana's economy strong.

Check Your Reading

1. Name two products that Indiana leads the nation in manufacturing.

2. Why is strip mining harmful to the environment?

3. **GEOGRAPHY SKILL:** Look at the map on page 227. How do you think Indiana's nearness to Lake Michigan helps in the making and selling of steel?

4. **THINKING SKILL:** Classify the goods mentioned in this lesson into the following groups: Transportation, Building Materials, and Products Used by Families.

Who Should Pay to Clean Up Acid Rain?

In Lesson 2 you read that the burning of coal causes pollution. When certain kinds of pollution in the air combine with moisture, such as rain, the result is acid rain. Acid rain is especially harmful because it damages trees, lakes, and streams. It also damages buildings and monuments.

Some studies have found that more than half of the pollution in acid rain comes from power plants in ten midwestern states, including Indiana. Winds from the west carry the pollution to northeastern states and to parts of Canada.

Many people say that the government should take responsibility for the acid rain problem. Since vehicles and industries across the nation are also sources of pollution, they argue that acid rain is a national problem, not just a problem for ten states.

Since power companies burn coal to produce electricity, other people think that the companies, not the government, should pay the cost of cleaning up acid rain. In 1989 President George Bush and others proposed that the power companies in those ten states responsible for more than half the damage should pay the costs to clean up acid rain.

Who should pay to clean up acid rain?

POINT ☆👉

State Governments Should Pay to Clean Up Acid Rain

Representative Philip R. Sharp from Muncie believes that acid rain is a national problem and that the cost of the cleanup should be shared by the entire country. He feels that those states responsible for most of the acid rain should pay their share but should not pay all of the cleanup costs. He points out that industries in some other states produce huge amounts of pollution. Sharp says:

> An intelligent national acid rain policy must be based on . . . fairness. The greater your state's contribution to the problem, the more your state should be required to contribute to the solution. The [ten] states will and should pay their share. Congress can make sure that the rest of the nation will do the same.

- How does Representative Sharp think that states should pay for the acid rain cleanup?

COUNTERPOINT 👈/☆

Power Companies Should Pay to Clean Up Acid Rain

Representative Gerry Sikorski of Minnesota is one member of Congress who wants power companies to pay for the cleanup of pollution that causes acid rain.

Sikorski and some other members of Congress say that many power companies that are responsible for pollution charge much lower rates than power companies in other parts of the country. They argue that these companies can afford to pay for the acid rain cleanup. Sikorski says:

> Electric rates in Indiana, Ohio, and a few other states are much lower than the national average. Our states should not have to pay for the cleanup of pollution caused by power plants that are not ours.

- Does Representative Sikorski feel that his state should have to pay for the acid rain cleanup?

UNDERSTANDING THE POINT/COUNTERPOINT

1. Why do some people think that all states should share in the costs of the acid rain cleanup?
2. Why do others feel that power companies should pay for cleaning up acid rain?
3. Which side do you think made the stronger case? Why?

231

3 Transportation and Trade

READ TO LEARN

Key Vocabulary

port
lock
import
export
international trade

Key Places

Southwind Maritime Centre
Burns Harbor
St. Lawrence Seaway
Indianapolis International
 Airport

Read Aloud

Give 'em a brake.

Have you ever seen these words on a sign beside a highway? The sign tells drivers to slow down for workers who are fixing our state's highways. In this lesson you will read about how good highways and other transportation systems help Indiana's economy.

Read for Purpose

1. **WHAT YOU KNOW:** Why is Indiana called the "Crossroads of America"?
2. **WHAT YOU WILL LEARN:** Which new forms of transportation help to keep Indiana an important crossroads today?

ON THE ROAD

"Honk!" As her father sounded the truck's horn, Rachel Simon waved happily at the children in a passing car. Rachel was excited. Today she was helping her dad transport a large load of corn from Terre Haute to Mount Vernon, a town near Evansville.

Rachel pelted her father with questions. "How are we getting to Mount Vernon, Dad?" "What's going to happen to the corn after we unload it?"

"Easy, Rachel," laughed her father. "We're going to take U.S. Route 41 and State Highway 62, just as I do every week. You'll see!"

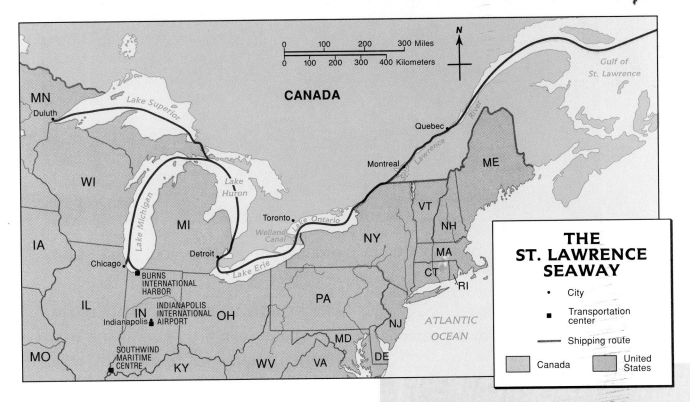

MAP SKILL: To which cities could a ship sail from Burns Harbor?

TRANSPORTATION LINKS

U.S. Route 41 and State Highway 62 are just two of the many highways that crisscross Indiana. Many of these highways follow the routes of old, bumpy roads that were built in the 1800s. These highways continue to make Indiana the "Crossroads of America."

Railroads also connect Indiana to other states and make trade possible. Trains are still important to Hoosier industries, just as they were in the 1800s.

SEA AND AIR HIGHWAYS

After driving for almost two hours, Jackie and her father arrived at the Southwind Maritime Centre in Mount Vernon. It is Indiana's largest port on the Ohio River. A port is a place where boats and ships can dock safely. You can take a tour of the Southwind Maritime Centre to see how a port works.

Ohio River ports are important to Hoosier trade today, just as they once were to Indiana's earliest traders. Burns Harbor is another big port on Lake Michigan. Ships carry goods from Burns Harbor to other ports through the St. Lawrence Seaway. The Great Lakes and the St. Lawrence River make up the seaway. It is deep enough for ocean-going ships.

Ships travel among the lakes through a system of canals. These canals are much bigger than the

233

Trucks transport goods such as milk, corn, and lumber in and out of our state.

ones that were used by Hoosiers in the 1800s. Locks help ships move through the canals. A lock is a part of a canal closed off by gates. The water in the lock can be raised or lowered. Find the seaway on the map on page 233.

Air travel is also an important part of our state's transportation system. Many planes fly into the Indianapolis International Airport every day. The airport makes it easier for Hoosiers to be involved in trade overseas.

Many Hoosier businesses use parts from other countries to make their goods. For example, imports from Asia help to make RVs. Imports are goods that are brought in from another country for sale or use. Exports are goods that are sent to other countries to be sold or traded. Indiana's main exports include electric equipment, farm goods, and buses.

Imports and exports are part of international trade, or trade with other countries. International trade allows Hoosiers to buy and sell many goods. Can you think of any imports that you use or eat?

IN TOUCH WITH THE WORLD

Good systems of transportation keep Indiana in touch with other countries. Roads, rivers, and airways help our state's products to reach places all over the world. Transportation also brings visitors into our state. In the next lesson you will read about the ways in which visitors help Indiana to grow.

Check Your Reading

1. What are two forms of transportation that link Indiana to the rest of the world?
2. Why is international trade important to Indiana?
3. **GEOGRAPHY SKILL:** Look at the map on page 233. Which river helps ships to get from Indiana to the Atlantic Ocean?
4. **THINKING SKILL:** Compare and contrast forms of transportation used today with forms of transportation used in the 1800s.

READ TO LEARN

■ Key Vocabulary

astronaut

■ Read for Purpose

1. **WHAT YOU KNOW:** What kinds of jobs do Hoosiers have?
2. **WHAT YOU WILL LEARN:** How did one Hoosier's job help others in our country?

INDIANA'S MAN IN SPACE

Virgil I. "Gus" Grissom was born on April 3, 1926, in Mitchell, a small town surrounded by rolling hills in southern Indiana. As a child Gus loved airplanes. When he became an adult, Gus joined the Air Force. He was awarded the Distinguished Flying Cross for flying missions during the Korean War. When Gus returned to the United States, he became an instructor in jet flying. Later he became a test pilot.

During the 1950s the United States and the Soviet Union both began to explore outer space. In 1958 the United States decided to choose men to train as its first astronauts. An astronaut is a person who travels into space. Because Grissom had an excellent background in flying, he was chosen to train for this new job along with six other men.

The training was scheduled to last two years. Learning to operate a spacecraft was very different from learning to fly airplanes. The new astronauts would be

Gus Grissom's training lasted almost two years.

traveling in space capsules. A capsule is the front part of the spaceship. It carries the instruments and astronauts. The capsule can separate from the rest of the rocket that pushes it into space. The six astronauts chosen to travel in these capsules were to be our country's first space pioneers. They would travel to a place where Americans had never been.

ASTRONAUT GUS GRISSOM

Through the window of his space capsule, Gus had a clear view of the clouds ahead. In a split second the capsule burst through them and into bright sunlight. The light blue sky turned dark blue. Then suddenly there was the blackness of space.

Gus was aboard the United States' Mercury capsule that he had named *Liberty Bell*. Mercury was the name of the model of the capsules used by the first astronauts. *Liberty Bell* lifted off from Cape Canaveral, Florida, on July 21, 1961. Gus was the second American to travel into space.

Liberty Bell glided silently on a carefully planned course. The object of the mission was to travel into space and then turn around and return to earth. From the capsule Gus could see the hazy outlines of the continents and oceans on the earth far below.

The flight was to be a short one—about 15 minutes. Soon Gus had to prepare for reentry into the earth's atmosphere. If the capsule was not positioned just right, it would burn up as it returned to earth.

After reaching a height of a little over 118 miles (189 km), *Liberty Bell* began its downward trip. It started to fall toward the earth. Then trouble began. The pressure on Gus's body began to feel like

Gus's view of the earth from space was a very special one.

BLAST OFF! for Gus and the *Liberty Bell*.

a great weight. As each second passed, the pressure became greater and greater. It was hard for him to breathe and to speak.

Soon, however, two parachutes popped out to slow the capsule's landing. After a few more seconds the capsule hit the water with a gentle shock. Gus was to open the hatch, or door, as soon as the helicopters hooked onto the capsule. The helicopters were based on a ship located 300 miles (480 km) from Cape Canaveral.

Suddenly, without warning, the hatch burst open. Water came rushing into the capsule. Quickly, Gus tore off his helmet and pulled himself up through the hatch. He knew that he had to get out of the capsule. If it filled with water, it would sink fast.

Soon Gus was floating in the ocean. Because his spacesuit was filled with air it held him up. But he became tangled in a line attached to the capsule. He knew that he had to free himself. If the capsule sank, he would be pulled down with it.

Just as the first helicopter arrived, he managed to free himself. By this time the capsule was sinking fast. Hurriedly a crewman from the helicopter hooked a line onto the capsule. But *Liberty Bell* was filled with water. It was too heavy for the helicopter to lift. It had to be cut loose.

The heat was intense as Gus began his re-entry into the atmosphere.

Meanwhile Gus was signaling for help. The water was so choppy that he could hardly move. Waves were splashing over his head. He felt as if he were going to drown. Nearly exhausted, he was picked up at last. It had been a close call. The space capsule was gone, but Gus was safe.

GUS FLIES AGAIN

Within the next two years after Gus's flight, four more Mercury capsules traveled into space. Each flight was made by a different astronaut. By this time the space pioneers were ready to fly in larger capsules. These capsules were named Gemini. Each one was built to carry two astronauts.

Gus was chosen to pilot the first Gemini flight into space. He was the first astronaut to make a second space flight. His copilot was a newly trained astronaut named John Young. The two astronauts took off from Cape Canaveral, which at that time was called Cape Kennedy, on March 23, 1965. Gus and John took pictures of the earth during the flight. It was a successful flight with an almost perfect landing. Eight more Gemini flights were made after this one.

Liberty Bell was lost but Gus was saved after an exciting space journey.

238

The goal of the next series of flights was to reach the moon. Gus was chosen to command the first Apollo flight. Edward White and Roger Chaffee were also chosen for the three-astronaut mission.

On January 27, 1967, the three astronauts were inside the capsule practicing for their flight. Suddenly there was a flash of fire. A problem with the wiring caused the terrible fire. All three astronauts were killed before they could escape. Gus was 40 years old.

This limestone monument in Mitchell stands as a proud reminder of Indiana's brave space pioneer.

GUS IS REMEMBERED

Gus is remembered as one of the great space pioneers. Hoosiers are proud that he came from our state. The Grissom Memorial is located at Spring Mill State Park, near his hometown of Mitchell. There is another memorial to Gus in Mitchell. It is a spaceship carved out of Indiana limestone. In northern Indiana Grissom Air Force Base was named in honor of Lieutenant Colonel Virgil I. "Gus" Grissom.

Gus worked hard to make his dream of flying come true. He was chosen as one of the first astronauts to travel into space. Gus's work as a space pioneer made it easier for other astronauts to travel safely into space.

Check Your Reading

1. What was there in Gus Grissom's background that made him a good choice as an astronaut?
2. Which two space capsules did Gus Grissom pilot?
3. What went wrong on Gus Grissom's flight aboard the *Liberty Bell*?
4. GEOGRAPHY SKILL: Look at the map of Indiana in the Atlas on page 295. Find Mitchell, Indiana.
5. THINKING SKILL: List three questions you would like to ask about space travel.

Reading Time Zone Maps

Key Vocabulary

time zone

In this chapter you have read about the different ways in which people work in Indiana. As in other states, some people here earn their living from farming. But when farmers in Indiana are just beginning their day, farmers in California are sound asleep. How is that possible?

Understanding Time Zones

The earth is divided into 24 **time zones**—one for each hour of the day. The difference in time between most neighboring time zones is exactly one hour.

Because the earth rotates from west to east, the time in zones east of you is always later than it is in your time zone. The time in zones west of you is always earlier than it is in your time zone. For example, suppose that it is 6:00 A.M. where you live. In the time zone just east of you, it is 7:00 A.M. In the time zone just west of you, it is 5:00 A.M.

Reading a Time Zone Map

The map on page 241 shows the time zones of the United States. How many time zones are there in our country? What is the name of the easternmost time zone?

Look at the clock for the Central Time Zone. It shows 6:00 A.M. What time is it in the Pacific Time Zone when it is 6:00 A.M. in the Central Time Zone?

Remember that the time in most time zones is one hour earlier or later than the time in the time zone next to it. If you know the time in one time zone, you can find the time anywhere by using these two rules:

1. Moving east, you must add an hour for each time zone you cross.
2. Moving west, you must subtract an hour for each time zone you cross.

Suppose that it is 3:00 P.M. in Chicago. Chicago is in the Central Time Zone. In New York City (one time zone to the east), it is 4:00 P.M. (3:00 P.M. + 1 hour = 4:00 P.M.). In Los Angeles (two time zones west), it is 1:00 P.M. (3:00 P.M. − 2 hours = 1:00 P.M.).

Differences in time can be important. Suppose that you live in Denver. You want to talk with your aunt in Anchorage. She gets home from work at 5:00 P.M. To reach her by phone at home, you would have to call after 7:00 P.M. your time.

As you can see from the map on page 241, most states in the United States are located in one time zone.

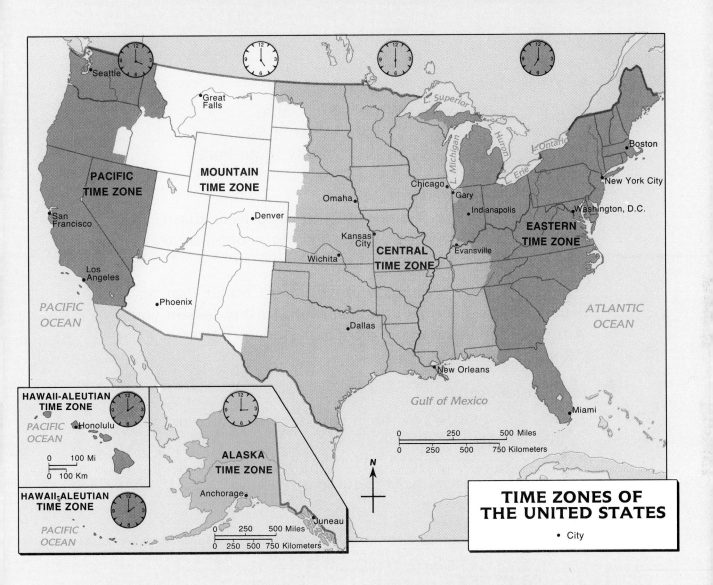

TIME ZONES OF
THE UNITED STATES

• City

However, some states are located in more than one time zone. Indiana is one of those states. You can see that most of Indiana is located in the Eastern Time Zone. However, one area in the northwestern corner of the state and one area in the southwestern corner of the state are located in the Central Time Zone.

Reviewing the Skill

1. What is a time zone?
2. When it is 5:00 A.M. in Phoenix, what time is it in Miami?
3. A friend in Seattle asked you to call at 7:00 P.M.. You live in Indianapolis. At what time should you call?
4. Why is it important to be able to use a time zone map?

241

4 Services

Key Vocabulary

tourist
service industry

Key Places

Whitewater Canal
  State Historic Site
Brown County State Park

Read Aloud

Some people think it must be strange to wear these clothes every day. But I enjoy showing people the way life in Indiana was long ago.

This is how a woman who works at Conner Prairie expressed her feelings about her job. In this lesson you will read about the many jobs that Hoosiers have helping people in our state.

Read for Purpose

1. **WHAT YOU KNOW:** What is your favorite place to visit in our state?
2. **WHAT YOU WILL LEARN:** How do tourism and other kinds of services help Indiana's economy?

VISITORS FROM OTHER STATES

"There's one from New York!"

"I see one from Minnesota!"

As they rode along Interstate 70, Susan and Kevin Hayes looked for license plates from other states.

"Why do so many people come to Indiana from other states?" Susan asked her mother.

"For the same reasons that you like to live here," answered Mrs. Hayes. "Because we have beautiful land, a varied climate, and many interesting sights to see."

A GREAT PLACE TO VISIT

Indiana has many interesting places for people to visit. Many tourists like to spend their vacations in Indiana. A tourist is someone who travels to learn about and to enjoy other places.

Where do tourists in Indiana like to go? The sandy shores of Indiana Dunes State Park are a popular choice for some tourists. Others come to enjoy the beauty of Fulton County and its famous round barns.

The map on page 244 shows some of the places that people find interesting and fun to visit. You can see why so many Hoosiers choose to spend their vacations right here in Indiana!

LEARNING ABOUT THE PAST

Many places in Indiana show how Hoosiers once lived. Would you like to be a pioneer for a day? At Conner Prairie you can see what it was like to live in a Hoosier village in 1836. You can talk to people who play the roles of various settlers living in the village.

If you go to the Whitewater Canal State Historic Site near Metamora, you can ride in a horse-drawn canal boat. As you walk through the town, you might feel as though you have gone back in time to the 1840s.

This Miami County round barn and Conner Prairie in Marion County are two of the many sites to visit in our state.

INDIANA: PLACES TO VISIT

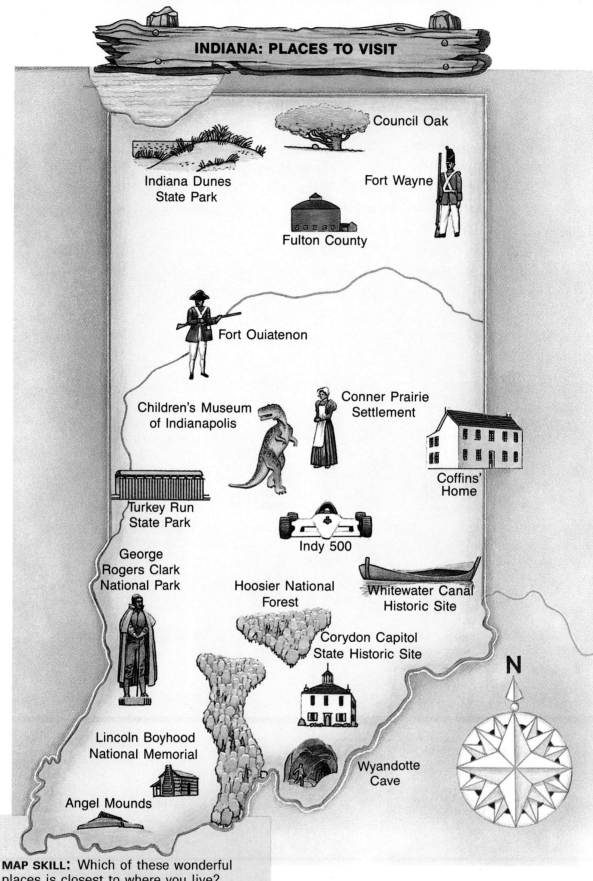

Council Oak

Indiana Dunes
State Park

Fort Wayne

Fulton County

Fort Ouiatenon

Children's Museum
of Indianapolis

Conner Prairie
Settlement

Coffins'
Home

Turkey Run
State Park

Indy 500

George
Rogers Clark
National Park

Hoosier National
Forest

Whitewater Canal
Historic Site

Corydon Capitol
State Historic Site

Lincoln Boyhood
National Memorial

Wyandotte
Cave

Angel Mounds

N

MAP SKILL: Which of these wonderful
places is closest to where you live?

These students are enjoying the Children's Museum of Indianapolis.

You can also learn about Indiana's past by visiting some of our state's museums. The most famous of these is the Children's Museum of Indianapolis. It is the world's largest museum for children. There you can climb on dinosaurs and do scientific experiments.

There are also many outdoor things to do in Indiana. Brown County State Park is Indiana's largest state park. In southern Indiana there are many caves to explore. In Bluespring Caverns, near Bedford, you can travel on an underground stream. The Wyandotte Caves near Corydon are also famous for their unusual rock formations.

People come from all over to see these interesting places. Over 30 million tourists spend their vacations here. Visitors help to make life in Indiana interesting. They also create new jobs and bring money into our state.

TOURISTS AND JOBS

Tourists shop in our stores, stay in our hotels, eat in our restaurants, and visit our museums. Shopkeepers, waiters, and hotel workers earn their livings, in part, because of tourism.

Those who serve the needs of tourists are part of a service industry. Service industries are different from manufacturing industries. Service workers do not make things. Instead, they do useful things that people need and want done.

Truck drivers, teachers, doctors, and government workers are all service workers. What are some other examples of service jobs?

Service industries are important to Indiana's economy. They make more money for the state than farming and manufacturing combined!

All these Hoosiers and the jobs they do are part of Indiana's **service industries**.

Look at the circle graph in the Indiana Almanac on page 317. It shows how much our state benefits from its industries. You can see how important service industries are to Indiana. Most Hoosiers today are service workers. In the future even more Hoosiers will probably be working in service industries.

JOBS FOR HOOSIERS

What do you want to do when you grow up? There are many different kinds of jobs to choose from in Indiana today. But our state's economy is always changing. Before you grow up, there will probably be new service and manufacturing industries in Indiana. There will probably be jobs to choose from that you can't even imagine now!

Check Your Reading

1. Name two places in our state that show how people once lived in Indiana.
2. How are service industries different from manufacturing industries?
3. **GEOGRAPHY SKILL:** Look at the map on page 244. Name a tourist spot located near the place in which you live.
4. **THINKING SKILL:** What effect does tourism have on Indiana's economy?

REVIEWING VOCABULARY

agriculture export tourist
economy industry

Number a sheet of paper from 1 to 5. Beside each number write the word from the list above that best matches each definition.

1. Any kind of goods sold to another country
2. All of the businesses that make one kind of product
3. The business of growing crops and raising animals
4. A person who travels for enjoyment
5. The way in which a place uses its resources to meet people's needs and wants

REVIEWING FACTS

Number a sheet of paper from 1 to 5. Beside each number write **T** if the statement is true. If the statement is false, rewrite it to make it true.

1. Wheat is Indiana's most important farm product.
2. Corn can be used to make fuel for automobiles.
3. More Hoosiers work in farming than in manufacturing.
4. International trade involves buying and selling goods inside our own country.
5. Teachers and truck drivers work in service industries.

✏ WRITING ABOUT MAIN IDEAS

1. **Writing a Travel Booklet:** Find out more about the Children's Museum of Indianapolis. Then write a travel booklet telling why tourists would enjoy visiting the museum. Describe the museum so that tourists who read your booklet would want to visit it.
2. **Researching a Person:** Research the life of one person who started a business in Indiana. You may wish to write about Eli Lilly, C. G. Conn, Madame C. J. Walker, or Orville Redenbacher. Write a short report about the person and present it to the class.

BUILDING SKILLS: READING TIME ZONE MAPS

1. What is a time zone?
2. Is all of Indiana in one time zone?
3. In which time zone do you live?
4. Suppose that you were flying from Indianapolis to Los Angeles, a trip that takes about four hours. If you leave Indianapolis at noon, what time will it be when you get to Los Angeles?
5. Describe two situations in which it would be helpful for you to understand time zones.

CHAPTER 13

INDIANA'S GOVERNMENT

▼ FOCUS

I want to be a lawyer because I like to help people. My grandfather was a lawyer in Korea and I would like to take after him.

Liz Yoon lives in Kokomo, the county seat of Howard County. In this chapter you will learn about how we make our laws and how our government works.

1 State Government

READ TO LEARN

Key Vocabulary

taxes
legislative branch
General Assembly
bill

executive branch
veto
judicial branch

Key People

Evan Bayh

Read Aloud

State government . . . operates a remarkable and diverse collection of colleges and universities. State government runs our prisons, our welfare offices, and our employment programs; it is responsible for public health, highways, ports, and parks.

These words by a governor of Indiana describe what Indiana's constitution says that government should do. The services he discussed provide for the peace, liberty, and happiness of Hoosiers. In this lesson you will learn how our state government works.

Read for Purpose

1. **WHAT YOU KNOW:** Who leads Indiana's government?
2. **WHAT YOU WILL LEARN:** How does the government of our state work?

OUR STATE AND YOU

Our state government is something you probably don't think about often. But did you know that the state government has a lot to do with the way you and other Hoosiers live every day?

In the last chapter you read about services. The state government provides many services, like fixing roads and taking care of parks. To pay for such services, it collects money from the people. This money is called taxes.

State government is mainly concerned with two things: services and taxes. It decides which services people should have and how much these services should cost taxpayers.

Look at the graph on this page to find out how each tax dollar is used by Indiana's government. Which service gets the most tax money?

In order to understand how state taxes are used, you first need to know how state government works.

THE LEGISLATIVE BRANCH

Our state government is based on the Constitution of 1851. It took the place of the Constitution of 1816, which you read about in Chapter 6.

In January 1990, fifth-grade students from a Muncie elementary school were studying their state government. They learned that Indiana's state government is divided into three parts, or branches. They also learned that the lawmaking branch, or legislative (lej' is lā tiv) branch, is the branch of government that writes the state's laws.

The class had an idea for a new law. They wanted a law to name the first week in October "Children's Career Week." During that week students all over the state would be told about future job opportunities. The students thought that a career week would be a great idea. But how could they make it a law?

They had to start with the legislative branch of Indiana's government, the General Assembly, which makes laws for the state. The Indiana General Assembly has two parts: the House of Representatives and the Senate. The students asked their local representative to write a bill, or plan for a law, about "Children's Career Week."

Their representative then wrote the bill and presented it to the House. The representatives voted for the bill. Next the bill had to go to the Senate.

If the members of the Senate did not agree with the members of the

GRAPH SKILL: How much of each tax dollar is spent on transportation?

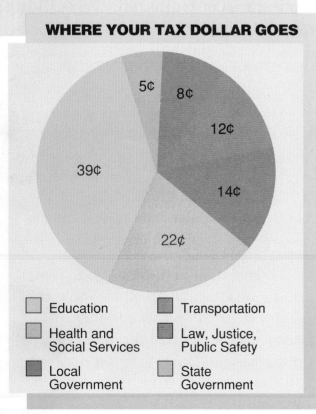

WHERE YOUR TAX DOLLAR GOES

5¢
8¢
12¢
14¢
39¢
22¢

- Education
- Health and Social Services
- Local Government
- Transportation
- Law, Justice, Public Safety
- State Government

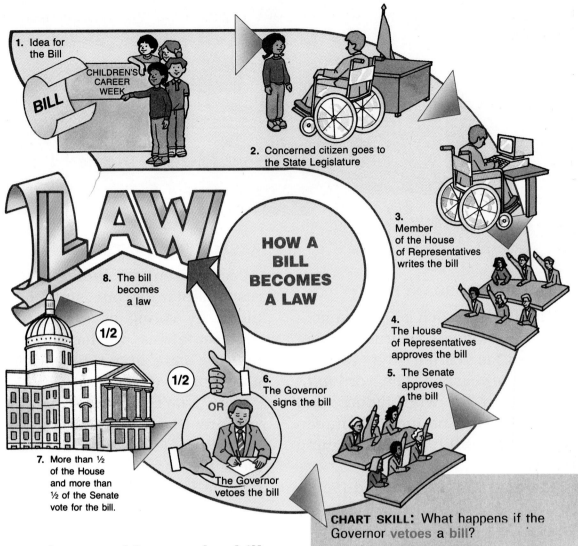

1. Idea for the Bill

CHILDREN'S CAREER WEEK

BILL

2. Concerned citizen goes to the State Legislature

3. Member of the House of Representatives writes the bill

HOW A BILL BECOMES A LAW

4. The House of Representatives approves the bill

5. The Senate approves the bill

6. The Governor signs the bill

OR

The Governor vetoes the bill

7. More than ½ of the House and more than ½ of the Senate vote for the bill.

8. The bill becomes a law

LAW

CHART SKILL: What happens if the Governor vetoes a bill?

House, they would vote the bill down. If they did agree, they would vote for the bill to be passed. If the bill were passed, it would be sent to the governor.

THE EXECUTIVE BRANCH

The governor is the head of the executive (eg zek′ yə tiv) branch of the state government. The executive branch makes sure that the laws of the state are carried out. The governor also plays a part in making laws.

If Governor Evan Bayh decided to sign the students' bill, it would become a law. If he decided not to sign their bill, then he would veto (vē′ tō) it. To veto means to refuse, or to say no. If a bill is vetoed, it goes back to the General Assembly. If more than half of the House and the Senate then vote in favor of the bill, it becomes a law. Look at the diagram on this page to see how the entire process works.

251

Governor Evan Bayh works in the State House in Indianapolis.

THE JUDICIAL BRANCH

The third branch of government that the students learned about in class is called the judicial (jü dish' əl) branch. The word *judicial* has to do with judges and courts of law. The judicial branch has responsibility for explaining the law.

Indiana has many different judges and courts. They decide the cases of people who may have broken the law. They also make sure that all state laws agree with the state constitution.

For example, the court might be asked to test the Muncie students' bill after it became a law. If a person thought that it went against the Indiana constitution, he or she could challenge the law in the courts. If the court decided that the law was against the state constitution, then the law would be thrown out. The court might decide, however, that the law should stand.

RESPONSIBLE CITIZENS

As citizens of Indiana, we are responsible for our state government. By voting or writing to our representatives, we let them know that we care about how well our government works.

You won't be able to vote until you are 18 years old, but you can still write letters to your government representatives. One day you may be serving in the state government—maybe even as governor!

Check Your Reading

1. How does our state get the money for government services?
2. What are the three branches of Indiana's government?
3. What can a governor do if he or she does not like a bill?
4. How can you get involved in your state government?
5. **THINKING SKILL:** List two questions you might ask a member of each of the three branches of our government.

2 Local Government

READND TO LEARN

Key Vocabulary

board of county
    commissioners
county council
county seat

common council
town board
mayor
Unigov

Read Aloud

People told me, "You can't run for mayor!" I said, "Why not? The constitution says I can, doesn't it?" . . . I ran for mayor because I believe that local government is a place where people can have a positive impact on their community. I wanted to be involved.

These words express the beliefs of Margaret Kuchta, who is mayor of Hobart, in Lake County. She strongly believes that people can work together to make their communities better places in which to live.

Read for Purpose

1. **WHAT YOU KNOW:** In which city or county do you live?
2. **WHAT YOU WILL LEARN:** Which services does your local government provide?

COUNTY GOVERNMENT

You read in the last lesson how laws are made by our state government. Some decisions, however, are the responsibility of local governments. Indiana's local governments include county, city, and town governments. The role of local government is to meet the different needs of each county, city, or town. For example, a county might want to build more hospitals. It is the job of county government to make this happen.

There are 92 counties in Indiana. Some include large cities while others are made up of small towns and

253

large farms. Look at the map on this page to find the county in which you live.

In each county voters elect members to a board of county commissioners and the county council. The board makes sure that the county's laws are carried out. The Council decides how much tax money the county should spend. It is also responsible for paying people who work for the county.

Local leaders meet in a town or city within their county, called the county seat. Look in the Almanac on page 313 to find a list of Indiana's county seats. What is your county seat?

CITIES AND TOWNS

Voters in cities elect members of common councils, which make their laws. Voters in towns elect members of town boards. One of the decisions that a common council or town board might make could be whether or not to increase the size of the local fire department.

Common councils and town boards are headed by mayors who are elected by the people. A mayor

MAP SKILL: Which of Indiana's 92 counties border on Lake Michigan?

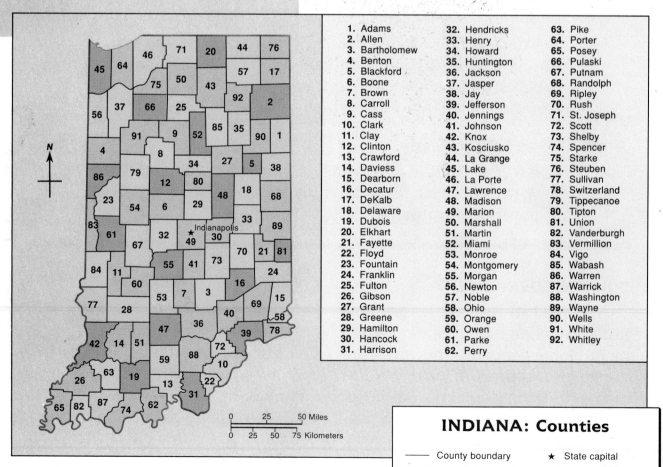

1. Adams	32. Hendricks	63. Pike
2. Allen	33. Henry	64. Porter
3. Bartholomew	34. Howard	65. Posey
4. Benton	35. Huntington	66. Pulaski
5. Blackford	36. Jackson	67. Putnam
6. Boone	37. Jasper	68. Randolph
7. Brown	38. Jay	69. Ripley
8. Carroll	39. Jefferson	70. Rush
9. Cass	40. Jennings	71. St. Joseph
10. Clark	41. Johnson	72. Scott
11. Clay	42. Knox	73. Shelby
12. Clinton	43. Kosciusko	74. Spencer
13. Crawford	44. La Grange	75. Starke
14. Daviess	45. Lake	76. Steuben
15. Dearborn	46. La Porte	77. Sullivan
16. Decatur	47. Lawrence	78. Switzerland
17. DeKalb	48. Madison	79. Tippecanoe
18. Delaware	49. Marion	80. Tipton
19. Dubois	50. Marshall	81. Union
20. Elkhart	51. Martin	82. Vanderburgh
21. Fayette	52. Miami	83. Vermillion
22. Floyd	53. Monroe	84. Vigo
23. Fountain	54. Montgomery	85. Wabash
24. Franklin	55. Morgan	86. Warren
25. Fulton	56. Newton	87. Warrick
26. Gibson	57. Noble	88. Washington
27. Grant	58. Ohio	89. Wayne
28. Greene	59. Orange	90. Wells
29. Hamilton	60. Owen	91. White
30. Hancock	61. Parke	92. Whitley
31. Harrison	62. Perry	

INDIANA: Counties

— County boundary ★ State capital

Firefighters, elected officials and teachers all provide services organized by local government.

sees that city or town laws are carried out. He or she is also in charge of the police department and helps to decide the number of police officers a city or town will hire.

UNIGOV

In 1970 the city government of Indianapolis and Marion County's government joined to form one local government called Unigov. Local leaders believed that it would help the city and the county run more smoothly. Under Unigov the borders of Indianapolis were expanded to take in most of Marion County. That change caused the city's population to double, making it one of the largest cities in the United States.

Indianapolis and Marion County now have one city-county council and one mayor. The city-county council decides how the area's tax money is to be spent.

GOVERNMENTS WORK TOGETHER

Indiana's county, city, and town governments work with and are helped by the state government. Indiana's state government also works with neighboring states and with the national government, as you will read in the next lesson.

 Check Your Reading

1. What are some of the services that local governments provide?
2. Which two kinds of local government joined to form Unigov?
3. How is the mayor's job similar to the job of the governor?
4. GEOGRAPHY SKILL: Look at the map on page 254. What county is Indianapolis in?
5. THINKING SKILL: How is Indianapolis's government different from other city governments?

3 Indiana and the National Government

READ TO LEARN

■ Key People

Jill Long   Birch Bayh
Richard Lugar   Dan Quayle
Dan Coats   George Bush

■ Read Aloud

Great lives do not go out—they go on.

Those words are carved on a statue of Benjamin Harrison, which stands in Indianapolis. Harrison was not only one of our state's senators, he was also our nation's twenty-third President. You will read in this lesson about Hoosiers who have served our national government and how the national government serves Indiana.

■ Read for Purpose

1. **WHAT YOU KNOW:** At which age will you be old enough to vote?
2. **WHAT YOU WILL LEARN:** What are the three branches of our national government?

OUR COUNTRY'S GOVERNMENT

The national government, like the state government, is divided into three branches. It has a legislative branch, an executive branch, and a judicial branch, as the diagram on page 257 shows. The national government, also called the federal government, is based on the United States Constitution. The Constitution is called the highest law in the land because all our other laws are based on it.

HOOSIER PRESIDENTS

The executive branch of the national government is led by the President. In the 1800s three Hoosiers became President of the United States.

THE THREE BRANCHES OF GOVERNMENT

EXECUTIVE BRANCH
President
Carries out laws

LEGISLATIVE BRANCH
Congress
Passes laws

JUDICIAL BRANCH
Supreme Court
Makes judgments about laws

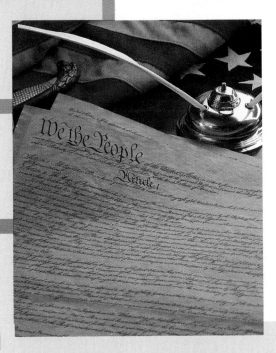

DIAGRAM SKILL: Our government is divided into three branches. What do they all have in common?

You read about William Henry Harrison in Chapter 6. In 1841, after serving as the Indiana Territory's governor, he became President. His grandson Benjamin Harrison was also President from 1889 to 1893. In Chapters 7 and 9 you read about Abraham Lincoln, who led our nation through one of its most difficult times. He is one of our most respected Presidents. In this lesson you will read more about the important role that Indiana has played in the national government, both in the past and in the present.

HOOSIERS IN CONGRESS

The capital of our national government is located in Washington, D.C. Congress, our national law-making branch, meets there in the Capitol building. Like Indiana's General Assembly, the U.S. Congress is made up of two parts: the House of Representatives and the Senate.

The number of people that Indiana sends to the House of Representatives depends on the size of our population. Today Indiana has ten representatives serving in the House. One of them is Congresswoman Jill Long, who represents the area around Ft. Wayne. She has served in the House since 1989.

Like every state, Indiana elects two senators to represent it in the Senate. A senator's term lasts six

257

years, and he or she can be reelected when the term is over. Senator Richard Lugar was first elected in 1976. Senator Lugar is a member of the Senate Foreign Relations Committee. This committee is concerned with the United States relations with other nations. Our other U. S. Senator is Dan Coats. He became a senator in 1989. One of Indiana's most famous senators was Birch Bayh, who served from 1963 to 1981. Governor Evan Bayh is Senator Bayh's son.

MR. VICE PRESIDENT

Another Hoosier in national government is our Vice President, Dan Quayle. Quayle was born in Indianapolis. He graduated from DePauw University and went to law school at Indiana University.

Representative Jill Long and Senator Richard Lugar represent Indiana in Congress. Birch Bayh was a famous Hoosier senator.

President George Bush and Vice President Dan Quayle are members of the executive branch of our national government.

Along with Senator Lugar, Dan Quayle represented Indiana in the Senate for four years before he was elected along with President George Bush to the executive branch of the national government in November 1988. Now this famous Hoosier serves the entire nation in his role as Vice President.

The national government also provides many jobs for a variety of Hoosiers. Did you know that your local mail carrier works for the national government? So do the people who work in our state's national parks. The national government affects our lives in many varied and interesting ways.

SERVING THE NATION

Hoosiers have shaped not only the history of our state but also that of our country. Their service has helped Indiana and the United States to prepare for a bright future, a future that includes you.

 Check Your Reading

1. How many senators does Indiana send to the United States Senate? How many representatives does it send to the House of Representatives?
2. To which office was Dan Quayle elected in 1988?
3. Name three types of work that people can do in the national government.
4. **THINKING SKILL:** Compare and contrast our local and national governments.

259

Reading Newspapers

Key Vocabulary

news article   headline

feature article   byline

editorial   dateline

In lesson 1 you read about the students in Muncie who wrote and presented a new bill to the Indiana legislature. How did people all over Indiana learn about the bill to set aside a children's career week? One way is through newspapers. Every large American city and many small towns have their own newspaper. The newspaper covers stories of local, state, and national interest.

The Parts of a Newspaper

Newspapers are divided into several parts. The front part usually has news articles. A news article reports recent events. Most newspapers also have feature articles. A feature article reports in detail on a person, subject, or event. For example, a local newspaper might have a feature article on recycling or about the town's early history.

Other parts of the newspaper include sports articles, cartoons, and editorials. An editorial is an article in which the editor gives opinions about an issue. An editor is the person who plans or runs the newspaper. Unlike a news article that includes only facts, an editorial gives opinions. For example, an editorial might urge readers to support plans to build a new library. An editorial might also support a political candidate who is running for local office, such as mayor.

Editorials often appear on a page with letters to the editor. These letters are written by the paper's readers. In them, readers give their opinions about an issue in the news. Through letters to the editor, readers can express many different opinions about one issue.

The Parts of a News Article

A news article always begins with a headline. The headline is printed in large type across the top of the article. It catches the reader's attention. Many news articles have a byline. The byline gives the name of the reporter who wrote the article. Some news articles also begin with a dateline. A dateline tells when and where the story was written.

A well-written news article begins by answering four questions: (1) *Who* was involved in the story? (2) *What* happened? (3) *When* did it happen? (4) *Where* did it happen? As you read

Students Write New Bill

by Joe Smith

INDIANAPOLIS (AP), January 10—A class of Muncie fifth graders has won the first round in getting a bill the pupils wrote through the Indiana Legislature.

The House Education Committee voted 8-0 Tuesday for House Bill 1016, which would name the first week in October as children's career week. The bill would encourage elementary and middle schools to broaden children's awareness of career opportunities.

The children have worked on the one-page bill as a school project. They convinced Representative Hurley Goodall, D-Muncie, to sponsor the bill. Next the bill goes to the full House.

"We accomplished something. We got a bill passed," said Gabe Aigner, one of the children, after the hearing.

"I was nervous—all those adults," said Kelly Buwalda, another student.

"They did a terrific job," said Theresa Greenwood, the children's teacher.

the news article above, decide if the reporter answered the *Who*, *What*, *When*, and *Where* questions.

Reviewing the Skill

1. Name three parts of a newspaper.
2. What does an editorial contain besides facts?
3. Write another headline for the news story about the students from Muncie.
4. Describe the events that happened in the story.
5. Why is it helpful to understand the different parts of a newspaper?

4 Looking Toward the Future

READ TO LEARN

■ Key Vocabulary

landfill   democracy
wetland

■ Read Aloud

Dear Senator:

I went to the landfill and I saw all kinds of stuff that could be recycled. We have all kinds of recycling bins at Osolo School where you can put paper, . . . glass, and aluminum cans. I think you can encourage all the schools of Indiana to have recycling bins.

Your friend,
Melody Lytell

Students like Melody and many other citizens across our state are concerned about protecting our environment. They want communities that will be safe and healthy places in which to live now and in the future.

■ Read for Purpose

1. **WHAT YOU KNOW:** What are some of the ways in which people pollute their environment?
2. **WHAT YOU WILL LEARN:** How can citizens and governments prepare for the future?

CLEAN AIR, CLEAN LAND, CLEAN WATER

Students from the University of Notre Dame in South Bend are studying ways in which to protect the environment. At the Environmental Center in Elkhart, once a landfill, the students and city workers are planning a park. A landfill is a huge pit into which garbage and trash are dumped.

Students have created a wetland at the old landfill. A wetland is a swamp, marsh, or other water-soaked area of land. Polluted water from the landfill often drains into the wetland. Here the pollution which could leak into wells and poison the drinking water is filtered out. Later, corn will be grown at the center. The corn will be used to make clean-burning ethanol fuel, which you read about in Chapter 12.

This project is one example of how people can make important changes to improve the environment. In this lesson you will read about other ways in which Hoosiers are preparing for a brighter future.

PROTECTING THE ENVIRONMENT

In the Point/Counterpoint on pages 230–231, you read two different opinions about the effects of acid rain. Hoosiers also have different ideas about other kinds of pollution that affect their lives now and will continue to do so in the future.

One hard problem is figuring out what to do with all the waste material that we produce, such as paper, some metals, and plastic. In most

University students are working hard in Elkhart to turn an ugly landfill once overflowing with garbage into a beautiful community park.

areas such waste is dumped at a landfill. Many of Indiana's landfills are almost completely used up—not only with our garbage but sometimes with garbage from other states as well. Some Indiana landfills have been leaking poisons into our water and land. Indiana, therefore, is running out of space to dump its garbage and trash.

Lawmakers and citizen groups believe that one answer to the problem is to recycle. Some factories have lessened their waste by recycling manufacturing materials. Another solution is for people to buy products that they can use again. The more materials we recycle, the less waste we will produce.

Many Hoosiers are asking their elected leaders to help find new ways to get rid of waste. If we are not able to keep our air and water clean, then we will not be able to use and enjoy such natural resources as our wetlands, lakes, and forests.

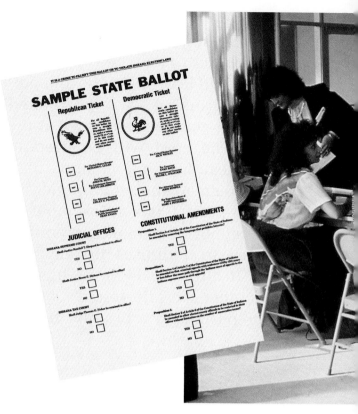

FUTURE DECISIONS

The future of our environment and of its resources depends upon citizens who know and who care about their communities. Such citizens are also able to make wise decisions about the people whom they elect to office.

Voting is an important responsibility in a **democracy**, or government that is run by the people it governs. In a democracy like ours every person's opinion and vote are important. In fact, some elections have been decided by only a handful of votes.

For example, in 1984 Frank McCloskey and Rick McIntyre were running for Congress from southwest Indiana. Both had strong support from citizens in the area. The total votes were so close that the election was declared a draw, or tie. When the votes were counted again, McCloskey had beaten McIntyre by only four votes!

Perhaps you will think about a close election such as this one when you are able to vote. Your vote could make a difference in whether the person you support wins or loses.

264

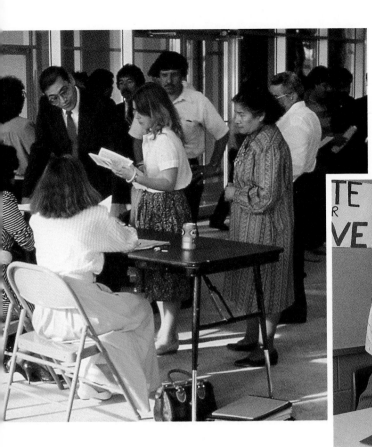

These people are voting in a state election. In school or club elections, students can learn about the importance of voting and living in a **democracy**.

AN EYE ON THE FUTURE

You have read about more than 300 years of Indiana's history, its land, and its people. Miami farmer, French trader, African-American freedman, Pennsylvania Quaker, Kentucky pioneer—all of these Hoosiers have made their mark on our wonderful state through the years. But the world that they lived in was a much different place from the world of today.

People have sometimes thought that Indiana has grown too fast for the good of the state. Still others have thought that growth and change in Indiana have occurred too slowly. You will have a chance to become a part of Indiana's future growth and change. You will also have a chance to make a difference in your state, your country, and the world. What do you think you can do today to prepare for the future?

 Check Your Reading

1. On which project are the students at the Environmental Center working?
2. What is happening to Indiana landfills?
3. Why is voting important?
4. **THINKING SKILL:** What do you think the future will be like if more people recycle and work to help the environment?

265

INVE$TING
IN · THE · FUTURE

"What do you want to be when you grow up?" is a familiar question. It is a question that Vernon Smith, the principal of Williams Elementary School in Gary, often asks the students in his school.

"When I first began asking students about their plans for the future, no one talked about going to college. The students did not realize that some jobs require a higher education," Smith said. "Even if they did, few could afford to pay for college."

Smith wanted to change that situation. "I'm from a poor family—the last of ten children—and we did not have the money for college," Smith says. "Many people helped me get the funds I needed. So I feel I should return something to my community. I believe if you see a need, you should try to do something about it."

Smith's first action was to take students to the Indiana University campus at Gary. Students had a chance to visit classrooms, walk through the campus, and see sporting events. "It was a way to develop an interest in college," Smith says.

But that was only the first step. The students would need money for college costs. Smith developed a program in which students could help themselves. The program is operated by the IU Dons, a group of Indiana University students. The Dons seek out needy high school freshmen to become Donzels, or younger members.

Students in the Donzel program learn about college opportunities and the benefits of a college education. They promise to stay in the program during their high school years.

The Donzels work for businesses in downtown Gary that are managed by the IU Dons. The money they earn is deposited into bank accounts to be saved for college expenses. A Donzel cannot withdraw money from the account until it is time for college.

The program helps young people to invest in their own future. Smith hopes that the students will remember to share what they have learned with others in their community.

REVIEWING VOCABULARY

bill	Unigov
mayor	veto
taxes	

Number a sheet of paper from 1 to 5. Beside each number write the word from the list above that best completes each sentence.

1. The government collects _____ to pay for government services.
2. If members of the House and Senate vote for a _____ and the governor signs it, it becomes a law.
3. A governor can _____ a bill to keep it from becoming a law.
4. A _____ is elected by the people to be in charge of a city or town.
5. Indianapolis and Marion County have a single government called _____.

REVIEWING FACTS

1. What are the three branches of our state's government and what does each branch do?
2. Name two types of governments that are found in Indiana other than the state government.
3. What does a county council do?
4. Name two United States Presidents who were Hoosiers.
5. How is the United States Congress similar to our state's General Assembly?

WRITING ABOUT MAIN IDEAS

1. **Writing a List of Elected Officials:** Find out who represents you in the different parts of government. Make a list of the names of your mayor or county officer, your governor, and your representatives in the Indiana General Assembly and the United States Congress.
2. **Writing an Advertisement:** Americans elect government officials, but some Americans do not vote. Write an advertisement urging people to vote in elections. Give reasons why people should vote. Also describe what can happen if people fail to vote.

BUILDING SKILLS: READING NEWSPAPERS

1. What is the difference between a news article and a feature article?
2. Read the article on page 261. Then answer the following questions.
   a. What is the headline?
   b. What information is provided in the byline?
3. Write the first paragraph of an editorial about the same subject as the article found on page 261.
4. Why is it helpful to know the parts of a newspaper article and to understand the types of articles that appear in a newspaper?

REVIEWING VOCABULARY

agriculture   pollution
democracy   taxes
environment

Number a sheet of paper from 1 to 5. Beside each number write the word from the list above that best matches the definition.

1. All of the conditions that surround and affect people and other living things
2. Anything that dirties the air, water, and soil
3. The business of growing crops and raising animals
4. Money collected from people to pay the costs of government
5. A form of government that is run by the people who are governed

WRITING ABOUT THE UNIT

1. **Preparing an Interview:** Prepare to interview someone who works in one of the industries described in this unit. Write at least five questions that you would ask the person in order to learn about his or her job.
2. **Writing a Paragraph:** Write a paragraph explaining why we need local government. Give at least one example to support your answer.

3. **Writing a Poem:** You have learned many things about Indiana. Make a list of the reasons that Indiana is a good place to live. Then use your ideas to write a poem that describes the good things in our state.

ACTIVITIES

1. **Researching Famous Hoosiers:** Research the lives and careers of several famous Hoosiers. They may be artists, athletes, business people, or government officials. Then prepare a chart that lists where each of them grew up and went to school, and how they became well known.
2. **Working Together to Make a Scrapbook:** With a classmate, prepare a scrapbook about one part of life in our state. You may wish to focus on Hoosier festivals, industries, or tourist sites. Present your findings in writing and drawings. Then arrange the pages to make a scrapbook.

BUILDING SKILLS: READING TIME ZONE MAPS

Study the map above to answer the following questions.

1. If you traveled to the neighboring time zone to the west of you, would it be earlier or later than in your own time zone?

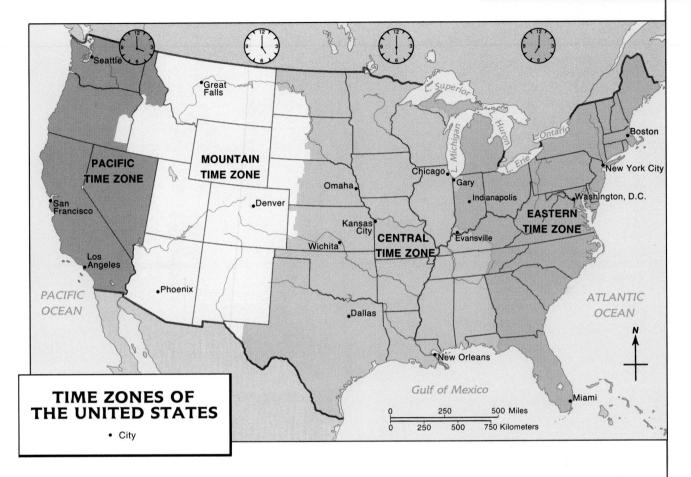

TIME ZONES OF THE UNITED STATES

• City

2. Suppose that you live in Indianapolis. If you wanted to telephone a friend in San Francisco when it was 8:00 A.M. there, what time would you have to make the call?

3. Suppose that you live in Gary. Your aunt in Omaha calls you when it is 5:00 P.M. in Omaha. What time is it in Gary?

4. Why do we have time zones?

LINKING PAST, PRESENT AND FUTURE

In the early 1900s the automobile and steel industries were two of the most important parts of Indiana's economy. Today they are less important than they once were. Which Hoosier industries do you think will become very important to our state's economy in the coming years? Why do you think so?

BARTHOLOMEW COUNTY

1. Geography of Our County
2. History of ___ County
3. Government ___ County
4. People of ___
5. Places ___ County

SPECIAL SECTION

EXPLORING YOUR COUNTY

FOCUS

In this book you have studied about our state's geography, climate, history, and government and about the life of Hoosiers today. Now let's apply what you have learned to your own county.

RICHARDS SCHOOL FOURTH GRADERS

When Mrs. Tibbetts's fourth graders in the W. D. Richards School came into their classroom one morning, they saw the name of their county written on the chalkboard: BARTHOLOMEW COUNTY. Mrs. Tibbetts asked them, "What do you know about our county?"

"That's easy," Josh said. "Bartholomew County is in Indiana."

"And Columbus is in Bartholomew County," Amanda added.

"Right," Mrs. Tibbetts said. "Now think of what you have learned about our state this year. You have studied our state's geography, history, and people. Next you are going to study your own county. What would you like to learn?"

ASKING QUESTIONS

Everyone thought for a moment. Troy asked if Columbus was the largest city in Bartholomew County. Ryan wanted to know how old Bartholomew County was. Melissa asked, "What happens in the county courthouse?"

Mrs. Tibbetts wrote all of the questions on the chalkboard. Then she asked, "Which of these questions belong together because they are about the same topic?"

SORTING QUESTIONS

The class discussed all of the questions. They sorted them into these five categories:

1. Geography of Our County
2. History of Our County
3. Government of Our County
4. People of Our County
5. Places to Visit in Our County

MAP SKILL: Mrs. Tibbetts's class is in Columbus. Name two other towns in Bartholomew County.

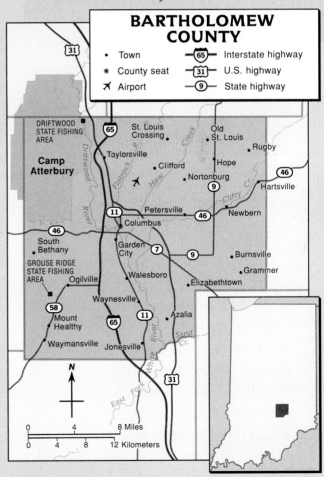

BARTHOLOMEW COUNTY

- • Town
- ◉ County seat
- ✈ Airport
- —65— Interstate highway
- —31— U.S. highway
- —9— State highway

Mrs. Tibbetts helped the students sort their questions about Bartholomew County into five categories.

Mrs. Tibbetts listed the five categories on the chalkboard, and the students read them carefully. Then they thought of even more questions that they wanted to ask. The students discovered that there was a lot they wanted to learn about Bartholomew County.

"The other two fourth-grade classes in the Richards School are going to study our county, too," Mrs. Tibbetts said. "Mrs. Carr's and Mrs. Kelly's classes are going to try and find answers to their own questions about Bartholomew County. Then we will share what we have learned with each other."

Mrs. Tibbetts said the three classes would work on projects to find out more about each of the five categories. She pointed to the geography category on the chalkboard. "That's our first topic," she said.

STUDYING GEOGRAPHY

Mrs. Tibbetts's class decided on several projects that would help them answer questions about Bartholomew County's landforms, rivers, towns, resources, and climate. The first project was to make a county map game.

MAKING A MAP GAME

Josh and Ryan volunteered to make the map game. But first they had to find out more about what their county looked like. Mrs. Tibbetts explained that the best way to get the information they needed was from an atlas. An atlas is a book or collection of maps. Your book has an atlas on pages 288–295.

Josh and Ryan got a large atlas from the school library. They found a map of Indiana and located Bartholomew County. Using the map scale, they figured out the size of the county's borders and made a large outline on posterboard.

Josh and Ryan created a map game about Bartholomew County. Their game was fun to play and helped the class to learn more about the county.

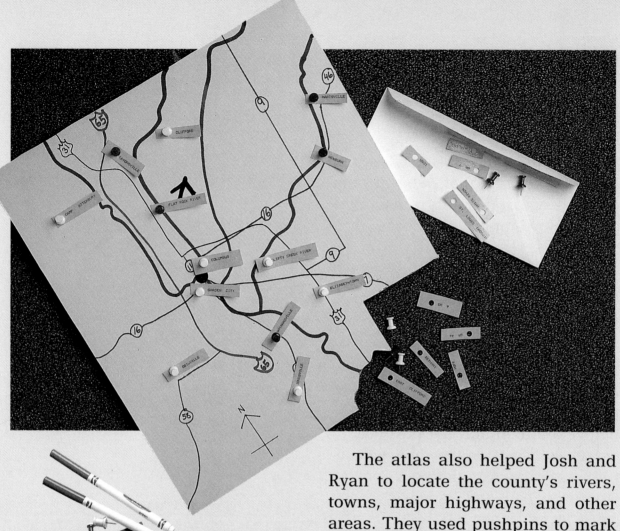

MAP SEARCH

Columbus	Grammer
Taylorsville	Burnsville
South Bethany	Petersville
Ogilville	Newbern
Mount Healthy	Nortonburg
Waymansville	Hartsville
Waynesville	Hope
Jonesville	Clifford
	St. Louis
Azalia	Crossing
Walesboro	Old St. Louis
Garden City	Rugby
Elizabethtown	

Sand Creek
Driftwood River
Clifty Creek
East Fork White River
Flatrock River
Haw Creek River
Grouse Ridge State Fishing Area
Driftwood State Fishing Area

Camp Atterbury
46 31 58
9   7
11 I-65

These are some of the tools that the students used to create their map game, shown above.

The atlas also helped Josh and Ryan to locate the county's rivers, towns, major highways, and other areas. They used pushpins to mark each one of these places on their county map.

The boys next made tags with the name of a Bartholomew County town, river, or highway on each one. Then they punched a hole through the corner of each tag. The goal of the game was for the players to find the correct position for each tag on the map and attach the tag to the correct pushpin.

Everyone in the class thought that the game was fun. In addition, Ryan said, "It helped me to learn where towns and other places are located in our county."

USING CHARTS

Amanda, Troy, and Carrie chose to work on a graph to show how many people lived in some of Bartholomew County's towns. The first thing they did was to look at a census report that showed how many people lived in each town in their county. The students used markers to draw vertical bars that represented these figures. Underneath the bars they wrote the names of the towns they had chosen to study. You can see their graph on this page. Which town on the graph has the most people?

Mrs. Tibbetts asked the class, "How do you think geography helped Columbus to become the largest city in the county?"

"One reason is that it's located where the Driftwood and the Flatrock rivers join to form the East Fork White River," Amy said.

"There's also an interstate highway nearby," Amanda said.

"The airport and the railroad help, too," Mrs. Tibbetts said.

The students decided that a good transportation system helps a town to grow. On the other hand, they realized that some towns may continue to have few people because most of the land around them is used for farming.

Troy, Amanda, and Carrie made a population graph of Bartholomew County's towns.

Decision Making

You read in Chapter 3 that making a decision means making a choice about something. You make choices every day. For example, you decide which clothes to wear, when to do your homework, and which books to read.

HELPING YOURSELF

The steps below review one way to make a decision.

1. Clearly state your goal.

2. Identify different actions you could take to reach your goal.

3. Identify what might happen as a result of each choice.

4. Choose the action that is most likely to help you reach your goal.

Applying the Skill

Now try the skill again. Suppose your county government is thinking about increasing taxes to buy new computers for county schools. Those who support the increase say that schools need the computers. Those who oppose the increase say that taxes are already too high and that the schools have enough computers for their needs. Would you support or oppose the increase?

Check yourself by answering the following questions.

1. To make a decision, you should first
   a. identify possible choices that are available.
   b. state your goal.
   c. ask someone to help you make the decision.
   d. make the decision without thinking about the results.

2. For each choice you have, you should
   a. consider the possible results of each choice.
   b. make a decision.
   c. do what other people want.
   d. make sure your friends agree.

Suppose your goal is to try to save money. Would you oppose or support the increase? Now suppose your goal is to have a strong computer education. Would you support or oppose the increase?

Reviewing the Skill

1. What is a decision?
2. Describe the steps you could follow to make good decisions.
3. What are two good decisions you have made recently? How do you know they were good?

3 County History

STUDYING HISTORY

While the students in Mrs. Tibbetts's class were working on their projects, Mrs. Carr's and Mrs. Kelly's classes were also studying their county. When they got to the history category, all three classes wrote out the questions that they wanted answered.

The teachers asked the students to research their questions. Some students worked in groups; others worked alone.

RESEARCHING

Where did the students find the answers to their questions? Some went to the county library, where they found articles in county history books and in old newspapers. They then made bibliographies, or lists of their sources.

Some students visited historical sites and took photographs of buildings or monuments. Julie visited an old theater in Columbus. "It's really exciting when you know you are in a building that was there long before you were born, and that you may be standing where history was made," Julie said.

Wherever it was that they went to find information, the students took notes on what they learned. Then the students in each class used their notes to write reports about the history of towns or about important people and events in their county's history.

Amanda, Michael, and Mike worked on their history reports in the county library.

CREATING A VIDEOTAPE

Mrs. Kelly's class rewrote their reports. Each student wrote his or her report as though he or she were a person in history. "I'll be Joseph Cox, one of Bartholomew County's first settlers," Suzanne said. "And I'll be Mary Cox!" said Laura.

The students made costumes for the time periods in which their characters lived. While they were in costume, the students read their first-person reports about the historical characters. Mrs. Kelly videotaped the students' performances and showed the tape to the other fourth-grade classes.

Mrs. Kelly filmed Suzanne and Laura in the roles of their historical characters.

Tracy, Debbie, and Christi hung the reports on their classroom's county history time line.

MAKING A TIME LINE

After the students in Mrs. Tibbetts's class had finished their reports on Bartholomew County's towns, they wanted to display them. "How shall we arrange them?" she asked the class.

"We can put them in the order in which the towns were founded and make a time line," Tracy said.

"Good idea," said Mrs. Tibbetts. "We'll make the time line from cardboard strips and put it up over the chalkboard. Then we can hang each report below the matching date on the time line."

When all the reports were in place, Christi said, "I really liked doing my report on Elizabethtown. I even took a trip there with my parents and the rest of my family."

"I'd like to know more about our city," Debbie said. "When are we going to begin to study more about Columbus?"

"Because the city of Columbus is the county seat, we will learn more about it in our study of county government—our next topic," Mrs. Tibbetts answered.

STUDYING GOVERNMENT

"Do you remember the question about the county courthouse?" Mrs. Tibbetts asked the next day. "Do you know why it is such a large building? Who works in the courthouse? What do they do?"

"Those are hard questions," said Hillary. "How can we find all of the answers?"

Mrs. Tibbetts suggested that the class review Chapter 13, which is about government, and study other books about Indiana's government in their library. "Then we'll visit the courthouse, the county jail, and the county library," she said.

MAKING A CIRCLE GRAPH

After doing their research and taking their field trip, the class made a list of some of the main functions of county government, such as providing police protection and library services and building roads and bridges. They discovered that one important job of government is collecting county taxes. "What happens to the money?" asked Chaz.

Mrs. Tibbetts called the county auditor and the county treasurer to get information about tax collection and spending. Chaz, Jason, Marleigha, and Hillary volunteered to show how county tax money is used.

"We'll make a circle graph," Hillary said.

They decided that the entire circle would stand for all the tax money collected in one year. But how would they show the different

Marleigha, Hillary, Chaz, and Jason made a circle graph of county taxes.

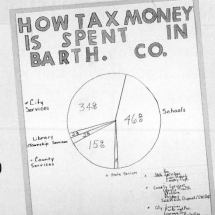

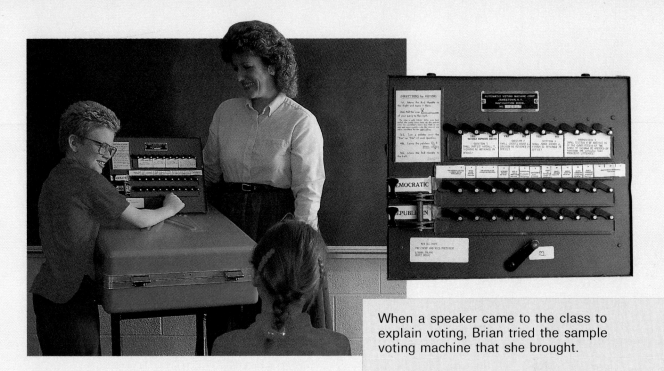

When a speaker came to the class to explain voting, Brian tried the sample voting machine that she brought.

ways the money was spent? The students used a calculator to figure out the percentage of tax money used for each service. They divided the circle to show these percentages and outlined each section of the circle with a black marker.

You can see their circle graph on page 280. How is most of the tax money collected in Bartholomew County spent?

Several students wondered who spent all the tax money that was collected. Mrs. Tibbetts explained that it was spent by their elected officials.

"I'd like to learn more about how people are elected," Amanda said.

BEING A VOTER

A representative from the Office of Voter Registration was invited to speak to the class. She explained that a person had to be 18 years old to vote and had to register to vote by filling out a special form.

A sample voting machine was brought to class. The names of the candidates for public office were listed at the top of the machine.

"How do you vote for the candidates?" Scott asked.

"I'll bet you move the levers on the machine," said Amanda. "Can we try it?"

Each student took a turn moving the lever next to the name of a candidate of his or her choice. "In a real election all the votes would be recorded on the machine, and the totals would be read by workers after the polls closed," Mrs. Tibbetts explained.

"I'll be glad when I can vote," Brian said. "Then I can help pick the people who spend our tax money!"

5 Our County's People

LEARNING ABOUT PEOPLE

"We know how many people live in Columbus. We also know how many people live in some other towns, like Hope and Clifford, in Bartholomew County," Mrs. Carr said to her class one morning. "What are some of the things that you want to know about the people who live in our county?"

"Where do people work?" Ben asked.

"What kinds of jobs do they do?" Jason wanted to know.

GRAPHING KINDS OF JOBS

Mrs. Carr suggested that students would find answers to their questions about jobs in a booklet prepared by the local chamber of commerce. The booklet showed the percentage of people who work in the county's various jobs. "We can make a large pictograph to display the information," Mrs. Carr told her students.

The class drew the pictograph on the chalkboard. First they made a key to explain their symbol, a figure of a person. Each figure represented 1 percent of the county's workers. Students took turns drawing the symbol on the graph.

When they had finished the graph, it was easy to see that most of Bartholomew County's people work in manufacturing jobs. The graph also showed that other people work in a variety of businesses that provide services, in government positions, and in agriculture.

Allen explains the class pictograph about county jobs.

GATHERING INFORMATION

Students in Mrs. Kelly's class wanted examples of what the people in their county do for fun.

"My family likes to go to the park," Julie said.

Mrs. Kelly showed the class a special map with the locations of all the parks in their town and county marked on it. She made a list of the parks on the chalkboard. "What kinds of things can you do in these parks?" she asked. As the students suggested activities, Mrs. Kelly wrote them on the chalkboard. Here are a few:

swimming	*basketball*
soccer	*hiking*
ice-skating	*baseball*
tennis	*picnicking*

Mrs. Kelly asked each student to choose a park and then design a booklet that would tell people about it. Erica chose Lincoln Park. Elizabeth wanted to make a booklet about Donner Park. Casey picked Westenedge Park.

After everyone had made a choice, each student wrote about the history of the park, where it was located, and the kinds of things a person could do in the park.

After the booklets were finished, students shared them with other classes. "These booklets tell a lot about our parks. I'd like to visit each one," Julie said.

The students' reports on county parks showed that people all over the county use and enjoy our parks in many different ways.

283

USING LOCAL RESOURCES

Karmen, Justin, Melissa, and Erin thought that they could learn more about their county if they could visit important county buildings and historical sites. But first they had to find the locations of these places. Where could they get this information?

"You could visit our Visitors Center, the local chamber of commerce, or the county historical society," Mrs. Carr said.

A few days later Melissa reported to the class: "We learned a lot about the buildings in our county. People at the Visitors Center told us that many visitors come to our town and our county to look at the architecture. Famous architects designed many of our county's public buildings, churches, and places of business. Even our school was designed by a famous architect!"

Some students labeled the photographs of the county sites they had visited on their tour.

TAKING A TOUR

Near the end of her class's study of Bartholomew County, Mrs. Carr suggested that students visit some county sites. They could walk to the historical places or important buildings that were nearby. "We can also take a bus tour of our county,"

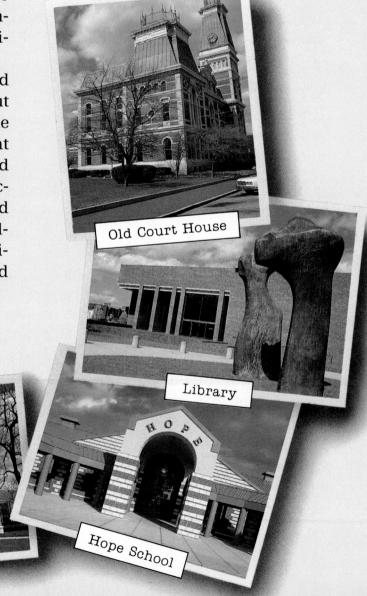

Old Court House

Library

Hope School

Visitors Center

she said. "All of our fourth-grade classes will be able to go."

Everyone was very excited as the classes set off on the tour. No one wanted it to end. When it was over, all the fourth graders had a lot to talk about.

"I loved visiting the Old Simmons School in Hope," Mariko said.

"I would like to tell everyone to visit our county," Jason said. "There are so many interesting things to see and do."

EXPLORING YOUR COUNTY

The fourth graders in the W. D. Richards School learned a lot about their county by doing their projects. As you have read, the students made maps, graphs, charts, time lines, and booklets. They also learned about their county government, how people vote in county elections, and what kinds of jobs they do.

You, too, can learn more about your county. What would you like to know? Think of some questions that you would ask to learn more about your county's geography, history, government, people, and places to visit. Which projects would help you to answer those questions?

By working on their projects, the fourth graders at the Richards School learned what makes their county special. As Rachel said, "I think my county is one of the best in Indiana." After you study your county, you may feel the same way about it. You will find out that your county is unlike any other.

The students at the W. D. Richards School were proud of the work they did in exploring their county.

YOU can make a difference

Throughout this book you have read about many people who make a difference. By going the extra mile, Beverly Stout, the "Smokey Lady," helps people to understand the hazards of forest fires. Joyce Marks Booth takes her responsibility as a citizen seriously by helping hundreds of homeless people in Indianapolis.

Jim Irvine turns his concern for the covered bridges in our state into action to save them for the future. The future is also on Vernon Smith's mind as he works to help young people save for a college education.

These are some of the people who have made an extra effort to help others. Chances are there is someone who has worked hard to solve a problem in your own community. Perhaps it was an adult. Perhaps it was a young person like you.

You may be too young to open a shelter for the homeless, but there are many ways you can help people in your community. Is there a park nearby that needs cleaning? A clean park helps everybody. Is there a senior citizen in your neighborhood who might enjoy a visit from a young person? Do you have a neighbor who needs help carrying groceries?

You might be able to help solve problems like these, or you might think of other ways to help your community. The important thing always to remember is that *you* can make a difference.

REFERENCE SECTION

ATLAS
THE WORLD
Political

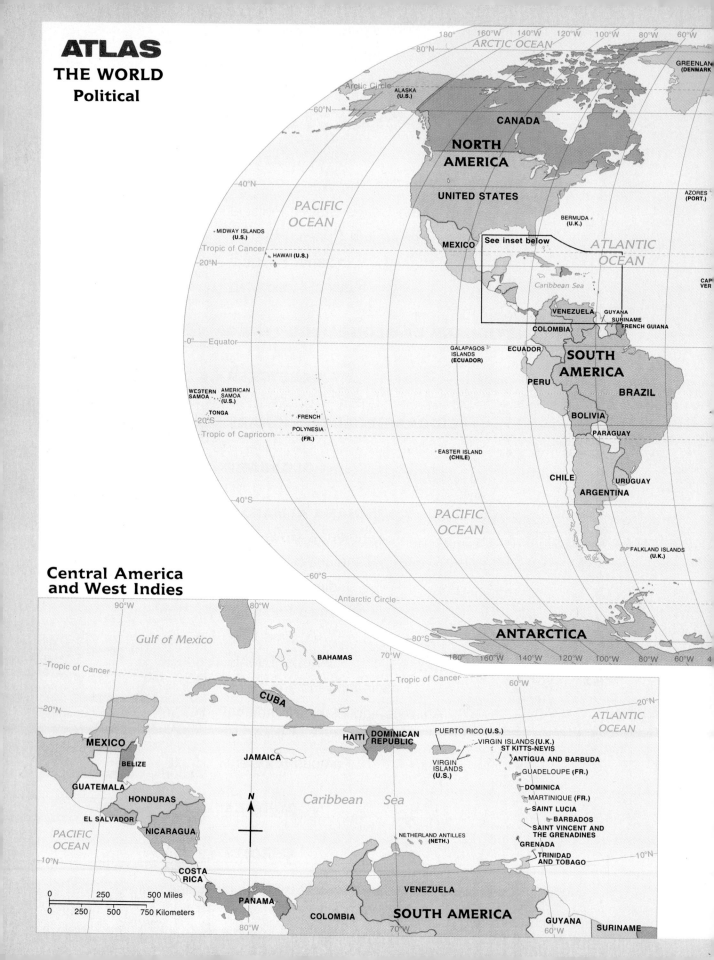

ARCTIC OCEAN

GREENLAND (DENMARK)

ALASKA (U.S.)

CANADA

NORTH AMERICA

UNITED STATES

PACIFIC OCEAN

BERMUDA (U.K.)

AZORES (PORT.)

MEXICO

See inset below

ATLANTIC OCEAN

Tropic of Cancer

HAWAII (U.S.)

Caribbean Sea

CAPE VERDE

MIDWAY ISLANDS (U.S.)

VENEZUELA
GUYANA
SURINAME
FRENCH GUIANA

COLOMBIA

Equator

GALAPAGOS ISLANDS (ECUADOR)

ECUADOR

SOUTH AMERICA

PERU

BRAZIL

WESTERN SAMOA

AMERICAN SAMOA (U.S.)

TONGA

FRENCH POLYNESIA (FR.)

Tropic of Capricorn

BOLIVIA

PARAGUAY

EASTER ISLAND (CHILE)

CHILE

URUGUAY

ARGENTINA

FALKLAND ISLANDS (U.K.)

Antarctic Circle

ANTARCTICA

Central America and West Indies

Gulf of Mexico

Tropic of Cancer

BAHAMAS

CUBA

MEXICO

BELIZE

GUATEMALA

HONDURAS

EL SALVADOR

NICARAGUA

PACIFIC OCEAN

HAITI

DOMINICAN REPUBLIC

JAMAICA

PUERTO RICO (U.S.)

VIRGIN ISLANDS (U.K.)
ST KITTS-NEVIS

VIRGIN ISLANDS (U.S.)

ANTIGUA AND BARBUDA

GUADELOUPE (FR.)

DOMINICA

MARTINIQUE (FR.)

SAINT LUCIA

BARBADOS

SAINT VINCENT AND THE GRENADINES

GRENADA

TRINIDAD AND TOBAGO

ATLANTIC OCEAN

Caribbean Sea

NETHERLAND ANTILLES (NETH.)

N

COSTA RICA

PANAMA

VENEZUELA

COLOMBIA

SOUTH AMERICA

GUYANA

SURINAME

| 0 | | 250 | | 500 Miles |
| 0 | 250 | | 500 | 750 Kilometers |

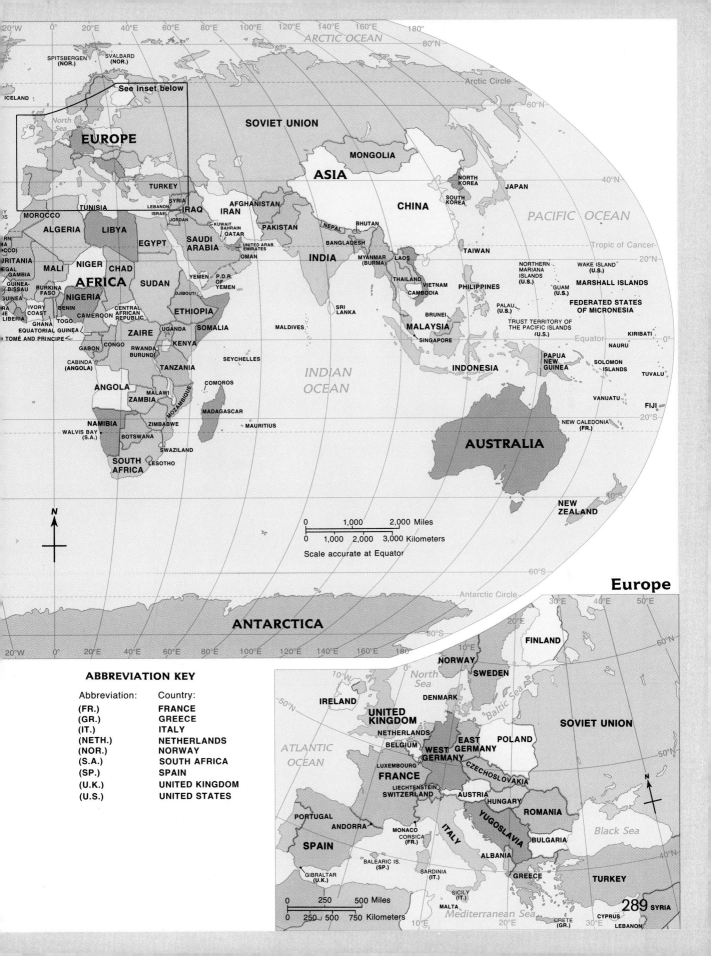

ARCTIC OCEAN

80°N

SPITSBERGEN
(NOR.)
SVALBARD
(NOR.)

Arctic Circle

ICELAND

60°N

See inset below

North
Sea

EUROPE

SOVIET UNION

ASIA

MONGOLIA

40°N

NORTH
KOREA

JAPAN

TURKEY

SYRIA

IRAQ

IRAN

AFGHANISTAN

CHINA

SOUTH
KOREA

PACIFIC OCEAN

LEBANON
ISRAEL

JORDAN

MOROCCO

TUNISIA

PAKISTAN

ALGERIA

LIBYA

EGYPT

SAUDI
ARABIA

KUWAIT
BAHRAIN
QATAR

NEPAL

BHUTAN

BANGLADESH

TAIWAN

Tropic of Cancer

20°N

UNITED ARAB
EMIRATES

INDIA

MYANMAR
(BURMA)

LAOS

WAKE ISLAND
(U.S.)

MAURITANIA

OMAN

NORTHERN
MARIANA
ISLANDS
(U.S.)

GUAM
(U.S.)

MARSHALL ISLANDS

MALI

NIGER

CHAD

YEMEN

P.D.R.
OF
YEMEN

THAILAND

VIETNAM

CAMBODIA

PHILIPPINES

FEDERATED STATES
OF MICRONESIA

GAMBIA

GUINEA-
BISSAU

AFRICA

NIGERIA

BURKINA
FASO

SENEGAL

SUDAN

DJIBOUTI

SRI
LANKA

BRUNEI

PALAU
(U.S.)

GUINEA

IVORY
COAST

BENIN

ETHIOPIA

MALAYSIA

TRUST TERRITORY OF
THE PACIFIC ISLANDS
(U.S.)

LIBERIA

GHANA

TOGO

CAMEROON

CENTRAL
AFRICAN
REPUBLIC

SINGAPORE

Equator

KIRIBATI

0°

EQUATORIAL GUINEA

SÃO TOMÉ AND PRINCIPE

ZAIRE

UGANDA

SOMALIA

MALDIVES

NAURU

GABON

CONGO

KENYA

SOLOMON
ISLANDS

TUVALU

CABINDA
(ANGOLA)

RWANDA
BURUNDI

TANZANIA

SEYCHELLES

INDONESIA

PAPUA
NEW
GUINEA

INDIAN
OCEAN

ANGOLA

MALAWI

COMOROS

VANUATU

NEW CALEDONIA
(FR.)

FIJI

ZAMBIA

MOZAMBIQUE

MADAGASCAR

20°S

NAMIBIA

ZIMBABWE

MAURITIUS

WALVIS BAY
(S.A.)

BOTSWANA

AUSTRALIA

SWAZILAND

SOUTH
AFRICA

LESOTHO

N

0   1,000   2,000 Miles

0   1,000   2,000   3,000 Kilometers

Scale accurate at Equator

NEW
ZEALAND

10°S

60°S

Antarctic Circle

ANTARCTICA

80°S

Europe

20°W   0°   20°E   40°E   60°E   80°E   100°E   120°E   140°E   160°E   180°

30°E   40°E   50°E

60°N

FINLAND

NORWAY

SWEDEN

IRELAND

North
Sea

DENMARK

Baltic
Sea

50°N

UNITED
KINGDOM

SOVIET UNION

NETHERLANDS

POLAND

ATLANTIC
OCEAN

BELGIUM

EAST
GERMANY

WEST
GERMANY

50°N

LUXEMBOURG

CZECHOSLOVAKIA

N

FRANCE

LIECHTENSTEIN
SWITZERLAND

AUSTRIA

HUNGARY

ROMANIA

PORTUGAL

ANDORRA

MONACO
CORSICA
(FR.)

ITALY

YUGOSLAVIA

Black Sea

BULGARIA

SPAIN

BALEARIC IS.
(SP.)

SARDINIA
(IT.)

ALBANIA

40°N

GIBRALTAR
(U.K.)

GREECE

TURKEY

SICILY
(IT.)

0   250   500 Miles

0   250   500   750 Kilometers

MALTA

Mediterranean Sea

CRETE
(GR.)

CYPRUS

SYRIA

LEBANON

10°E

20°E

30°E

ABBREVIATION KEY

Abbreviation:	Country:
(FR.)	FRANCE
(GR.)	GREECE
(IT.)	ITALY
(NETH.)	NETHERLANDS
(NOR.)	NORWAY
(S.A.)	SOUTH AFRICA
(SP.)	SPAIN
(U.K.)	UNITED KINGDOM
(U.S.)	UNITED STATES

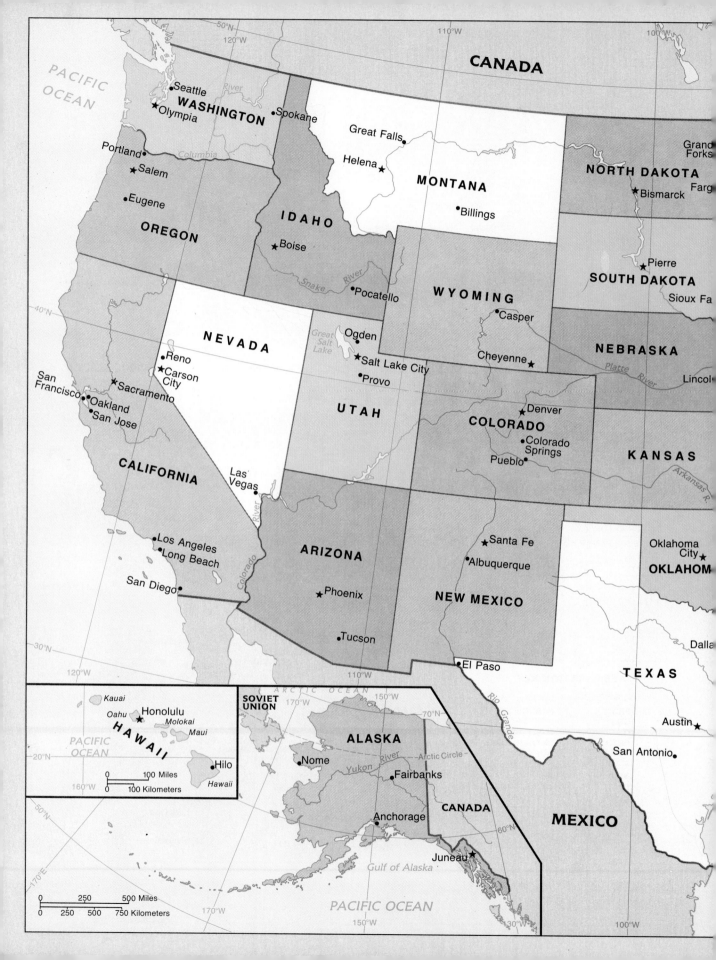

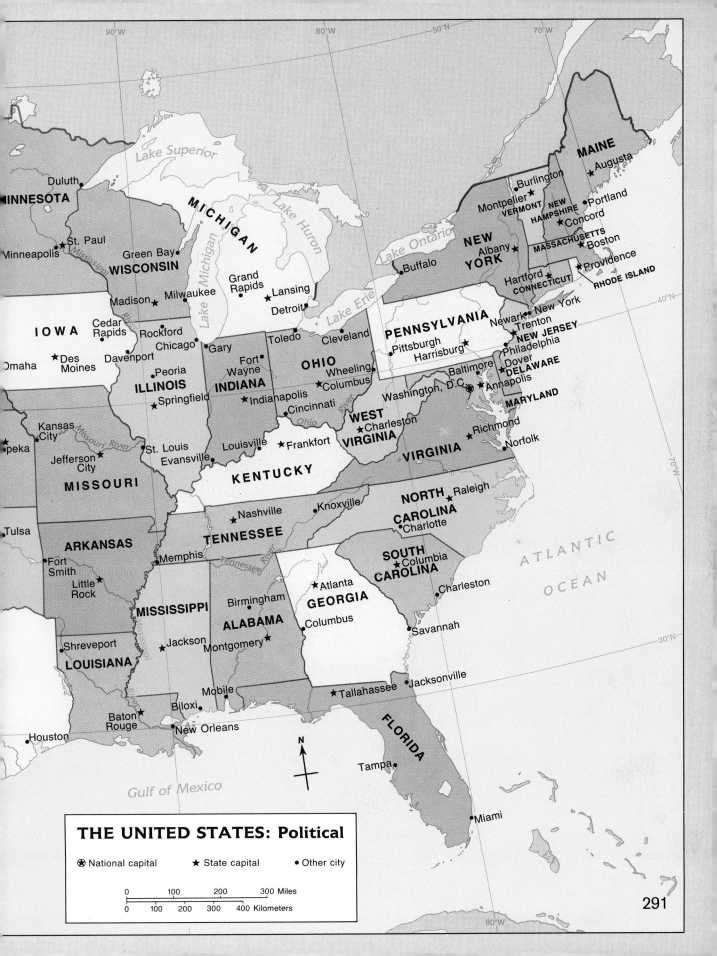

THE UNITED STATES: Political

⊛ National capital   ★ State capital   • Other city

| 0 | 100 | 200 | 300 Miles |
| 0 | 100 | 200 | 300 | 400 Kilometers |

291

Strait of
Juan de Fuca
Vancouver
Island

Puget
Sound

Columbia River

PACIFIC
OCEAN

Cape
Mendocino

40°N

San
Francisco
Bay

120°W

30°N

Gulf of
California

292

Coast Ranges
Cascade Range
COLUMBIA PLATEAU

Snake River

Sacramento River

Sierra Nevada
CENTRAL VALLEY

San Joaquin River

Lake
Tahoe

Mt. Whitney
14,494 ft
(4,418 m)

DEATH
VALLEY

MOJAVE
DESERT

Salton
Sea

SONORA
DESERT

GREAT
BASIN

Great
Salt
Lake

GREAT
SALT
LAKE
DESERT

Lake
Mead

Colorado River

Gila River

R O C K Y

Teton
Range

Range

Wasatch
Range

Green River

COLORADO
PLATEAU

M O U N T A I N S

Missouri River

Yellowstone River

Black
Hills

Cheyenne River

River

Platte River

G R E A T   P L A I N S

INTERIOR

Rio Grande

Pecos River

Brazos River

Colorado River

EDWARDS
PLATEAU

MEXICO

PACIFIC
OCEAN

160°W

Kauai

Oahu

Maui

Hawaii

HAWAII

20°N

100 Miles
0   100 Kilometers

Mauna Kea
13,796 ft.
(4,205 m)

N

Point Barrow

ARCTIC
OCEAN

70°N

ALASKA

Brooks Range

Yukon River

Alaska Range

Mt. McKinley
20,320 ft.
(6,193 m)

N

CANADA

Bering Strait

Bering
Sea

50°N

170°W

PACIFIC
OCEAN

Aleutian Islands

160°W

Gulf of
Alaska

150°W

0   250   500 Miles
0   250   500   750 Kilometers

140°W

CANADA

Lake of
the Woods

Mesabi Range

Lake Superior

GREAT

LAKES

Lake Huron

Lake Michigan

St. Lawrence River

White Mts.

Bay of
Fundy

Green Mts.

Adirondack
Mts.

Lake Ontario

Hudson River

Cape
Cod

Mississippi

CENTRAL

PLAINS

River

Lake Erie

ALLEGHENY
PLATEAU

40°N

Long Island

Wabash River

Susquehanna River

Delaware R.

Delaware Bay

70°W

Missouri

Ohio

River

River

River

Allegheny Mountains

Potomac R.

Chesapeake Bay

PLAINS

OZARK

PLATEAU

Kentucky
Lake

Mississippi River

Tennessee River

APPALACHIAN MOUNTAINS

PIEDMONT

ATLANTIC COASTAL PLAIN

Cape Hatteras

ATLANTIC

OCEAN

nsas

River

**Ouachita
Mountains**

Alabama River

Chattahoochee River

Savannah River

Red

River

30°N

GULF COASTAL PLAIN

Mobile Bay

Galveston Bay

Mississippi Delta

Gulf of Mexico

Lake
Okeechobee

90°W

N

THE UNITED STATES
Physical

0   100   200   300 Miles

0   100   200   300   400 Kilometers

Florida Keys

Straits of Florida

80°W

WEST INDIES

293

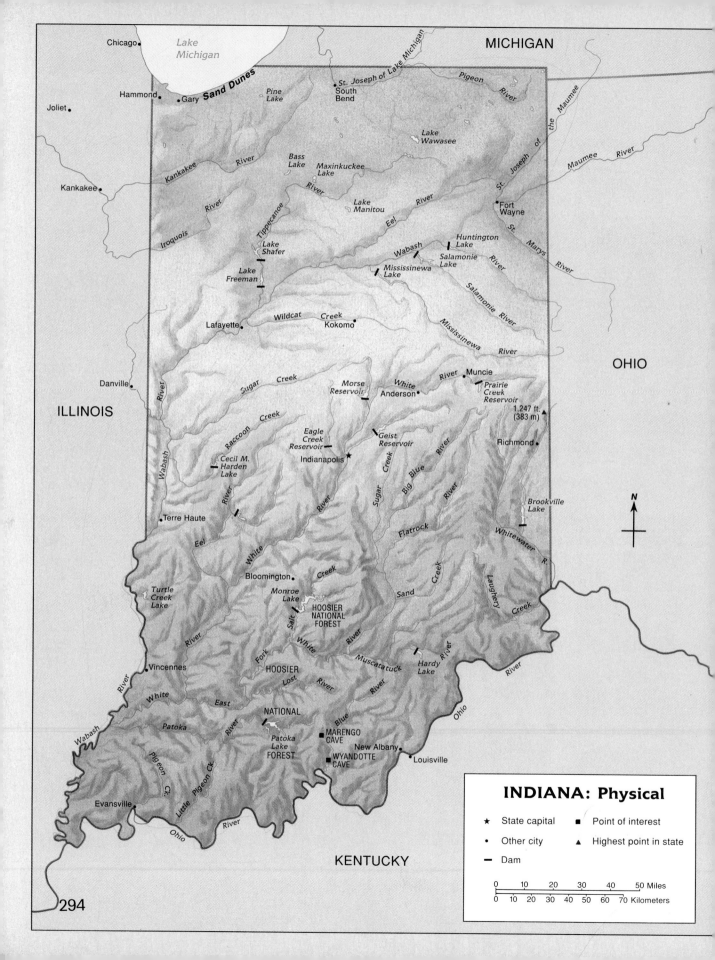

Chicago

Lake
Michigan

MICHIGAN

Joliet

Hammond   Gary **Sand Dunes**   Pine   St. Joseph of Lake Michigan   Pigeon   River
Lake   South
Bend

Lake
Wawasee

Maumee   River

Kankakee   *Kankakee*   *River*   Bass   Maxinkuckee   *River*
Lake   Lake
River   Lake   St. Joseph of
Manitou   *Eel*   *River*   Fort
Wayne

Iroquois   *River*   *Tippecanoe*   Lake   Wabash   Huntington
Shafer   Lake
Lake   Mississinewa   Salamonie
Freeman   Lake   Lake

St. Marys   River

Lafayette   Wildcat   *Creek*   Kokomo   *Mississinewa*   *River*   Salamonie   *River*

OHIO

Danville   *River*   Sugar   *Creek*   Morse   White   *River*   Muncie   Prairie
Reservoir   Anderson   Creek
Reservoir

ILLINOIS   *Raccoon*   *Creek*   Eagle   Geist   1,247 ft.
Creek   Reservoir   (383 m)
Reservoir

Wabash   Cecil M.   Indianapolis   *Sugar*   *Big*   *Blue*   *River*   Richmond
Harden
Lake   *Creek*

Terre Haute   *River*   Flatrock   Brookville
Lake
Eel   White   *Creek*   *Whitewater*   *R.*

Bloomington   *Creek*   *Sand*   *Creek*   *Laughery*
Turtle   *N*
Creek   Monroe   *River*   *Creek*
Lake   Lake   HOOSIER
NATIONAL
River   FOREST
Salt   *White*   *River*
HOOSIER   *Muscatatuck*   Hardy   *River*
Vincennes   *Fork*   *River*   *River*   Lake
Lost   Blue   Ohio   *River*
White   *East*
Patoka   NATIONAL   *Blue*
River   MARENGO
Wabash   Patoka   CAVE
Lake   FOREST   New Albany
Pigeon   WYANDOTTE   Louisville
Ck.   CAVE
Evansville   *Little Pigeon Ck.*
River   KENTUCKY
Ohio

294

INDIANA: Physical

★ State capital   ■ Point of interest

• Other city   ▲ Highest point in state

— Dam

0   10   20   30   40   50 Miles
0 10 20 30 40 50 60 70 Kilometers

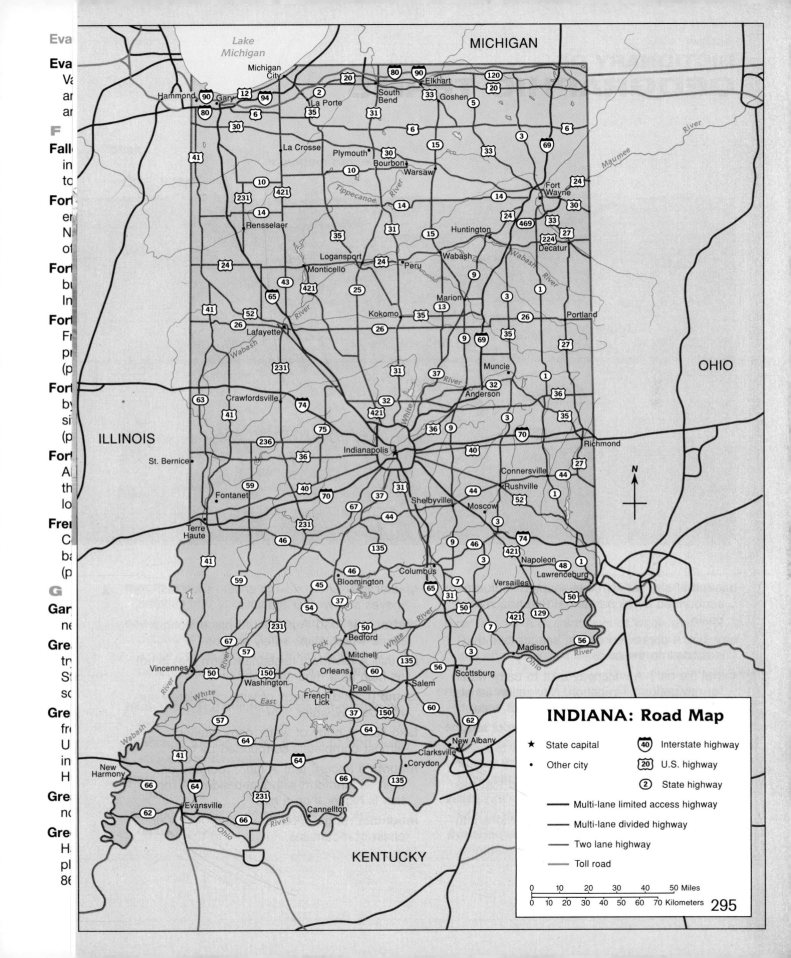

INDIANA: Road Map

- ★ State capital
- • Other city
- ⬡40 Interstate highway
- ⬡20 U.S. highway
- ⬡2 State highway
- ——— Multi-lane limited access highway
- ——— Multi-lane divided highway
- ——— Two lane highway
- ——— Toll road

N

0 10 20 30 40 50 Miles
0 10 20 30 40 50 60 70 Kilometers

295

MICHIGAN

OHIO

ILLINOIS

KENTUCKY

Lake Michigan

Michigan City
Hammond · Gary
La Porte
South Bend · Goshen · Elkhart
La Crosse
Plymouth · Bourbon · Warsaw
Rensselaer
Logansport · Peru · Wabash · Huntington · Fort Wayne · Decatur
Monticello
Lafayette
Kokomo · Marion · Portland
Crawfordsville
St. Bernice · Indianapolis · Muncie · Anderson · Richmond
Fontanet
Terre Haute · Shelbyville · Connersville · Rushville · Moscow
Vincennes · Bloomington · Columbus · Versailles · Napoleon · Lawrenceburg
Washington · Bedford · Mitchell · Madison
New Harmony · Orleans · Paoli · French Lick · Salem · Scottsburg
Evansville · Cannellton · New Albany · Clarksville · Corydon

L

Lafayette (laf ē et′) The county seat of Tippecanoe County and the home of Purdue University; 40°N, 87°W. (p. 83)

Little Pigeon Creek (lit′ əl pij′ ən krēk) The place in southern Indiana where Abraham Lincoln lived; 38°N, 87°W. (p. 137)

Lost River (lôst riv′ ər) A river in southern Indiana that "disappears" into sinkholes. (p. 32)

M

Madison (mad′ ə sən) The county seat of Jefferson County, once known as "Porkopolis" because it was a major shipping point for pork along the Ohio River; 39°N, 85°W. (p. 155)

Marion County (mer′ ē ən koun′ tē) The county in which Indianapolis is located. (p. 255)

Metamora (met ə môr′ ə) Home of the Whitewater Canal State Historic Site in eastern Indiana; 39°N, 85°W. (p. 154)

Michigan (mish′ i gən) A state in the middle-western United States, located just north of Indiana. (p. 20)

Michigan Road (mish′ i gən rōd) A large road built in the 1820s that connected northern and southern Indiana. Today it is a part of U.S. Route 421. (p. 152)

Mississippi River (mis ə sip′ ē riv′ ər) One of the longest rivers in North America. It flows from north to south in the central United States. (p. 66)

Mounds State Park (moundz stāt pärk) A state park near Anderson with prehistoric Indian mounds; 40°N, 86°W. (p. 64)

Muncie (mun′ sē) The county seat of Delaware County, in eastern Indiana, and the home of Ball State University; 40°N, 85°W. (p. 197)

N

National Road (nash′ ə nəl rōd) A road built in the 1830s from Maryland to Illinois that crossed through Indiana. Today it is a part of U.S. Route 40. (p. 152)

New Albany (nü ôl′ bə nē) The county seat of Floyd County in southern Indiana, on the Ohio River; 38°N, 86°W. (p. 20)

New France (nü frans) The land in North America controlled by France during the 1600s and 1700s. (p. 80)

New Harmony (nü här′ mə nē) A town in Posey County in southwestern Indiana that was bought by Robert Owen in 1824 and renamed New Harmony; 38°N, 88°W. (p. 143)

North America (nôrth ə mer′ i kə) A continent in the Northern and Western hemispheres. (p. 62)

Northwest Territory (nôrth west′ ter′ i tôr ē) The United States territory created in 1787 that was bounded by the Ohio River, the Great Lakes, and the Mississippi River. (p. 104)

O

Ohio (ō hī′ ō) A state in the middle-western United States, located just east of Indiana. (p. 19)

Ohio River (ō hī′ ō riv′ ər) A river that flows from the Appalachian Mountains to the Mississippi River and forms the southern boundary of Indiana. (p. 21)

P

Prophetstown (prof′ its toun) A village on the Tippecanoe River where Tecumseh and Tenskwatawa lived in the early 1800s, near the present-day city of Lafayette; 40°N, 87°W. (p. 126)

S

St. Joseph River (sānt jō′ zəf riv′ ər) Two rivers of this name flow through Indiana. One begins at Lake Michigan and flows southwest, near South Bend. Another flows in the northwestern part of the state, near Fort Wayne. (p. 25)

St. Lawrence River (sānt lôr′ əns riv′ ər) A river that forms part of the border between the United States and Canada. It begins in Lake Ontario and flows into the Atlantic Ocean. (p. 80)

St. Lawrence Seaway (sānt lôr′ əns sē′ wā) The waterway that makes it possible for ships to travel between the Great Lakes and the Atlantic Ocean. (p. 233)

St. Marys River (sānt mâr′ ēz riv′ ər) A river that begins in northwestern Ohio, flows into northeastern Indiana, and joins the St. Joseph River at Fort Wayne. (p. 25)

GAZETTEER

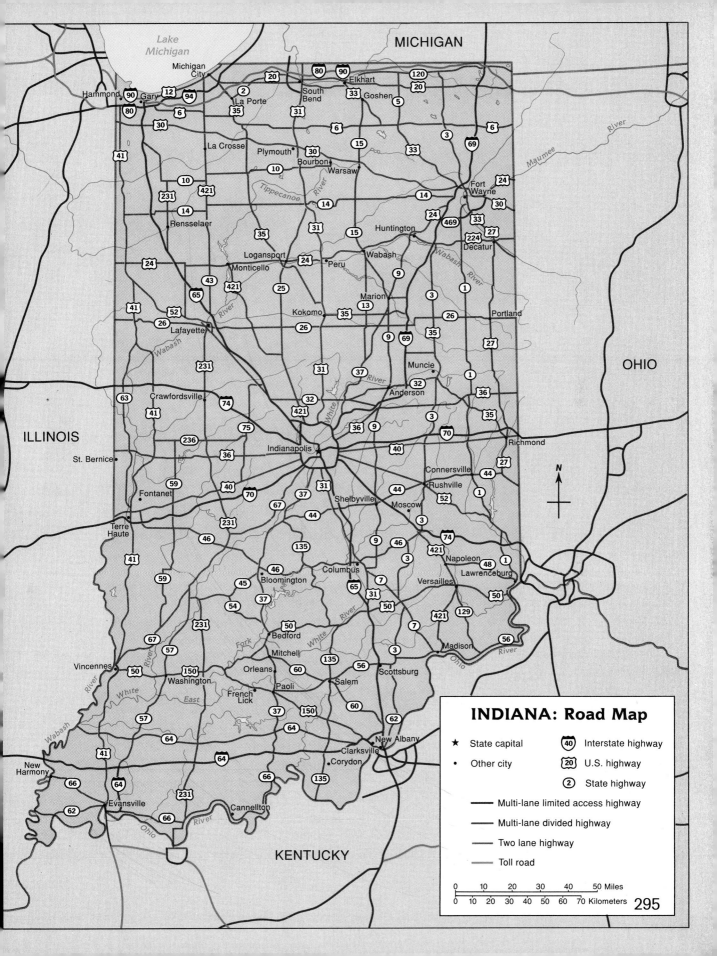

INDIANA: Road Map

★ State capital

• Other city

⑳ U.S. highway

② State highway

⑩ Interstate highway

— Multi-lane limited access highway

— Multi-lane divided highway

— Two lane highway

— Toll road

| 0 | 10 | 20 | 30 | 40 | 50 Miles |
| 0 | 10 20 | 30 40 | 50 | 60 | 70 Kilometers |

295

DICTIONARY OF
GEOGRAPHIC TERMS

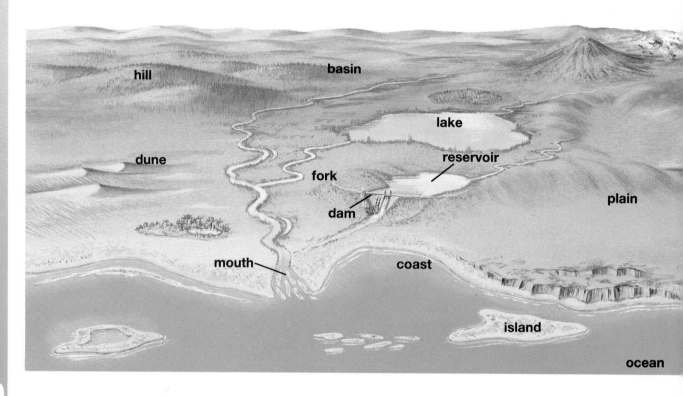

hill   basin   lake   reservoir   plain

dune   fork   dam   mouth   coast   island   ocean

basin (bā′ sin) A low, bowl-shaped landform surrounded by higher lands. *See also* **river basin**.

bay (bā) A part of an ocean, sea, or lake that extends into the land.

canal (kə nal′) A waterway built to carry water for navigation or irrigation. Navigation canals usually connect two other bodies of water.

coast (kōst) The land along an ocean or sea.

dam (dam) A wall built across a river to hold back flowing water.

dune (dün) A mound or ridge of sand that has been piled up by the wind.

fork (fôrk) The place where a river divides into branches.

glacier (glā′ shər) A large sheet of ice that moves slowly over the land.

harbor (här′ bər) A protected place along a shore where ships safely anchor.

hill (hil) A rounded, raised landform that is not as high as a mountain.

island (ī′ lənd) A body of land completely surrounded by water.

lake (lāk) A body of water completely or almost completely surrounded by land.

mountain (moun′ tən) A high, rounded or pointed landform with steep sides. A mountain is higher than a hill.

mountain range (moun′t ən rānj) A row or chain of mountains.

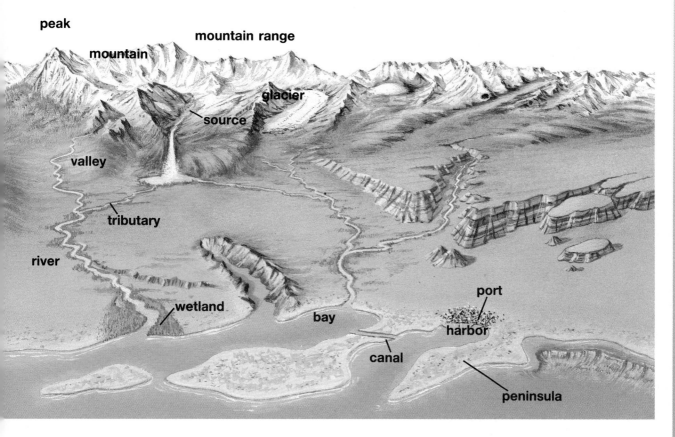

mouth (mouth) The part of a river where it empties into another body of water.

ocean (ō′ shən) One of the earth's four largest bodies of water. The four oceans are really a single connected body of salt water that covers about three fourths of the earth's surface.

peak (pēk) The pointed top of a mountain or hill.

peninsula (pə nin′ sə lə) A body of land nearly surrounded by water.

plain (plān) A large area of flat or nearly flat land.

port (pôrt) A place where ships load and unload goods.

reservoir (rez′ ər vwär) A natural or artificial lake used to store water.

river (riv′ ər) A large stream of water that flows in a natural channel across the land and empties into a lake, ocean, or another river.

river basin (riv′ ər bā′ sin) All the land drained by a river and its tributaries.

source (sôrs) A spring, lake, or other body of water where a river or stream begins.

tributary (trib′ yə tär ē) A river or stream that flows into a larger river or stream.

valley (val′ ē) An area of low land between hills or mountains.

wetland (wet′ land) An area of swamp, marsh, or other wet surface.

GEOGRAPHIC TERMS

GAZETTEER

This Gazetteer is a geographical dictionary that will help you to pronounce and locate the places discussed in this book. Latitude and longitude are given for cities and some other places. The page number tells you where each place appears in the text for the first time.

PRONUNCIATION KEY

a	cap	hw	**wh**ere	oi	c**oi**n	ü	m**oo**n
ā	c**a**ke	i	b**i**b	ôr	f**or**k	ū	c**u**te
ä	f**a**ther	ī	k**i**te	ou	c**ow**	ûr	t**er**m
är	c**ar**	îr	p**ier**ce	sh	**sh**ow	ə	**a**bout, tak**e**n,
âr	d**are**	ng	so**ng**	-th	**th**in		penc**i**l, apr**o**n,
ch	**ch**ain	o	t**o**p	th	**th**ose		helpf**u**l
e	h**e**n	ō	r**o**pe	u	s**u**n	ər	lett**er**, doll**ar**,
ē	m**e**	ô	s**aw**	ù	b**oo**k		doct**or**

A

Africa (af′ ri kə) A continent located in the Eastern and Southern hemispheres. (p. 9)

Angel Mounds State Historic Site (ān′ jəl moundz stāt hi stôr′ ik sīt) A historic site near Evansville with Native American mounds; 38°N, 88°W. (p. 64)

Appalachian Mountains (ap ə lā′ chē ən moun′ tənz) The low, rounded mountains that range over much of the eastern United States. (p. 91)

Asia (ā′ zhə) The largest continent, located in the Eastern and Northern hemispheres. (p. 9)

Atlantic Ocean (at lan′ tik ō′shən) The ocean that borders the eastern United States. (p. 9)

B

Beringia (bə rinj′ ē ə) The land bridge that once connected Asia and North America. (p. 62)

Bloomington (blü′ ming tən) The county seat of Monroe County and the home of Indiana University; 39°N, 87°W. (p. 64)

Brown County State Park (broun koun′ tē stāt pärk) Indiana's largest state park; 39°N, 86°W. (p. 245)

Buffalo Trace (buf′ ə lō trās) An old animal path that connected New Albany and Vincennes in southern Indiana. (p. 152)

Burns Harbor (bûrnz här′ bər) A large port on Lake Michigan; 42°N, 87°W. (p. 233)

C

Canada (kan′ ə də) The country in North America that borders the northern United States. (p. 24)

Clarksville (klärks′ vil) A town in Clark County, on the Ohio River, named for George Rogers Clark; 38°N, 86°W. (p. 105)

Corn Belt (kôrn belt) The region in the middle-western United States, including Indiana, that has the right climate for growing corn. (p. 223)

Conner Prairie (kon′ ər prâr′ ē) The place near Indianapolis at which the life of early pioneers is recreated; 40°N, 86°W. (p. 243)

Corydon (kôr′ ē dən) The territorial and state capital of Indiana from 1813 to 1825; 38°N, 86°W. (p. 130)

D

Deaf Man's Village (def manz vil′ ij) The village where Frances Slocum lived with her husband, located on the banks of the Mississinewa River. (p. 110)

E

East Fork White River (ēst fôrk hwīt riv′ ər) A branch of the White River that flows through southern Indiana. (p. 30)

Evansville (ev′ ənz vil) The county seat of Vanderburgh County in southwestern Indiana and home of the University of Southern Indiana; 38°N, 88°W. (p. 41)

F

Fallen Timbers (fôl′ ən tim′ bərz) The place in Ohio where the Battle of Fallen Timbers took place in 1794. (p. 106)

Fort Greenville (fôrt grēn′ vil) A fort in eastern Ohio at which Anthony Wayne and Native American leaders signed the Treaty of Greenville in 1795. (p. 106)

Fort Miami (fôrt mī am′ ē) An old French fort built in 1715 near Kekionga, in northeastern Indiana; 41°N, 85°W. (p. 83)

Fort Ouiatenon (fôrt wē ôt′ ə non) A former French fort on the Wabash River, near the present-day town of Lafayette; 40°N, 87°W. (p. 83)

Fort Sackville (fôrt sak′ vil) A fort captured by George Rogers Clark in 1779, near the site of present-day Vincennes; 39°N, 87°W. (p. 101)

Fort Wayne (fôrt wān) The county seat of Allen County, in northeastern Indiana, where the Miami village of Kekionga was once located; 41°N, 85°W. (p. 66)

French Lick (french lik) A town in Orange County, in southern Indiana, where basketball player Larry Bird was born; 39°N, 87°W. (p. 217)

G

Gary (gâr′ ē) A city in Lake County located near Lake Michigan; 42°N, 87°W. (p. 20)

Great Britain (grāt brit′ ən) The island country in Europe against which the United States fought the American Revolution; sometimes called England. (p. 79)

Great Lakes (grāt lāks) The world's largest freshwater lakes, located between the United States and Canada. The Great Lakes include: Lake Superior, Lake Michigan, Lake Huron, Lake Erie, and Lake Ontario. (p. 23)

Great Lakes Plain (grāt lāks plān) The northern region of Indiana. (p. 22)

Greenfield (grēn′ fēld) The county seat of Hancock County in central Indiana and birthplace of poet James Whitcomb Riley; 40°N, 86°W. (p. 211)

Grouseland (grous′ lənd) The house built by William Henry Harrison in Vincennes when he was governor of the Indiana Territory; 39°N, 87°W. (p. 119)

H

Harmonie (här′ mə nē) The town in southwestern Indiana built by George Rapp and his followers in 1814 and later renamed New Harmony; 38°N, 88°W. (p. 143)

Hoosier National Forest (hü′ zhər nash′ ə nəl fôr′ ist) Indiana's largest forest, located in southern Indiana. (p. 48)

I

Illinois (il ə noi′) A state in the middle-western United States, located just west of Indiana. (p. 19)

Indiana (in dē an′ ə) The state in the middle-western United States that is the subject of this book. (p. 19)

Indiana Dunes State Park (in dē an′ ə dünz stāt pärk) A national park on the shores of Lake Michigan; 42°N, 87°W. (p. 25)

Indiana Territory (in dē ān′ ə ter′ i tôr ē) The area established as the western part of the Northwest Territory in 1800. It originally included the present-day states of Indiana, Illinois, Wisconsin, and parts of Minnesota and Michigan. (p. 118)

Indianapolis (in dē ə nap′ ə lis) The capital of Indiana since 1825, located in the center of the state; 40°N, 86°W. (p. 132)

K

Kankakee River (kang kə kē′ riv′ ər) A river that begins in northern Indiana and flows southwest into Illinois. (p. 80)

Kekionga (kēk ē ong′ ə) A Miami village in northeastern Indiana that later became the site of Fort Wayne; 41°N, 85°W. (p. 66)

Kentucky (kən tuk′ ē) A state in the southeastern United States, located just south of Indiana. (p. 20)

Knob Creek (nob krēk) The place in Kentucky that Abraham Lincoln's family left to move to Indiana. (p. 135)

Kokomo (kō′kə mō) The county seat of Howard County; 41°N, 86°W. (p. 20)

GAZETTEER

L

Lafayette (laf ē et′) The county seat of Tippecanoe County and the home of Purdue University; 40°N, 87°W. (p. 83)

Little Pigeon Creek (lit′ əl pij′ ən krēk) The place in southern Indiana where Abraham Lincoln lived; 38°N, 87°W. (p. 137)

Lost River (lôst riv′ ər) A river in southern Indiana that ''disappears'' into sinkholes. (p. 32)

M

Madison (mad′ ə sən) The county seat of Jefferson County, once known as ''Porkopolis'' because it was a major shipping point for pork along the Ohio River; 39°N, 85°W. (p. 155)

Marion County (mer′ ē ən koun′ tē) The county in which Indianapolis is located. (p. 255)

Metamora (met ə môr′ ə) Home of the Whitewater Canal State Historic Site in eastern Indiana; 39°N, 85°W. (p. 154)

Michigan (mish′ i gən) A state in the middle-western United States, located just north of Indiana. (p. 20)

Michigan Road (mish′ i gən rōd) A large road built in the 1820s that connected northern and southern Indiana. Today it is a part of U.S. Route 421. (p. 152)

Mississippi River (mis ə sip′ ē riv′ ər) One of the longest rivers in North America. It flows from north to south in the central United States. (p. 66)

Mounds State Park (moundz stāt pärk) A state park near Anderson with prehistoric Indian mounds; 40°N, 86°W. (p. 64)

Muncie (mun′ sē) The county seat of Delaware County, in eastern Indiana, and the home of Ball State University; 40°N, 85°W. (p. 197)

N

National Road (nash′ ə nəl rōd) A road built in the 1830s from Maryland to Illinois that crossed through Indiana. Today it is a part of U.S. Route 40. (p. 152)

New Albany (nü ôl′ bə nē) The county seat of Floyd County in southern Indiana, on the Ohio River; 38°N, 86°W. (p. 20)

New France (nü frans) The land in North America controlled by France during the 1600s and 1700s. (p. 80)

New Harmony (nü här′ mə nē) A town in Posey County in southwestern Indiana that was bought by Robert Owen in 1824 and renamed New Harmony; 38°N, 88°W. (p. 143)

North America (nôrth ə mer′ i kə) A continent in the Northern and Western hemispheres. (p. 62)

Northwest Territory (nôrth west′ ter′ i tôr ē) The United States territory created in 1787 that was bounded by the Ohio River, the Great Lakes, and the Mississippi River. (p. 104)

O

Ohio (ō hī′ ō) A state in the middle-western United States, located just east of Indiana. (p. 19)

Ohio River (ō hī′ ō riv′ ər) A river that flows from the Appalachian Mountains to the Mississippi River and forms the southern boundary of Indiana. (p. 21)

P

Prophetstown (prof′ its toun) A village on the Tippecanoe River where Tecumseh and Tenskwatawa lived in the early 1800s, near the present-day city of Lafayette; 40°N, 87°W. (p. 126)

S

St. Joseph River (sānt jō′ zəf riv′ ər) Two rivers of this name flow through Indiana. One begins at Lake Michigan and flows southwest, near South Bend. Another flows in the northwestern part of the state, near Fort Wayne. (p. 25)

St. Lawrence River (sānt lôr′ əns riv′ ər) A river that forms part of the border between the United States and Canada. It begins in Lake Ontario and flows into the Atlantic Ocean. (p. 80)

St. Lawrence Seaway (sānt lôr′ əns sē′ wā) The waterway that makes it possible for ships to travel between the Great Lakes and the Atlantic Ocean. (p. 233)

St. Marys River (sānt mâr′ ēz riv′ ər) A river that begins in northwestern Ohio, flows into northeastern Indiana, and joins the St. Joseph River at Fort Wayne. (p. 25)

GAZETTEER

South Bend (south bend) The county seat of St. Joseph County, in northern Indiana, and home of the University of Notre Dame; 42°N, 86°W. (p. 80)

Southern Hills and Lowlands (su<u>th</u>′ ərn hilz and lō′ landz) The southern region of Indiana. (p. 22)

Southwind Maritime Centre (south′ wind mar′ i tīm sen′ tər) Indiana's largest port on the Ohio River, located in Mount Vernon; 38°N, 88°W. (p. 233)

Spencer County (spen′ sər koun′ tē) County in southern Indiana in which Abraham Lincoln and his family lived. (p. 137)

T

Terre Haute (ter ə hōt′) The county seat of Vigo County and the home of Indiana State University; 39°N, 87°W. (p. 29)

Thames River (temz riv′ ər) The river in Canada, near Lake Erie, where the Battle of the Thames was fought in 1813. (p. 127)

Till Plain (til plān) The central region of Indiana. (p. 22)

Tippecanoe River (tip ē kə nü′ riv′ ər) The river in northern Indiana where the Battle of Tippecanoe was fought in 1811. (p. 126)

Toledo (tə lē′ dō) A city in Ohio located along the shores of Lake Erie. In the 1850s it was the starting point for the Wabash and Erie Canal. (p. 154)

Turkey Run State Park (tûr′ kē run stāt pärk) One of the nation's first state parks, located in Parke County in western Indiana; 40°N, 87°W. (p. 181)

U

United States (ū nī′ tid stāts) A country that has 49 states in North America and the state of Hawaii in the Pacific Ocean. (p. 19)

V

Vincennes (vin senz′) The county seat of Knox County in southwestern Indiana and the first capital of the Indiana Territory; 39°N, 87°W. (p. 83)

Virginia (vər jin′ yə) A state in the southeastern United States. (p. 135)

W

Wabash and Erie Canal (wô′ bash ənd î′ rē kə nal′) America's longest canal, completed in 1853; it connected Lake Erie with the Wabash River and the Ohio River. (p. 154)

Wabash Lowland (wô′ bash lō′ land) A fertile area in southwestern Indiana. (p. 32)

Wabash River (wô′ bash riv′ ər) The longest river in Indiana, beginning in western Ohio and ending in southwestern Indiana. (p. 21)

Wabash Valley (wô′ bash val′ ē) The valley formed by the Wabash River. (p. 66)

Washington, D.C. (wô′ shing tən dē sē) The capital of the United States. (p. 132)

White River (hwīt riv′ ər) A tributary of the Wabash River that flows in southern Indiana. (p. 30)

Whitewater Canal State Historic Site (hwīt′ wô tər kə nal′ stāt hi stôr′ ik sīt) The place at Metamora where part of the Whitewater Canal is preserved. (p. 154)

Whitewater River (hwīt′ wô tər riv′ ər) A river in southeastern Indiana near the border with Ohio. (p. 32)

Wyandotte Caves (wī ən dot′ kāvz) The caves near Corydon known for their unusual rock formations; 38°N, 86°W. (p. 244)

---

a cap; ā cake; ä father; är car; âr dare; ch chain; e hen; ē me; hw where; i bib; ī kite; îr pierce; ng song; o top; ō rope; ô saw; oi coin; ôr fork; ou cow; sh show; th thin; <u>th</u> those; u sun; ù book; ü moon; ū cute; ûr term; ə about, taken, pencil, apron, helpful; ər letter, dollar, doctor

GAZETTEER

BIOGRAPHICAL DICTIONARY

The Biographical Dictionary will help you to pronounce the names of and to identify the Key People in this book. The page number tells you where each name first appears in the text.

PRONUNCIATION KEY

a	cap	hw	**wh**ere	oi	c**oi**n	ü	m**oo**n
ā	cake	i	bib	ôr	fork	ū	cute
ä	father	ī	kite	ou	c**ow**	ûr	term
är	car	îr	p**ier**ce	sh	**sh**ow	ə	about, taken,
âr	dare	ng	so**ng**	th	**th**in		pencil, apron,
ch	**ch**ain	o	top	<u>th</u>	**th**ose		helpful
e	hen	ō	rope	u	sun	ər	letter, dollar,
ē	me	ô	saw	ù	b**oo**k		doctor

B

Bayh, Birch (bī), 1928– United States senator from Indiana who served in Congress from 1963 to 1981. (p. 258)

Bayh, Evan (bī), 1955– Elected governor of Indiana in 1988. He is the son of Birch Bayh. (p. 251)

Bird, Larry (bûrd), 1956– Famous professional basketball player from French Lick. (p. 217)

Brokenburr, Robert L. (bro′ kən bûr), 1886–1974 African-American state senator who fought for the passage of a civil rights law in Indiana. (p. 189)

Bush, George (bùsh) Elected President of the United States in 1988. (p. 259)

C

Carmichael, Hoagy (kär′ mī kəl), 1899–1981 Songwriter from Indianapolis who is best known for his song "Star Dust." (p. 213)

Clark, George Rogers (klärk), 1752–1818 Frontier fighter who defeated the British at Vincennes and gained control of the Northwest Territory for the United States during the American Revolution. (p. 101)

Coats, Dan (kōts), 1943– Hoosier who became a United States senator in 1989. (p. 258)

Coffin, Catherine (kô′ fin), 1803–1881 One of Indiana's most famous Underground Railroad conductors, also known as "Aunt Katy." (p. 167)

Coffin, Levi (kô′ fin), 1789–1877 An Underground Railroad conductor who, along with his wife Catherine, helped over 3,000 slaves to reach freedom. (p. 167)

Conn, C. G. (kôn), 1844–1931 Businessman who started one of America's largest musical instrument companies in Elkhart after the Civil War. (p. 228)

D

Dreiser, Theodore (drī′ sər), 1871–1945 Famous writer from Indiana who wrote novels about the problems of greed and dishonesty in American life. (p. 212)

H

Hamilton, Henry (ham′ əl tən), about 1740–1796 British general who headed the British army in the West during the American Revolution. He was defeated at Vincennes by George Rogers Clark. (p. 100)

Harper, Ida H. (här′ pər), 1851–1931 State and national leader in the struggle for women's voting rights. (p. 187)

Harris, Chapman (har′ is), An African-American Hoosier who ferried many slaves across the Ohio River to freedom. (p. 166)

Harrison, William Henry (har′ ə sən), 1773–1841 Governor of the Indiana Territory from 1800 to 1812. He signed many treaties with Indians and also fought battles with them. In 1841 he became President. (p. 118)

Harroun, Ray (hâr′ ün), 1878–1968 First winner of the Indy 500 in 1911. (p. 215)

Hatcher, Richard (hach′ ər), 1933– Mayor of Gary from 1967 to 1987. He was the first African-American mayor of a large American city. (p. 189)

Haynes, Elwood (hānz), 1857–1925 Hoosier from Kokomo who invented one of the first automobiles. (p. 179)

J

Jennings, Jonathan (jen′ ingz), 1784–1834 Elected the first governor of Indiana in 1816. He was also one of the main authors of Indiana's Constitution of 1816. (p. 130)

K

Knight, Bobby (nīt), 1940– Coach of the Indiana University basketball team since 1971. (p. 216)

L

La Salle, Robert (lə sal′), 1643–1687 Frenchman who was the first known European to explore what is now Indiana. (p. 80)

Lilly, Eli (lil′ ē), 1839–1898 Businessman who started one of the world's largest pharmaceutical companies in Indianapolis in 1876. (p. 228)

Lincoln, Abraham (ling′ kən), 1809–1865 Brilliant United States President who grew up at Little Pigeon Creek, Indiana. (p. 135)

Little Turtle (lit′ əl tûr′ təl), 1752–1812 Chief of the Miami Indians who defeated American troops at Kekionga in 1791. (p. 105)

Lugar, Richard (lü′ gər), 1932– United States senator from Indiana. (p. 258)

M

McNutt, Paul V. (mək nut′), 1891–1955 Governor of Indiana during the Great Depression. (p. 182)

Morgan, John Hunt (môr′ gən), 1825–1864 Confederate general who led troops into southern Indiana during the Civil War. (p. 172)

Morton, Oliver P. (môrt′ ən), 1823–1877 Governor of Indiana during the Civil War. (p. 171)

O

Oliver, James (ol′ ə vər), 1823–1908 South Bend Hoosier born in Scotland who invented the chilled plow. (p. 159)

Owen, Robert (ō′ ən), 1771–1858 Wealthy man from Scotland who bought Harmonie in 1824 and renamed it New Harmony. (p. 143)

P

Pontiac (pōn′ tē ak), 1720–1769 Ottawa chief who led an Indian attack on British forts in 1763. (p. 90)

Porter, Cole (pôr′ tər), 1893–1964 Famous songwriter from Peru, Indiana. (p. 213)

Porter, Gene Stratton (pôr′ tər), 1868–1924 Famous Hoosier writer whose books reflect her love of the outdoors. (p. 212)

Pyle, Ernie (pīl), 1900–1945 Newspaper writer from Dana who wrote about the experiences of soldiers and sailors in World War II. (p. 183)

Q

Quayle, Dan (kwāl), 1947– Hoosier elected Vice President of the United States in 1988. (p. 258)

R

Rapp, George (rap), 1757–1847 A preacher from Germany who, with his followers, built the community of Harmonie in 1814. (p. 142)

Redenbacher, Orville (red′ ən bä kər), 1907– Businessman from Brazil, Indiana, who began one of the biggest popcorn businesses in America. (p. 223)

BIOGRAPHICAL DICTIONARY

Richardson, Jr., Henry J. (rich′ ərd sən), 1902–1983   African-American lawyer who led the fight against school segregation in Indiana. (p. 189)

Riley, James Whitcomb (rī lē′), 1849–1916   Famous writer from Greenfield known as the "Hoosier Poet." (p. 211)

Robertson, Oscar (rob′ ərt sən), 1938–   First Hoosier basketball player to score 25,000 points in his career. (p. 217)

Rockne, Knute (rok′ nē), 1888–1931   Coach of the Notre Dame football team in the early 1900s. (p. 218)

Roosevelt, Franklin D. (rōz′ velt), 1882–1945   President of the United States during the Great Depression and most of World War II. (p. 182)

Rudolph, Wilma (rü′ dôlf), 1940–   Track and field champion who overcame serious illnesses to win three gold medals in the 1960 Olympics. (p. 218)

S

Stephenson, D. C. (stē′ vən sən), 1892–1966   Ku Klux Klan leader who was arrested and jailed for murder in 1924. (p. 188)

Studebaker, Clem (stüd′ ə bā kər), 1831–1901   South Bend businessman who opened a wagon shop with his brother in 1852. Later their company became a famous manufacturer of automobiles. (p. 178)

Studebaker, Henry (stüd′ ə bā kər), 1826–1895   Cofounder, with his brother Clem, of the Studebaker Company. (p. 178)

T

Tarkington, Booth (tär′ king tən), 1869–1946   Famous writer from Indianapolis. (p. 211)

Tecumseh (tə kum′ sə), about 1768–1813   Indian leader who fought against William Henry Harrison's efforts to buy Indian land. (p. 124)

Tenskwatawa (ten skwot′ ə wo), about 1778–1837   The brother of Tecumseh who was known as "the Prophet." (p. 124)

W

Washington, George (wô′ shing tən), 1732–1799   Leader of an attack that marked the beginning of the French and Indian War. Later he became the first President of the United States. (p. 89)

Wayne, Anthony (wān), 1745–1796   American general who defeated the Miami in the Battle of Fallen Timbers in 1794. (p. 105)

White Beaver (hwīt bē′ vər), Mohegan guide who led Robert La Salle into present-day Indiana in 1679. (p. 80)

---

a cap; ā cake; ä father; är car; âr dare; ch chain; e hen; ē me; hw where; i bib; ī kite; îr pierce; ng song; o top; ō rope; ô saw; oi coin; ôr fork; ou cow; sh show; th thin; th those; u sun; u̇ book; ü moon; ū cute; ûr term; ə about, taken, pencil, apron, helpful; ər letter, dollar, doctor

BIOGRAPHICAL DICTIONARY

GLOSSARY

This Glossary will help you to pronounce and understand the meanings of the Key Vocabulary in this book. The page number at the end of the definition tells where the word or term first appears.

PRONUNCIATION KEY

a	cap	hw	**wh**ere	oi	**c**o**in**	ü	m**oo**n
ā	cake	i	bib	ôr	fork	ū	cute
ä	father	ī	kite	ou	c**ow**	ûr	term
är	**c**ar	îr	**p**ierce	sh	**sh**ow	ə	about, taken,
âr	dare	ng	so**ng**	th	**th**in		pencil, apron,
ch	**ch**ain	o	top	th	**th**ose		helpful
e	hen	ō	rope	u	sun	ər	letter, dollar,
ē	me	ô	saw	u	book		doctor

A

agriculture (ag′ ri kul chər) The science or business of raising crops and farm animals. (p. 221)

American Revolution (ə mer′ i kən rev ə lü′ shən) The war fought from 1776 to 1783 between American colonists and Britain in which America gained independence. (p. 100)

archaeologist (är kē ol′ ə jist) A scientist who searches for and studies artifacts. (p. 61)

artifact (är′ tə fakt) Something made by people, such as a tool or simple object, used in ancient times. (p. 61)

astronaut (as′ trə nôt) A person who travels into space. (p. 235)

B

basin (bā′ sin) A low, bowl-shaped landform surrounded by higher lands. (p. 24)

Battle of Fallen Timbers (bat′ əl əv fô′ lən tim′ bərz) The battle fought on August 20, 1794, between American soldiers, led by General Anthony Wayne, and Miami warriors, led by Little Turtle. (p. 106)

Battle of the Thames (bat′ əl əv thə temz) The battle fought in Canada during the War of 1812 in which Tecumseh died and William Henry Harrison defeated the British and the Indians. (p. 127)

Battle of Tippecanoe (bat′ əl əv tip ē kə nü′) The battle fought on November 7, 1811, in which William Henry Harrison and his men attacked Tecumseh's followers. (p. 126)

bill (bil) A plan for a law. (p. 250)

board of county commissioners (bôrd əv koun′ tē kə mish′ ə nərz) A group of people elected by county voters to see that the county's laws are carried out. (p. 254)

byline (bī′ līn) The line in a newspaper story that tells who wrote the article. (p. 260)

bypass (bī′ pas) A road that turns off the main road. (p. 156)

C

canal (kə nal′) A waterway for ships dug across land. (p. 154)

cardinal directions (kär′ də nəl di rek′ shənz) The four main directions of the compass: north, south, east, and west. (p. 11)

cause (kôz) Something that makes something else happen. (p. 122)

census (sen′ səs) An official count of the people living in a country or district. (p. 120)

centennial (sen ten′ ē əl) A one-hundredth anniversary. (p. 180)

circle graph (sûr′ kəl graf) A drawing that shows how something is divided into parts. (p. 185)

civil rights (siv′ əl rīts) The rights of all people to be treated equally under the law. (p. 186)

Civil War (siv′ əl wôr) The war between the Union and the Confederate states that lasted from 1861 to 1865. (p. 171)

clan (klan) A group of families united by the belief that they are all descended from the same ancestor. (p. 67)

climate (klī′ mit) The weather that an area usually has over a long period of time. (p. 38)

colony (kol′ ə nē) A place that is ruled by another country. (p. 79)

common council (kom′ ən koun′ səl) A group of people elected by city voters to make city laws. (p. 254)

compass rose (kum′ pəs rōz) A small drawing with lines showing direction. (p. 11)

Confederacy (kən fed′ ər ə sē) The states of the southern United States that formed their own country during the Civil War. (p. 171)

conservation (kon′ sər vā′ shən) The protection and wise use of natural resources. (p. 49)

constitution (kon sti tü′ shən) A plan of government. (p. 130)

continent (kon′ tə nənt) One of the seven large bodies of land on the earth. (p. 9)

corduroy road (kôr′ də roi rōd) A road made of logs laid side by side across the roadbed. (p. 153)

county council (koun′ tē koun′ səl) A group of people elected by county voters to decide how to spend tax money. (p. 254)

county seat (koun′ tē sēt) The town or city that is the center of government for a county. (p. 254)

custom (kus′ təm) The usual practice or actions of a group of people. (p. 113)

D

dateline (dāt′ līn) The line in a newspaper story that tells when and where the article was written. (p. 260)

decision (di sizh′ ən) A choice. (p. 74)

Declaration of Independence (dek lə rā′ shən əv in di pen′ dəns) The document written in 1776 that stated that American colonists were no longer under British rule. (p. 100)

degree (di grē′) A measure of distance between lines of latitude or longitude. (p. 42)

delegate (del′ i gāt) A person who is elected to speak or act for others. (p. 130)

democracy (di mok′ rə sē) A government run by the people it governs. (p. 264)

dictionary (dik′ shə ner ē) A reference book that gives the meanings of words and their pronunciations. (p. 87)

discrimination (di skrim ə nā′ shən) An unfair difference in treatment. (p. 186)

E

economy (i kon′ ə mē) The way a state or country uses its resources to meet people's needs and wants. (p. 221)

editorial (ed i tôr′ ē əl) A newspaper article in which the editors give their opinions. (p. 260)

effect (i fekt′) What happens as a result of something else. (p. 122)

elevation (el ə vā′ shən) The height of a place above sea level. (p. 26)

Emancipation Proclamation (i man sə pā′ shən prok lə mā′ shən) The announcement issued by President Abraham Lincoln in 1863 that all slaves in Confederate states held by the Union army were free. (p. 173)

encyclopedia (en sī klə pē′ dē ə) A book or set of books that contains information on many subjects. (p. 86)

environment (en vī′ rən mənt) The surroundings in which people, plants, or animals live; the air, land, and water. (p. 229)

equator (i kwā′ tər) An imaginary line that lies halfway between the North Pole and the South Pole. (p. 10)

erosion (i rō′ zhən) The wearing away of rock and soil by water, wind, or ice. (p. 33)

GLOSSARY

executive branch (eg zek′ yə tiv branch) The part of a government that makes sure the laws are carried out. (p. 251)

explorer (ek splôr′ ər) A person who travels to unknown lands. (p. 80)

export (eks′ pôrt) A good that is sent to another country for sale or trade. (p. 234)

F

fact (fakt) A statement that can be proven true. (p. 140)

feature article (fē′ chər är′ ti kəl) A newspaper story that reports in detail about a person, subject, or event. (p. 260)

ferry (fer′ ē) A boat used to carry people, cars, and goods across a river or other narrow body of water. (p. 136)

fertile (fûr′ təl) Land that is good for growing crops. (p. 28)

flatboat (flat′ bōt) A boat with a flat bottom and square ends for traveling downstream with the river current. (p. 153)

fork (fôrk) A branch of a river. (p. 30)

free state (frē stāt) Any state in the United States in which it was not legal to own slaves. (p. 165)

French and Indian War (french ənd in′ dē ən wôr) The war fought in North America between France and its Indian allies and Great Britain that lasted from 1754 until 1763. (p. 89)

frontier (frun tîr′) The land at the edge of a settled area. (p. 99)

fuel (fū′ əl) Something that is burned to produce heat or energy. (p. 47)

fur trader (fûr tra′ dər) A person who collected furs to be sold. (p. 81)

G

General Assembly (jen′ ər əl ə sem′ blē) The lawmaking body of the Indiana government. (p. 250)

geography (jē og′ rə fē) The study of the earth's land, water, plants, animals, and people. (p. 21)

glacier (glā′ shər) A large sheet of ice that moves slowly over the land. (p. 24)

global grid (glō′ bəl grid) The lines of latitude and longitude on a world map that make it possible to locate places. (p. 44)

Grange (grānj) An organization for farmers in the United States. (p. 162)

graph (graf) A drawing that shows the changes of and the relationship between two or more things. (p. 184)

Great Depression (grāt di presh′ ən) The period of bad times during the 1930s when many businesses in America failed and people lost their jobs. (p. 181)

grid map (grid map) A map made up of two sets of lines that cross each other to make squares. (p. 14)

ground water (ground wô′ tər) Water that has seeped below the earth's surface and is stored naturally among rocks and soil. (p. 48)

growing season (grō′ ing sē′ zən) The time of year when the weather is warm enough for crops to grow. (p. 41)

guide words (gīd wûrds) The words that tell which part of the alphabet is covered in a volume of an encyclopedia. In a dictionary they tell the first and last words that are defined on a page. (p. 86)

H

Harmonist (här′ mə nist) A follower of George Rapp. (p. 142)

headline (hed′ līn) The title to a newspaper article, printed at the top of the story. (p. 260)

hemisphere (hem′ i sfîr) One half of the earth. (p. 9)

a cap; ā cake; ä father; är car; âr dare; ch chain; e hen; ē me; hw where; i bib; ī kite; îr pierce; ng song; o top; ō rope; ô saw; oi coin; ôr fork; ou cow; sh show; th thin; th those; u sun; ù book; ü moon; ū cute; ûr term; ə about, taken, pencil, apron, helpful; ər letter, dollar, doctor

GLOSSARY

heritage (her′ i tij) A group's history and traditions. (p. 68)

humidity (hū mid′ i tē) The moisture or dampness in the air. (p. 39)

I

immigrant (im′ i grənt) A person who comes to another country to live. (p. 178)

import (im′ pôrt) A good that is brought in from another country for sale or use. (p. 234)

industry (in′ də strē) All the businesses that make one kind of product or provide one kind of service. (p. 225)

integration (in ti grā′ shən) The bringing together of different groups of people; the elimination of racial segregation. (p. 189)

interdependent (in tər di pen′ dənt) Depending on one another to help meet needs and wants. (p. 161)

intermediate directions (in tər mē′ ldē it di rek′ shənz) The directions of a compass that lie halfway between the cardinal directions. (p. 11)

international trade (in tər nash′ ə nəl trād) Trade, or exchange of goods, with other countries. (p. 234)

interpreter (in tûr′ prit ər) A person who helps people who speak different languages to understand one another. (p. 113)

interstate highway (in′ tər stāt hī′ wā) A wide road running between two or more states. (p. 156)

Iron Brigade (ī′ ərn bri gād′) A group of soldiers from Indiana and neighboring states that fought as a unit in the Civil War. (p. 171)

J

judicial branch (jü dish′ əl branch) The part of a government composed of the courts. (p. 252)

K

Ku Klux Klan (kü′ kluks klan′) A secret group whose members are united by their hatred of people who are different from themselves. (p. 188)

L

land bridge (land brij) An area of land connecting two larger land masses. During the Ice Age a land bridge connected Asia and North America. (p. 62)

landfill (land′ fil) A huge pit into which garbage and trash are dumped. (p. 262)

landform (land′ fôrm) A shape on the earth's surface, such as a mountain or a valley. (p. 21)

land-use map (land′ ūs map) A map that shows the main natural resources and products of an area. (p. 208)

latitude (lat′ i tüd) An imaginary line on a map or globe that measures degrees north or south of the equator. (p. 42)

lean-to (lēn′ tü) An open shelter with a sloping roof formed of branches and twigs. (p. 136)

legislative branch (lej′ is lā tiv branch) The part of a government that makes the laws. (p. 250)

limestone (līm′ stōn) A kind of rock used for building and making lime. (p. 33)

line graph (līn graf) A drawing that shows changes over a period of time. (p. 184)

livestock (līv′ stok) Animals that are raised on a farm for profit. (p. 221)

log cabin (lôg kab′ in) A home built out of logs that are stacked. (p. 136)

longitude (lon′ ji tüd) An imaginary line on a map or globe that measures degrees east or west of the prime meridian. (p. 43)

M

mammoth (mam′ əth) A huge, woolly animal of the past that looked something like an elephant. (p. 62)

manufacturing (man yə fak′ chər ing) The making of large numbers of products in factories. (p. 177)

map key (map kē) A guide that explains the meaning of each symbol used on a map. (p. 12)

mayor (mā′ ər) The person who is the official head of a city or town government. (p. 254)

meridian (mə rid′ ē ən) A line of longitude. (p. 43)

mineral (min′ ər əl) A natural substance found in the earth. (p. 47)

missionary (mish′ ə ner ē) A person who teaches his or her religion to others who have different beliefs. (p. 81)

monument (mon′ yə mənt) Something that is built in honor of a person or an event. (p. 51)

moraine (mə rān′) A pile or mound of rocks, gravel, clay, and dirt left behind by a glacier. (p. 24)

mound (mound) A hill or heap of earth. (p. 63)

mouth (mouth) The part of a river where it empties into another body of water. (p. 29)

myth (mith) A story that explains the beliefs of a group. (p. 69)

N

natural feature (nach′ ər əl fē′ chər) A part of the earth that is made by nature. (p. 21)

natural resource (nach′ ər əl re sôrs′) Something found in nature that is useful to people. (p. 46)

navigable (nav′ i gə bəl) Wide and deep enough for ships and boats to travel in. (p. 154)

news article (nüz är′ ti kəl) A newspaper story that gives facts about a recent event. (p. 260)

nomad (nō′ mad) A person who moves from place to place in search of food. (p. 62)

Northwest Ordinance (nôrth west′ ôr′ də nəns) The law passed in 1787 that provided a way to divide and settle the Northwest Territory. (p. 117)

O

ocean (ō′ shən) The whole body of salt water that covers nearly three fourths of the earth's surface. (p. 9)

opinion (ə pin′ yən) A person's belief or feeling about something. (p. 140)

Ordinance of 1785 (ôr′ də nəns əv sev′ ən tēn′ ā′ tē fīv) The law that provided a way for settlers to buy land and establish schools in the Northwest Territory. (p. 117)

Owenite (ō′ ən īt) A follower of Robert Owen. (p. 144)

P

parallel (par′ ə lel) A line of latitude. (p. 42)

pharmaceutical (fär mə sü′ ti kəl) Having to do with medicines that are sold in drugstores. (p. 228)

pioneer (pi ə nîr′) One of the first people of a group to move into an area. (p. 105)

plain (plān) A large area of flat or gently rolling land. (p. 24)

plank road (plangk rōd) A road made by placing flat planks across a path. (p. 153)

pollution (pə lü′ shən) The things that make the air, soil, or water dirty. (p. 229)

Pontiac's Rebellion (pōn′ tē aks ri bel′ yən) The Indian attack on British forts west of the Appalachian Mountains in 1763. (p. 90)

population (pop yə lā′ shən) The number of people who live in an area. (p. 119)

population map (pop yə lā′ shən map) A map that shows where people live or how many people live in different areas. (p. 208)

port (pôrt) A place where ships load and unload goods. (p. 233)

portage (pôr′ tij) A path where boats and goods can be carried from one body of water to another. (p. 66)

preacher (prē′ chər) A person who speaks about religious ideas. (p. 142)

precipitation (pri sip i tā′ shən) Snow, rain, or any other form of water that falls to earth. (p. 39)

prehistoric (prē his tôr′ ik) Of the time before people could write history. (p. 62)

a cap; ā cake; ä father; är car; âr dare; ch chain; e hen; ē me; hw where; i bib; ī kite; îr pierce; ng song; o top; ō rope; ô saw; oi coin; ôr fork; ou cow; sh show; th thin; <u>th</u> those; u sun; ů book; ü moon; ū cute; ûr term; ə about, taken, pencil, apron, helpful; ər letter, dollar, doctor

GLOSSARY

prime meridian (prīm mə rid′ ē ən) The imaginary line on maps or globes that serves as the starting point for measuring lines of longitude. (p. 10)

Proclamation of 1763 (prok lə mā′ shən əv sev′ ən tēn′ siks′ tē thrē) The British law that stated that British colonists could not settle west of the Appalachian Mountains. (p. 91)

publicity (pu blis′ i tē) The means used to bring a person or thing to the attention of the public. (p. 194)

R

reaper (rē′ pər) A machine used for cutting grain. (p. 159)

recreation (rek rē ā′ shən) The activities that people do to relax and enjoy themselves. (p. 214)

recycling (rē sī′ kling) Using something over again. (p. 182)

reference book (ref′ ər əns bùk) A book that has facts about different subjects. (p. 86)

region (rē′ jən) A large area with common features that set it apart from other areas. (p. 22)

religion (ri lij′ ən) The way people worship the God or gods they believe in. (p. 81)

road map (rōd map) A map that shows how to get from one place to another by using roads and highways. (p. 156)

rural (rùr′ əl) Of or from the country. (p. 205)

S

sand dune (sand dün) A hill of sand that has been piled up by the wind. (p. 22)

scale (skāl) The relationship between the distances shown on the map and the real distances on the earth. (p. 13)

secede (si sēd′) To withdraw from a group, organization, or nation. (p. 171)

segregation (seg ri gā′ shən) A forced separation; the act of separating one group of people from other groups. (p. 187)

self-sufficient (self′ sə fish′ ənt) Able to provide for one's own needs. (p. 158)

service industry (sûr′ vis in′ də strē) A group of businesses that provides useful services but does not make any goods. (p. 245)

silt (silt) Tiny bits of sand, clay, or dirt picked up and deposited by rivers and streams. (p. 31)

sinkholes (singk′ hōlz) Holes that water has worn in rocks, especially in limestone. (p. 32)

slave (slāv) A person who is owned by another person. (p. 118)

slave state (slāv stāt) A state in the United States in which slavery was legal until the end of the Civil War. (p. 165)

source (sôrs) A spring, lake, or other body of water where a river or stream begins. (p. 29)

steamboat (stēm′ bōt) A boat that moves under the power of a steam engine. (p. 154)

stockade (sto kād′) An area closed off by a fence made of strong posts that are set upright. (p. 84)

strip mining (strip mīn′ ing) The use of huge machines to strip away earth so that coal or other minerals can be mined. (p. 229)

symbol (sim′ bəl) Something that stands for something else. (p. 12)

T

taxes (taks′ əz) The money that the government collects from people to pay for government services. (p. 249)

technology (tek nol′ ə jē) The use of scientific ideas to meet people's needs. (p. 159)

temperature (tem′ pər ə chər) How hot or cold something is. (p. 38)

territory (ter′ i tôr ē) Land that is owned by a country. (p. 104)

till (til) The rocks, gravel, and dirt left by glaciers on low or uneven land. (p. 24)

time line (tīm līn) A diagram that shows when events took place. (p. 108)

time zone (tīm zōn) One of the 24 divisions of the earth used to measure time. (p. 240)

tornado (tôr nā′ dō) A dangerous storm that whirls in a swift, funnel-shaped cloud. (p. 40)

tourist (tùr′ ist) A person who travels for enjoyment. (p. 242)

town board (toun bôrd) A group of people elected by the voters of a town to make the town's laws. (p. 254)

GLOSSARY

trace (trās) A trail made by animals through the forest. (p. 152)

trade goods (trād gůdz) Goods that are exchanged for other goods.(p. 81)

trading post (trād′ ing pōst) A place on the frontier where people met to exchange goods. (p. 81)

transportation (trans pər tā′ shən) A method of moving goods and people from place to place. (p. 151)

transportation map (trans pər tā′ shən map) A map showing different ways to travel from one place to another. (p. 14)

treaty (trē′ tē) An agreement between nations. (p. 106)

Treaty of Greenville (trē′ tē əv grēn′ vil) The agreement made in 1795 that stated that Indians would move from the eastern part of the Northwest Territory. (p. 106)

Treaty of Paris (trē′ tē əv par′ is) The agreement signed in 1763 that ended the French and Indian War. (p. 89)

tributary (trib′ yə ter ē) A stream or river that flows into a larger river or stream. (p. 30)

U

Underground Railroad (un′ dər ground′ rāl′ rōd) The secret escape routes used by slaves to escape to the North. (p. 166)

Unigov (ū′ ni guv) A single system of local government for the city of Indianapolis and Marion County that was formed in 1970. (p. 255)

Union (ūn′ yən) The northern states that remained part of the United States during the Civil War. (p. 171)

V

veto (vē′ tō) To refuse to agree to. (p. 251)

W

War of 1812 (wôr əv ā′ tēn′ twelv) The war fought between the United States and Great Britain between 1812 and 1815. (p. 126)

weather (we<u>th</u>′ ər) How hot, cold, wet, or dry a place is. (p. 37)

wetland (wet′ land) An area of swamp, marsh, or other wet surface. (p. 262)

wigwam (wig′ wom) A house made of long, bent poles covered with bark. (p. 67)

World War I (wûrld wôr wun) The war fought between 1914 and 1918 in which the United States joined countries fighting against Germany and other countries. (p. 181)

World War II (wûrld wôr tü) The war fought all over the world between 1939 and 1945 that America entered after Pearl Harbor was bombed by Japan in 1941. (p. 182)

a cap; ā cake; ä father; är car; âr dare; ch chain; e hen; ē me; hw where; i bib; ī kite; îr pierce; ng song; o top; ō rope; ô saw; oi coin; ôr fork; ou cow; sh show; th thin; <u>th</u> those; u sun; ů book; ü moon; ū cute; ûr term; ə about, taken, pencil, apron, helpful; ər letter, dollar, doctor

GLOSSARY

INDIANA ALMANAC

An almanac is a collection of important and interesting information. The Indiana Almanac will help you to learn more about your state.

INDIANA'S GOVERNORS

GOVERNOR	TERM
Jonathan Jennings	1816-1822
Ratliff Bon	1822
William Hendricks	1822-1825
James B. Ray	1825-1831
Noah Noble	1831-1837
David Wallace	1837-1840
Samuel Bigger	1840-1843
James Whitcomb	1843-1848
Paris C. Dunning	1848-1849
Joseph A. Wright	1849-1857
Ashbel P. Willard	1857-1860
Abram A. Hammond	1860-1861
Henry Smith Lane	1861
Oliver P. Morton	1861-1867
Conrad Baker	1867-1873
Thomas A. Hendricks	1873-1877
James D. Williams	1877-1880
Issac P. Gray	1880-1881
Albert G. Porter	1881-1885
Issac P. Gray	1885-1889
Alvin P. Hovey	1889-1891
Ira Joy Chase	1891-1893
Claude Matthews	1893-1897
James A. Mount	1897-1901
Winfield T. Durbin	1901-1905
J. Frank Hanly	1905-1909

GOVERNOR	TERM
Thomas R. Marshall	1909-1913
Samuel M. Ralston	1913-1917
James P. Goodrich	1917-1921
Warren T. McCray	1921-1924
Emmett Forest Branch	1924-1925
Ed Jackson	1925-1929
Harry G. Leslie	1929-1933
Paul V. McNutt	1933-1937
M. Clifford Townsend	1937-1941
Henry F. Schricker	1941-1945
Ralph F. Gates	1945-1949
Henry F. Schricker	1949-1953
George N. Craig	1953-1957
Harold W. Handley	1957-1961
Matthew E. Welsh	1961-1965
Roger D. Branigin	1965-1969
Edgar D. Whitcomb	1969-1973
Otis R. Bowen	1973-1981
Robert D. Orr	1981-1989
Evan Bayh	1989-

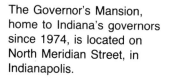

The Governor's Mansion, home to Indiana's governors since 1974, is located on North Meridian Street, in Indianapolis.

INDIANA'S COUNTIES

County Name	County Seat	County Population*	Population Rank	Area in Square Miles (Sq Km)	Area Rank	Year Formed
Adams	Decatur	31,500	45	340 (880)	72	1836
Allen	Fort Wayne	303,900	3	659 (1706)	1	1824
Bartholomew	Columbus	64,800	22	409 (1059)	35	1821
Benton	Fowler	9,800	88	407 (1053)	40	1840
Blackford	Hartford City	14,500	81	166 (429)	89	1839
Boone	Lebanon	39,000	33	424 (1097)	28	1831
Brown	Nashville	13,200	84	312 (807)	76	1836
Carroll	Delphi	19,300	71	372 (964)	62	1828
Cass	Logansport	39,900	32	414 (1073)	31	1829
Clark	Jeffersonville	89,100	15	376 (974)	60	1801
Clay	Brazil	25,100	60	360 (933)	70	1825
Clinton	Frankfort	31,800	44	405 (1049)	41	1830
Crawford	English	10,200	87	307 (794)	79	1818
Daviess	Washington	28,900	50	432 (1120)	26	1817
Dearborn	Lawrenceburg	38,100	35	307 (796)	80	1803
Decatur	Greensburg	24,100	61	373 (965)	61	1822
De Kalb	Auburn	35,500	41	364 (942)	68	1837
Delaware	Muncie	120,100	10	392 (1015)	51	1827
Dubois	Jasper	36,700	38	429 (1112)	27	1818
Elkhart	Goshen	151,100	6	466 (1207)	16	1830
Fayette	Connersville	27,200	55	215 (558)	87	1819
Floyd	New Albany	64,600	23	150 (388)	91	1819
Fountain	Covington	18,300	76	398 (1031)	46	1826
Franklin	Brookville	20,200	68	385 (996)	55	1811
Fulton	Rochester	18,700	74	369 (956)	64	1836
Gibson	Princeton	33,000	43	490 (1268)	13	1813
Grant	Marion	75,800	19	415 (1075)	30	1832
Greene	Bloomfield	30,800	46	546 (1414)	4	1821

313

County Name	County Seat	County Population*	Population Rank	Area in Square Miles (Sq Km)	Area Rank	Year Formed
Hamilton	Noblesville	102,300	14	398 (1032)	47	1823
Hancock	Greenfield	45,700	27	307 (795)	81	1828
Harrison	Corydon	29,500	49	486 (1259)	14	1808
Hendricks	Danville	76,800	18	409 (1059)	36	1824
Henry	New Castle	49,300	25	395 (1022)	50	1822
Howard	Kokomo	82,600	17	293 (759)	82	1844
Huntington	Huntington	36,600	38	366 (948)	66	1834
Jackson	Brownstown	37,200	37	514 (1330)	8	1816
Jay	Portland	21,400	66	384 (1996)	66	1836
Jasper	Rensselaer	26,200	58	561 (1454)	3	1838
Jefferson	Madison	29,900	48	363 (939)	69	1811
Jennings	Vernon	23,200	63	378 (980)	59	1817
Johnson	Franklin	85,800	16	321 (832)	75	1823
Knox	Vincennes	40,600	30	520 (1346)	6	1790
Kosciusko	Warsaw	65,400	21	540 (1398)	5	1837
La Grange	La Grange	28,900	51	380 (984)	58	1832
Lake	Crown Point	487,900	2	501 (1297)	12	1837
La Porte	La Porte	105,600	12	600 (1555)	2	1832
Lawrence	Bedford	43,000	28	452 (1171)	20	1818
Madison	Anderson	131,800	7	453 (1173)	19	1823
Marion	Indianapolis	791,900	1	396 (1026)	49	1822
Marshall	Plymouth	41,800	29	444 (1511)	24	1836
Martin	Shoals	11,300	86	339 (877)	73	1820
Miami	Peru	37,600	36	369 (956)	65	1834
Monroe	Bloomington	103,100	13	385 (996)	55	1818
Montgomery	Crawfordsville	35,500	41	505 (1308)	10	1823
Morgan	Martinsville	54,900	24	409 (1060)	37	1822
Newton	Kentland	13,800	82	401 (1038)	44	1859
Noble	Albion	38,600	33	413 (1069)	32	1836
Ohio	Rising Sun	5,500	92	87 (226)	92	1844
Orange	Paoli	19,300	71	408 (1057)	38	1816
Owen	Spencer	17,700	77	386 (1001)	53	1819

314

County Name	County Seat	County Population*	Population Rank	Area in Square Miles (Sq Km)	Area Rank	Year Formed
Parke	Rockville	15,300	80	444 (1511)	24	1821
Perry	Cannelton	18,900	73	381 (988)	57	1814
Pike	Petersburg	12,900	84	341 (883)	71	1817
Porter	Valparaiso	124,300	9	419 (1084)	29	1836
Posey	Mount Vernon	26,300	57	410 (1061)	34	1814
Pulaski	Winamac	13,300	83	435 (1126)	25	1839
Putnam	Greencastle	30,200	47	482 (1248)	15	1822
Randolph	Winchester	27,600	54	454 (1175)	18	1818
Ripley	Versailles	25,300	59	447 (1158)	23	1818
Rush	Rushville	18,400	75	408 (1057)	39	1822
St. Joseph	South Bend	244,200	4	459 (1189)	17	1830
Scott	Scottsburg	20,900	67	192 (496)	88	1820
Shelby	Shelbyville	40,200	31	412 (1068)	33	1822
Spencer	Rockport	20,200	68	400 (1036)	45	1818
Starke	Knox	22,200	65	309 (801)	77	1850
Steuben	Angola	28,100	52	308 (798)	78	1837
Sullivan	Sullivan	20,200	68	452 (1171)	21	1817
Switzerland	Vevay	7,400	90	224 (579)	86	1814
Tippecanoe	Lafayette	125,400	8	502 (1299)	11	1826
Tipton	Tipton	16,300	79	261 (675)	83	1844
Union	Liberty	6,900	91	163 (421)	90	1821
Vanderburgh	Evansville	166,400	5	236 (611)	85	1818
Vermillion	Newport	17,500	78	260 (674)	84	1824
Vigo	Terre Haute	104,800	11	405 (1048)	41	1818
Wabash	Wabash	35,600	40	398 (1032)	48	1835
Warren	Williamsport	8,400	89	366 (949)	67	1827
Warrick	Boonville	46,400	26	391 (1013)	52	1813
Washington	Salem	23,200	63	516 (1336)	7	1814
Wayne	Richmond	72,300	20	404 (1046)	43	1811
Wells	Bluffton	26,400	56	370 (959)	63	1837
White	Monticello	23,700	62	506 (1311)	9	1834
Whitley	Columbia City	27,900	53	336 (870)	74	1839

*Population figures are based on 1988 estimate.

INDIANA'S CLIMATE

116° F.
47° Celsius
The highest temperature ever recorded in Indiana was on July 14, 1936, at Collegeville.

-35° F.
-37° Celsius
The lowest temperature ever recorded in Indiana was on February 2, 1951, at Greensburg.

107 inches
272 centimeters
The largest annual snowfall ever recorded in Indiana was in 1929 at La Porte

AVERAGE MONTHLY TEMPERATURE IN EVANSVILLE AND SOUTH BEND

Degrees Fahrenheit

80
70
60
50
40
30
20
10
0

Degrees Celsius

27
21
16
10
4
-1
-7
-12
-18

JAN   MAR   MAY   JULY   SEPT   NOV

—•— Evansville   —•— South Bend

INDIANA ALMANAC

INDIANA'S ECONOMY

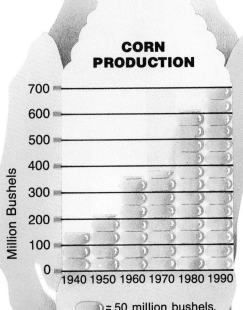

CORN PRODUCTION

Million Bushels

700
600
500
400
300
200
100
0

1940 1950 1960 1970 1980 1990

= 50 million bushels.
A bushel is a dry
measure equal to
32 quarts.

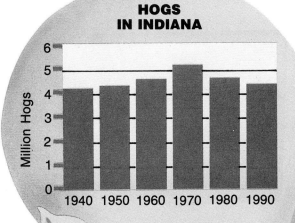

HOGS IN INDIANA

Million Hogs

6
5
4
3
2
1
0

1940 1950 1960 1970 1980 1990

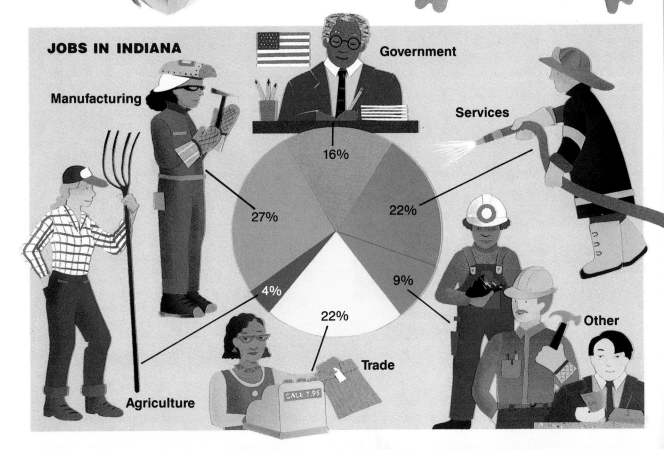

JOBS IN INDIANA

Manufacturing

Government

Services

16%

27%

22%

4%

9%

22%

Trade

Agriculture

Other

SALE 1.95

INDIANA TIME LINE

1679 Robert La Salle becomes the first known European to explore the Indiana region

1779 George Rogers Clark and his men capture Fort Sackville at Vincennes

1785 Ordinance of 1785 is passed

1732 The French build Fort Miami at portage between Wabash and Maumee rivers

2000 years ago Mound builders live in Indiana

1787 Northwest Ordinance is passed

1600s

1700s

10,000 years ago Nomadic hunters and gatherers are living throughout North and South America

1754-63 The French and Indian War

1763 Pontiac's Rebellion occurs; Proclamation of 1763 is issued

1795 Treaty of Greenville is signed

1700s Various Native American groups settle in Indiana

1791 American soldiers are defeated at Kekionga by Miami chief Little Turtle

1794 "Mad" Anthony Wayne wins the Battle of Fallen Timbers

1968 Richard Hatcher is first African-American elected as mayor of large city: Gary, Indiana

1811 Governor Harrison's troops win the Battle of Tippecanoe

1870s James Oliver invents a new steel plow

1980s and 1990s Indiana Legislature increases state support of education

1816 Indiana becomes the nineteenth state

1920 American women gain right to vote

1863 Emancipation Proclamation is issued

1917 The U.S. enters World War I

1939-45 World War II

1861 Civil War begins

1800s

1900s

1800 Congress establishes the Indiana Territory

1847 Madison and Indianapolis Railroad is completed

1918 World War I ends

1909 Gary becomes a center for the steel industry

1949 Indiana legislature makes school segregation illegal

1865 Civil War ends

1929 Great Depression begins

1830s Underground Railroad begins; National Road is built

1916 Indiana celebrates its centennial

319

ANNUAL EVENTS IN INDIANA

SUMMER

JUNE
Clay City Pottery Festival, Clay City
Festival of the Wild Rose Moon, Middlebury
Adena-Hopewell Rendezvous, Anderson
Greentown Glass Festival, Greentown
North Judson Mint Festival, North Judson
Indiana International Airshow, Mt. Comfort
Freedom Festival, Evansville
Richmond Area Rose Festival, Richmond
Abe Martin Festival, Nashville

JULY
Oldenburg Freudenfest, Oldenburg
Madison Regatta, Madison
Old Settlers' Day, Corydon
City of South Bend Ethnic Festival, South Bend
Annual Steel City Festival, Gary
Festival of the Dunes, Chesterton
Shoals Catfish Festival, Shoals
Fourth of July Celebration, Roachdale
Indiana Black Expo, Indianapolis

AUGUST
Village Art Festival, Nappanee
Antique Gas and Tractor Show, Portland
Reins of Life Rendezvous, Mishawaka
Indiana Avenue Jazz Festival, Indianapolis
Swiss Wine Festival, Vevay

WINTER

DECEMBER
Christmas Candlelight Tours, New Harmony
Festival of Lights, Santa Claus
Connor Prairie by Candlelight, Noblesville

JANUARY
Porter County Winter Carnival, Valparaiso
Midwinter Fest, Union City
Indiana Special Olympic Games, Paoli

FEBRUARY
Parke County Maple Fair, Rockville

FALL

SEPTEMBER
Little Italy Festival, Clinton
Daviess County Turkey Trot Festival, Montgomery
Annual Dale Fall Festival, Dale
Paoli Indian Summer Festival, Paoli
Persimmon Festival, Mitchell
Tipton County Pork Festival, Tipton
Johnny Appleseed Festival, Fort Wayne
Kee-Boon-Mein-Kaa Festival, South Bend
Duneland Harvest Festival, Porter
Greek Festival, Indianapolis
Fiesta, Indianapolis
Steamboat Days Festival, Jeffersonville
Feast of the Hunters' Moon, Lafayette

OCTOBER
Mississinewa 1812, Marion
Indian Trails Festival, Anderson
Canal Days—Traders Rendezvous, Metamora
Columbus Ethnic Expo, Columbus
College Corner Halloween Celebration, College Corner

NOVEMBER
Festival of Trees and Lights, Muncie
Knox Peppermint Candy Cane Parade, Knox
Nights Before Christmas Candlelight Tour, Madison
Old-Fashioned Christmas Walk, Metamora

SPRING

MARCH
Maple Sugarbush Weekend, Evansville
APRIL
Heritage Week, New Harmony
Little 500 Weekend, Bloomington
Renaissance Faire, Terre Haute
MAY
Studebaker Festival, South Bend
500 Festival, Indianapolis
Whistle-Stop Days, Hesston
Gene Stratton-Porter Days, Geneva

FASCINATING INDIANA FACTS

Raggedy Ann and Raggedy Andy™ were created in Indianapolis, in Marion County by a man named John Gruelle. He made them by fixing up old dolls that were found in the attic. He later wrote forty books about them for children.

The largest flag in the world is the United States flag made in Evansville, in Vanderburgh County. It measures 210 feet (64 meters) by 411 feet (125 meters). Eight People worked for six weeks to construct it. It was completed in 1980.

A dog once traveled from Wolcott, Indiana, to Silverton, Oregon, in search of its owners, a distance of 2,000 miles (3,218 km). The dog, a collie named Bobbie, was lost by its owners in Wolcott, White County, in 1923, but turned up at their new home in Oregon six months later.

Sarah Parke Morisson, from Salem, in Washington County, was the first woman in the nation to graduate from a state university. She received a degree from Indiana University at Bloomington in 1869.

Johnny Appleseed is buried in Fort Wayne, in Allen County. Every year a Johnny Appleseed Festival is held there in Johnny Appleseed Park. Thousands come to this pioneers day festival that re-enacts the way people lived in Johnny Appleseed's time.

Peru, in Miami County, home of the Circus Hall of Fame, is often called the circus capital of the nation. Every summer children of all ages perform in the circus shows there, or on the road in traveling circuses.

321

INDIANA ALMANAC

1. Tulip tree
2. Great horned owl
3. Red oak
4. Tiger swallowtail
   butterfly
5. Trillium
6. Violet
7. Jack-in-the-pulpit
8. Squirrel corn
9. Spring beauty
10. Quail
11. Fox squirrel
12. Fox
13. White tailed deer
14. Downy woodpecker
15. Sycamore
16. Shag bark
    hickory
17. Canada goose
18. Paw paw
19. Groundhog
20. Raccoon
21. Beaver
22. Timber rattler
23. Bull frog
24. Rabbit
25. Peppermint
26. Cardinal
27. Indigo bunting
28. Peony
29. Sarvice bush
30. Dogwood
31. Red cedar

INDIANAPOLIS 500 WINNERS

YEAR	DRIVER	Mph	Kph	YEAR	DRIVER	Mph	Kph
1911	Ray Harroun	74.59	120.04	1953	Bill Vukovich	128.74	207.19
1912	Joe Dawson	78.72	126.69	1954	Bill Vukovich	130.84	210.57
1913	Jules Goux	75.93	122.20	1955	Bob Sweikert	128.21	206.33
1914	Rene Thomas	82.47	132.72	1956	Pat Flaherty	128.49	206.78
1915	Ralph De Palma	89.84	144.58	1957	Sam Hanks	135.60	218.23
1916	Dario Resta	84.00	135.18	1958	Jimmy Bryan	133.79	215.31
1919	Howdy Wilcox	88.05	141.70	1959	Rodger Ward	135.86	218.65
1920	Gaston Chevrolet	88.62	142.62	1960	Jim Rathmann	138.77	223.33
1921	Tommy Milton	89.62	144.23	1961	A.J. Foyt	139.13	223.91
1922	Jimmy Murphy	94.48	152.05	1962	Rodger Ward	140.29	225.77
1923	Tommy Milton	90.95	146.37	1963	Parnelli Jones	143.14	230.36
1924	L.L. Corum and			1964	A.J. Foyt	147.35	237.14
	Joe Boyer	98.23	158.09	1965	Jim Clark	150.69	242.51
1925	Peter De Paolo	101.13	162.75	1966	Graham Hill	144.32	232.26
1926	Frank Lockhart	95.90	154.34	1967	A.J. Foyt	151.21	243.35
1927	George Souders	97.55	156.99	1968	Bobby Unser	152.88	246.04
1928	Louis Meyer	99.48	160.10	1969	Mario Andretti	156.87	252.46
1929	Ray Keech	97.59	157.06	1970	Al Unser, Sr.	155.75	250.66
1930	Billy Arnold	100.45	161.66	1971	Al Unser, Sr.	157.74	253.86
1931	Louis Schneider	96.63	155.51	1972	Mark Donohue	162.96	262.26
1932	Frederick Frame	104.14	167.60	1973	Gordon Johncock	159.04	255.95
1933	Louis Meyer	104.16	167.63	1974	Johnny Rutherford	158.59	255.22
1934	Bill Cummings	104.86	168.76	1975	Bobby Unser	149.21	240.13
1935	Kelly Petillo	106.24	170.98	1976	Johnny Rutherford	148.73	239.36
1936	Louis Meyer	109.07	175.53	1977	A.J. Foyt	161.33	259.64
1937	Wilbur Shaw	113.58	182.79	1978	Al Unser, Sr.	161.36	259.68
1938	Floyd Roberts	117.20	188.62	1979	Rick Mears	158.90	255.72
1939	Wilbur Shaw	115.04	184.14	1980	Johnny Rutherford	142.86	229.87
1940	Wilbur Shaw	114.28	183.92	1981	Bobby Unser	139.08	223.83
1941	Mauri Rose and			1982	Gordon Johncock	162.03	260.76
	Floyd Davis	115.12	185.27	1983	Tom Sneva	162.12	260.90
1946	George Robson	114.82	184.78	1984	Rick Mears	163.61	263.30
1947	Mauri Rose	116.34	187.23	1985	Danny Sullivan	152.98	246.20
1948	Mauri Rose	119.81	192.82	1986	Bobby Rahal	170.72	274.75
1949	William Holland	121.33	195.26	1987	Al Unser, Sr.	162.18	261.00
1950	Johnny Parsons	124.00	199.56	1988	Rick Mears	144.81	233.00
1951	Lee Wallard	126.24	203.16	1989	Emerson Fittipaldi	167.58	269.64
1952	Troy Ruttman	128.92	207.48				

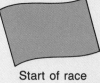
Start of race

Stop

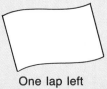
One lap left

Car leaving race

Car in trouble

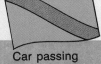
Car passing

End of race

FAMOUS HOOSIERS

Marshall (Major) Taylor born in Indianapolis in 1878; died in 1932; Bicyclist; world champion 1899

Amelia Earhart born in Atchison, Kansas in 1898; died in 1937; aviator; 1935-1937 Counselor in Careers for Women, Purdue University

John Wesley Hardrick born in Indianapolis in 1891; died in 1968; artist; known for his life-sized portraits of important Indianapolis citizens

Don Mattingly born in Evansville in 1961; baseball player; has played first base for the Yankees since 1983

Joshua Bell born in Bloomington in 1967; violinist; one of the youngest professional violinists in the world

Wilbur Shaw born in Shelbyville in 1902; died in 1954; race-car driver; three-time winner of the Indianapolis 500

Jim Davis born in Marion in 1945; cartoonist; author and illustrator of the comic strip "Garfield"

John Cougar Mellencamp born in Seymour in 1951; musician; best known for his albums *American Fool, Scarecrow,* and *The Lonesome Jubilee*

Theodore C. Steele born in Owen county in 1847; died in 1926; artist; part of "The Hoosier Group"; painted nine of the portraits in the Governors' Portraits Collection

Shelley Long born in Fort Wayne in 1949; movie and television actress; best known for her role on the television show "Cheers"

Michael Jackson born in Gary in 1958; musician; brother of Janet Jackson; winner of eleven Grammy awards

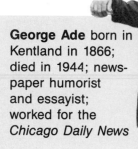

George Ade born in Kentland in 1866; died in 1944; newspaper humorist and essayist; worked for the *Chicago Daily News*

Kurt Vonnegut born in Indianapolis in 1922; writer; author of numerous books, including *Slaughterhouse-Five,* and *Cat's Cradle*

Robert Indiana born in Indianapolis in 1928; artist; best known for his 1966 painting "LOVE"

James Dean born in Marion in 1931; died in 1955; actor; best known for roles in *East of Eden, Giant,* and *Rebel Without a Cause*

Kevin Pugh born in Indianapolis in 1960; ballet dancer; principal dancer for the National Ballet of Canada

Jane Pauley born in Indianapolis in 1950; television newscaster

Ryan White born in 1971; died in 1990; worked to educate people throughout the state and country about AIDS

Jessamyn West born in Jennings County in 1902; died in 1984; writer; author of numerous books, including *Friendly Persuasion, The Big Country,* and *The Massacre at Fall Creek*

David Letterman born in Indianapolis in 1947; comedian; host of the popular "Late Night with David Letterman" television show

INDEX

Page references in italic type that follow an *m* indicate maps. Those following a *p* indicate photographs, artwork, or charts.

INDEX

INDEX

333

CREDITS

COVER:
Photography: **John Maxwell**

MAPS: **R. R. Donnelley and Sons Company Cartographic Services**

ILLUSTRATION CREDITS: Jolynn Alcorn: 316–317, 321. **Lori Anderson:** 111–114. **Len Ebert:** 58–59, 148–149. **Allan Eitzen:** 224, 226. **Joe Forte:** 318–319. **Steve Fuller:** 236–238. **Simon Galkin:** 212, 244. **Linda Graves:** 70–73. **Diana Magnuson:** 192–194. **Ann Neumann:** 4–5, 320, 322–323. **Hima Pamoedjo:** 160, 324. **Joel Snyder:** 67–68, 84, 138–139, 174. **Patrick Gnan:** 16–17. **Fred Winkowski:** 2–3. The names and the depictions of Raggedy Ann and Raggedy Andy are trademarks of Macmillan, Inc.

PHOTO CREDITS: ALLEN COUNTY-FORT WAYNE HISTORICAL SOCIETY: 187L. ALLEN COUNTY-FORT WAYNE PUBLIC LIBRARY, HISTORICAL GENEALOGY DEPARTMENT: 188 (inset). J. C. ALLEN & SON, INC.: 181T, 182B, 182L. ANDRES ALONSO: 36, 78, 96, 116, 134, 176, 204, 234. AMERICAN MUSEUM OF NATURAL HISTORY: 62. ARTSTREET: 173L (inset). BALL STATE UNIVERSITY: 188B. GWEN BERGHORN: 32BL, 32BR, 48, 49B (inset), 243L. THE BETTMANN ARCHIVE: 136R, 182R, 183L, 189R, 201R. BLACK STAR: Miami Herald Cross, 184; Jim Pickerell, 51M. BLOOMINGTON COUNTY CONVENTION AND VISITORS' CENTER: 217BL. BOSTON BALLET: Jack Mitchell, 327MR. ED BREEN: 33B, 33TL. BUTLER UNIVERSITY: Rare Book/Special Collections, 217BR. CALUMET REGIONAL ARCHIVES: 179L, 189L. CAMERAMANN INTERNATIONAL LTD.: 226BL, 226M. CINCINNATI ART MUSEUM, Subscription fund purchase; "The Underground Railroad" by Charles T. Webber, 167. CONNOR PRAIRIE HISTORICAL SITE: 159R. CORYDON CAPITOL STATE HISTORIC SITE: 131L (inset). CULVER PICTURES: 183R, 212TL, 212TR, 212BL, 213MR, 325TL, 326BL. DANADJIEVA & KOENIG ASSOCIATES, ARCHITECTS: 53M, 54R. DAN DEEM: 216BL. COURTESY OF THE DETROIT INSTITUTE OF THE ARTS: 90. FRANK DRIGGS COLLECTION: 213ML. DUOMO: Bryan Yablonsky, 325ML. PHOTOGRAPH COURTESY EITELJORG MUSEUM OF AMERICAN INDIAN AND WESTERN ART: Thomas Gentry, Photographer, 82R. FRANK ESPICH: 54L. CHARLENE FARIS: 162R, 312. RICHARD FIELDS: 18, 25R (inset), 32T, 33TR, 52L, 153, 220. FOCUS ON SPORTS: 215B. GAMMA-LIASION: Penelope Breese, 258MR (inset); Yvonne Hemsey, 326BR. GEORGE ROGERS CLARK NATIONAL HISTORICAL PARK: 101. GRANT HEILMAN: 41B, 49T; Isaac Geib, 223. RICHARD HAYNES, JR.: 60, 76, 86, 121L, 150, 164, 198T, 246BR, 248, 255M, 255R, 265R (inset), 270, 272–275, 277–286. MICHAL HERON: 190T. HISTORIC NEW HARMONY: 143B. HISTORICAL PICTURES SERVICE: 80L, 100, 107L, 125T, 125B, 144R, 161R, 171L, 173R; H. E. Robinson, 119L. J. FRED HOUSEL: 53L. THE IMAGE BANK: André Gallant, 128B. INDIANA HIGH SCHOOL ATHLETIC ASSOCIATION: 216BR. INDIANA HISTORICAL BUREAU: 102L, 131R (inset). COURTESY OF THE INDIANA HISTORICAL SOCIETY AND THE GLENN A. BLACK LABORATORY OF ARCHAEOLOGY: 64. INDIANA STATE LIBRARY: 105, 128 (insets), 131M, 178L, 181R (inset), 187R, 327BR; Picture Collection, Indiana Division, 162L. INDIANA STATE MUSEUM: The Museum Shop, 203BL. INDIANA UNIVERSITY ARCHIVES: 326ML. INDIANA UNIVERSITY AUDITORIUM: 140. THE INDIANAPOLIS NEWS: Mike Fender, 152R. © INDY 500 PHOTOS: 215 (inset), 325BR. JAMES WHITCOMB RILEY HOUSE AND MUSEUM: Nagley, 211R. ERIC JOHNSON: 261. DARRYL JONES: 30. LGI: Douglas Dobler, 326MM; Roger Jones, 326TR; Dave Hogan, 326MR. LIBRARY OF CONGRESS: 201L. LILLY LIBRARY, INDIANA UNIVERSITY, BLOOMINGTON, INDIANA: Niles MSS., Manuscripts Dept., 161L, 213R. LIMBERLOST STATE HISTORIC SITE: 212BR. MACMILLAN PUBLISHING CO.: 87. MADAM WALKER URBAN LIFE CENTER: 195. JOHN MAXWELL: 202TL. MIAMI COUNTY HISTORICAL SOCIETY: 213L. MOVIE STILL ARCHIVES: 327TR. HANS NAMUTH: 327TL. NASA: 236TL, 236TR. NATIONAL BALLET OF CANADA: 327MM. NORTH WIND PICTURE ARCHIVES: 159L. THE PALLADIUM-ITEM/PALLADIUM PUBLISHERS CORP.: 152L. PAWS, INC.: 326TL. DAVID PHILLIPS: 8. PHOTO RESEARCHERS: Philip Boyer, 203BR; Bill Dyer, 203T; Chester Higgins Jr., 190B; Susan McCartney, 255L; Larry Miller, 39. THOMAS A. POTTER: 20T, 41R. DAVE REPP: 20BL, 29, 33L (inset), 52R, 63BL, 206, 218, 239R, 263T. ELEANOR ROACH: 34, 121R, 243R, 266. SID RUST: 252L. ANDREW SACKS: 222R. SPORTS ILLUSTRATED: Tony Rice, 217MR. BILL STALIONS: 25L. JOHN STARKY: 53R. CHRISTIAN STEINER: 325BL. STOCK BOSTON: Bob Daemmrich, 264–265. STOCK MARKET: Berenholtz, 51R; Gabe Palmer, 257; Wes Thompson, 258B.

STUDEBAKER NATIONAL MUSEUM, INC.: 178R. SUPERSTOCK: 102R, 136L, 207L, 211L, 259R (inset); William Hamilton, 179R. SYGMA; 327ML; Theo Westenberger, 327BL. TIPPECANOE COUNTY HISTORICAL ASSOCIATION: 85; R. Woods, 207R. COLLECTION MRS. ROWENA H. TUCKER: 325MR. TSW-CLICK/CHICAGO: Frank Cezus, 20BR; Dawson Jones, 226R; Cathlyn Melloon, 40-41; James P. Rowan, 63T, 63BR. UNIPHOTO: A. Pierce Bounds, 51L. © 1978 UNITED FEATURES SYNDICATE, INC.: 326TM. UPI/BETTMANN NEWSPHOTOS: 258TR (inset), 259, 325TR. MICHAEL VAUGHN: 222L, 252R. JOE VIESTI: 198B, 202C, 228, 229, 230, 243B, 245, 246TR, 263B. VINCENNES UNIVERSITY: 197. WASHINGTON AND LEE UNIVERSITY, Lexington, VA.: Washington/Curtis/Lee Collection, 89. MARK WICK: 216ML, 216T. LEO DE WYS: Arthur Hustwitt, 202BL, 202BR.